LINCOLN CHRISTIAN UNIVERSITY

Nurturing Knowledge

Susan B. Neuman
University of Michigan

Kathleen Roskos
John Carroll University

with

Tanya S. Wright
University of Michigan

Lisa Lenhart
University of Akron

SCHOLASTIC

New York • Toronto • London • Auckland • Sydney
Mexico City • New Delhi • Hong Kong • Buenos Aires

DEDICATION

To Benjamin and Rebekah who nurture our knowledge of early childhood.

To Starboy who strives to know with imagination and heart.

Scholastic Inc. grants teachers permission to photocopy the reproducible pages in this book only for personal classroom use. No other part of this publication may be reproduced in whole or in part, or stored in a retrieval system, or transmitted in any form or by any means, electronic, mechanical, photocopying, recording, or otherwise, without written permission of the publisher. For information regarding permission, write to Permissions Department, Scholastic Inc., 557 Broadway, New York, NY 10012.

Cover design: Maria Lilja
Interior design: LDL Designs
Illustrations: Michelle Dorenkamp
Cover photo: Ellen Senesi
Interior photos: pp. 7, 16, 39, 41, 67, 80, 121, 151, 169, 180, 183: James Levin, © Scholastic;
p. 21 (top): © Mary White; pp. 21 (bottom two), 26, 30, 31, 32, 33, 156: © James F. Christie;
p. 32: © Lisa Lenhart; p. 55: © Keith Levit/IndexOpen; pp. 69, 102, 135: John Fortunato © Scholastic;
p. 87: © Wendy Saio/Shutterstock; p. 105: © FogStock LLC/IndexOpen;
pp. 139, 148: © Lauren Leon; p. 166: © Sean Justice/Getty Images.

ISBN-13: 978-0-439-82130-8
ISBN-10: 0-439-82130-4
Copyright © 2007 by Susan B. Neuman and Kathleen Roskos
All rights reserved. Published by Scholastic Inc.
Printed in the U.S.A.
6 7 8 9 10   40   16 15 14 13 12

CONTENTS

ACKNOWLEDGMENTS

We wish to thank the following early education sites for their generosity and cooperation. We truly appreciate the opportunity to photograph their settings and to collect examples of children's work.

* Arizona Centers for Early Literacy Excellence, Yuma, Arizona
* Aurora Co-Op Nursery School, Aurora, Ohio
* Carrol Nursery School, Shaker Heights, Ohio
* Hathaway Brown Preschool, Shaker Heights, Ohio
* Kenston Early Learning Center, Bainbridge, Ohio

By Jim Trelease

*I*n case you don't already know it, the ship of early childhood education is now enveloped in the "perfect storm." The elements that make the storm so severe are winds, high tides, atmospheric pressure, and freezing temperatures.

These "winds" are none other than politicians who believe that we can achieve higher student scores by legislating increasingly higher standards, sometimes without regard to student differences or developmental stages. This is like thinking you can improve your popularity by simply taking another poll.

The "high tides" are corporate leaders who are trying to meet international competition by demanding that schools adopt a business paradigm of assessment and accountability for all, often forgetting that children are not trains or planes, that they do not all arrive and take off on time.

The increasing "atmospheric pressures" take the form of insecure parents who succumb to the pressures of the marketplace (or their neighborhood) and are duped into thinking they have to raise a baby Einstein (though I hope they'd think twice about it if they knew how unhappy his childhood was). Living in an age when nearly 30 percent of 3-year-olds are watching nearly three hours of television a day, these parents don't realize that it's the number of words they speak into their child's ear that count the most, not the number of words you speak into your cell phone.

And finally there are the "freezing temperatures," by which I mean the culture from which we draw the teachers who sail the ship of early education. It's a culture in which more video games were bought last year than Major League Baseball, NFL, or NBA tickets combined. At a time when there has never been so much information—either handheld or wall-sized—available to each person, this culture makes *People* magazine its periodical of choice and Britney Spears its most googled term.

That's the perfect storm. And all the surfing, downloading, uploading, podding, blogging, e-mailing, googling, instant-messaging, and wikiing in the world will not quell the storm. But this book could.

It could be the closest thing to a perfect answer for the perfect storm, our best hope for navigating the ship through today's shoals.

Thanks to the findings of modern research, we know more than ever before which factors count the most in students' success and which count the most in their failure. For example, long-term studies show us that families speaking the most words, reading the most books, playing the most games, and making the most visits to libraries are the ones whose children succeed best in school.

The above fact is true not only nationally but also internationally. For example, Finland's students consistently lead the world in academic achievement, despite the fact that they delay the start of school until age 7. Their success is largely based on families that do many of the right things much of the time. Given the huge diversity of American families (unlike Finland's), how can we expect U.S. children to come to formal education with equal skills? Almost half of our children are in remediation on day one of kindergarten.

One solution is in this book, *Nurturing Knowledge*. What these four education experts have done is to tap the research of the last 25 years and create a classic model for early childhood education based on what we know about successful families. It stands to reason that if you can't change the homes, then you should change the classroom where children are going to spend almost a thousand hours a year. In other words, imitate these model families.

The long-standing concern about early childhood education centers is their inconsistency. We standardize our electrical appliances, our weights and measures, speed limits, auto emissions, and handicapped access, but our early childhood centers are as different from one another as night and day. How can we tolerate that as a nation? If and when we get around to a national early education standard, the regulators need look no further than this book for guidance.

For me, there are two factors that stand out above all the others in this volume. To begin with, unlike those storm elements rocking the boat, these authors truly understand child development. That is, unlike the forces trying to legislate "play" out of preschool and kindergarten, the authors recognize its infinite value to learning. That's not to suggest the authors flaunt or ignore government standards. To the contrary, they note the standards and demonstrate exactly how to reach them through play, student-generated interest, and organized instruction.

The second outstanding factor is that the authors provide a teaching curriculum that is not based on lofty, untried theories or idealized classrooms. Instead, it comes from real-life teachers and their students. There are no golden, unreachable goals here.

And finally, it might be helpful to remind ourselves that no storm lasts forever, that politicians often have short attention spans when riding bandwagons, and that today's parents eventually will be replaced by the children we have now in our early childhood centers. If we do right by them, they'll change the climate for the next generation of teachers and children.

CHAPTER 1

Knowledge Seekers: Young Children Learning About Literacy

"Guess what?" 4-year old Benjamin runs to tell his teacher on Monday morning. "Killer whales are bigger than sharks," he exclaims. "And guess what?" he goes on. "Killer whales are different than sharks." "They are? How so?" his teacher inquires. "Killer whales are mammals and sharks are fish. And guess what?" he continues. "What?" she patiently replies. "Killer whales don't bite people, but sharks sometimes do." After several more "Guess whats," his teacher finally asks, "Benjamin, how did you learn so much about killer whales?" He shrugs, "Oh, I don't know—my dad and I read about it a lot." And he runs off to share this fascinating information with his friends.

Children are natural knowledge seekers—whether "cooking" in the classroom kitchen, drawing, playing on a slide, or gathering whale facts like Benjamin. They want to learn about their world, and they're eager to share their ideas and experiences with others. They'll search for opportunities to discover new information, as they aspire to become more and more expert on a topic. Chances are that Benjamin, known to his class as the "orca whale expert," and his dad have been reading, talking, watching videos, and playing all sorts of games about whales and sharks for the last few days, and that Benjamin's knowledge and vocabulary have grown exponentially with each new encounter and engaging experience.

What we now know is that in the course of learning about whales, Benjamin is learning about literacy. Children's search for knowledge and the vocabulary words to express their ideas are integrally intertwined with learning to read and write. As children acquire knowledge, they become fascinated to learn about the tools of communication—reading and writing—and what they can do with them. They'll often pretend to read a book on spiders, or use a combination of writing and drawing to describe the worms they discover in their backyard. Recent research (Bransford, Brown, & Cocking, 2000) in the cognitive sciences powerfully demonstrates that children's ultimate success in reading—their ability to read for understanding—requires a great deal of vocabulary and knowledge along with the skills of reading. You simply can't have one without the other.

Yet the press for academic success has recently overwhelmed voices that call for the interplay of knowledge and skills. Curriculum packages, adorned with the trappings of early childhood puppets and playthings, provide hours of activities, all targeted to learning basic sounds and letter skills. Described as compensatory programs, these preschool programs presumably play catch-up, helping children who are considered less fortunate develop the skills that children from more privileged circumstances are learning.

But here's the tragic irony. Reading achievement in the earliest years may look like it's just about letters and sounds—but it's not. Successful reading, as will become abundantly clear by grades 3 and 4, consists of knowing a relatively small store of unconscious procedural skills, accompanied by a massive and slowly built-up store of conscious content knowledge. It is knowledge and the disposition to want to learn more that encourage children to question, discover, evaluate, and invent new ideas and that enable them to become successful readers.

Therefore, meaning—not sounds or letters—drives children's earliest experiences with print. Four-year-old Edward repeatedly asks his teacher to reread a favorite book not because he's driven to learn about print concepts. Rather, it's what's inside the book that matters to him. Fascinated with

Meaning drives children's earliest experiences with print.

"trash trucks," he wants to read in order to learn how they work. In the same way, Rebekah asks her teacher to reread a book about "the very hungry caterpillar," not to learn about color names, but to understand how an animal can transform into a beautiful butterfly. Content and the desire to know many things is what drive Edward and Rebekah to learn about reading and writing.

We wrote this book with Benjamin, Edward, Rebekah, and their friends in mind. It's a practical guide for linking early literacy skills and content knowledge. It will help teachers connect children's genuine desire for making meaning with ways to help them formulate and communicate their ideas. When their minds are engaged, children become motivated to better understand why literacy is important and how it serves to function in their day-to-day activities, and in their lifelong pursuit of learning.

About the Book

Children's knowledge and skills don't just develop magically overnight. Teachers need to purposefully plan experiences and intentionally engage children in knowledge-building experiences and rich conversations and interactions to support their learning. Given the sheer amount of content that children need to know and the challenge of providing developmentally appropriate learning experiences, such planning and preparation may sometimes seem overwhelming.

To make things easier, we've developed a framework that emphasizes the most powerful research-based literacy practices. Each of these five essential practices is strongly linked to children's achievement (Dickinson & Neuman, 2006; Neuman & Dickinson, 2001). They are

* A supportive learning environment
* Reading aloud to children
* Singing, rhyming, and word play
* Developmental writing
* Literacy-related play activities

In Chapters 2 through 6, we'll focus on each of these essential practices in depth, highlighting the research base and proven strategies to implement in the classroom. Then, in Chapters 7 through 11, we'll show you how to put the five essentials into practice to promote children's content learning. Chapters on math, science, social studies, the arts, and physical education will describe what children need to know and be able to do—the content standards and benchmarks established by experts for helping children get ready for school. Using the five essentials listed above, we'll then focus on guiding children's developing understandings, showing you how to integrate content and communication in ways that support children's interests and ideas.

We think you'll find that literacy learning can be meaningful, useful, and great fun for children as they explore, discover, and develop new knowledge of the world around them. And we hope you'll communicate this information with parents by sharing the ideas in Chapter 12, knowing that parent involvement is an important key to children's learning and development.

The Foundation of Reading and Writing— Language!

Before we jump right into the topic of literacy, let's first address its foundation—language. Literacy is based on a solid foundation of oral language development. Whether we are speaking or writing, we are using language to share our ideas with others. Whether we are listening or reading, we are trying to understand the meaning of someone else's words. Children who have well-developed language skills will be able to apply this knowledge as they learn to read and write.

The early years from birth to age 5 are critically important for language development. Research

(Biemiller, 2003) strongly confirms that children who know more words can learn more rapidly from their environment, whether someone is speaking to them, reading to them, or later when they are reading independently. Strong comprehension skills in elementary school, therefore, are built upon the foundation of oral language skills that develop during a child's first five years. From their first words, children learn language from those around them. So, whether they are at home or at school, children need to be surrounded by adults who speak with them as much as possible. It is imperative that we are intentional in helping the children in our classrooms to develop their listening, comprehending, and speaking skills to prepare them for school and for life.

How Do I Create Knowledge-Building Language Experiences?

Understand how important you are in this process. Children are always listening to the adults around them. The words and phrases that you use often will quickly become a part of the children's vocabularies. Sometimes, it's very funny to hear children parrot the little teacher phrases that you use. During play, you might hear one child say to another, "Listen carefully, everyone" or "Please sit crisscross applesauce." You'll realize that even when you don't know it, children are listening to and learning from your language.

At the same time, it's important to remember that children can't learn or understand language that they have never heard. Sometimes teachers and parents worry that children won't understand big words, so they choose not to use them. You might explain that animals go to sleep during the winter but choose not to use the word *hibernate* out of concern that this word is too difficult. If you stop and remember that your words are one of the main sources for giving a child new knowledge, you'll realize that skipping the big word is a missed opportunity. PreK teachers who want their students to develop strong oral language skills and new ideas must model complex vocabulary and grammar to help children learn.

Look for opportunities to expose children to words and concepts that they may not know, and take advantage of these teachable moments. For example, try to use language that is challenging, always remaining attentive to whether or not a child can comprehend what you are saying. Give explanations and examples, particularly when you are teaching a new word or phrase. "When an animal goes to sleep for the winter, we say it is *hibernating*." Then, provide opportunities for children to practice their new language: "Do you remember what we call it when animals go to sleep for the winter? We call it *hibernating*." Incidental comments like these begin to build a storehouse of new words and knowledge.

By exposing children to complex language, you will begin to help them learn to express thoughts, feelings, and ideas. There is a big difference between the child who only has the language to say, "I want a cookie," and the child who can explain to you all about the cookies his class had for snack, such as "I like the white parts of oreo cookies because it's delicious and covers my mouth with sweets!" Descriptive words like *delicious* help children articulate their feelings and convey much more information.

It's also helpful to provide gentle feedback when children mispronounce words or use language incorrectly. Children's misuse or mispronunciation of language can be charming. Often, adults think this is so delightful that they hesitate to model the correct usage or they may even encourage a child to continue making the same mistake. In the long run, however, it's not helpful to the child. When Erica said, "I *renember* the pumpkin farm," her teacher responded by modeling the correct pronunciation of the word. "Erica, I'm glad you *re-**mem**-ber* that trip. We had so much fun." Helping children to use their new words, however, is far more helpful than correcting their pronunciation. As young language learners, it's important for them to feel comfortable in giving their new words a "go" without having to worry that they are making mistakes.

Once you pay attention to your own use of language, you'll realize that opportunities to strengthen children's language and create knowledge-building opportunities are available at almost every moment of the day (Neuman & Roskos, 2005). Your day is filled with moments for you to "give language" by using new words or by modeling appropriate grammar and usage. In each chapter, we'll provide helpful hints for using language to support children's vocabulary development and content knowledge.

How Do I Know Children Are Learning? Informing Instruction

How do we know children are learning? Knowing how to pace instruction and how to support children's learning requires informed instructional decision making and a plan of action. This is the heart of assessment—the process of observing, recording, and documenting what children know and are able to do (Neuman & Roskos, 2005).

Effective assessment (Neuman, Copple, & Bredekamp, 2000) should enable teachers to do the following:

* Monitor and document children's progress over time
* Ensure that instruction is responsive and appropriately matched to children's needs
* Identify children who might need additional instruction
* Inform and involve parents

Therefore, in this approach, teaching and assessment are really complementary processes; in fact, one activity informs the other. In our work, we have adhered to the five principles listed on page 12:

Throughout the book, we'll provide informal strategies for assessing children's progress. You'll see opportunities to take stock of what children are learning to help examine benchmarks of progress for linking literacy and content learning. We'll suggest different forms of assessment, including documentation, retellings, portfolios, checklists, and observation activities, in Chapters 7 through 11.

But we need to remember that assessment is a means and not an end in itself. As such, it must be conducted by responsible and informed adults to benefit children's learning, with the ultimate goal of helping to nurture their knowledge and understanding.

FIVE ASSESSMENT PRINCIPLES

1. Assessment should support children's development. Good assessment helps to identify children's strengths, needs, and progress toward learning goals. This information can be used for program planning and decision making to ensure that instruction is responsive to and appropriate for children's current level.

2. Assessment should use a variety of tools, including collections of children's work (such as inventions, writings, and drawings) and records of conversations with children. Multiple methods ensure a more valid and reliable assessment of a children's program in its many dimensions and forms.

3. Assessment should encourage children to observe and reflect on their own progress. Asking for children's input can be a key factor in helping them learn and take ownership of their successes.

4. Assessment must avoid cultural bias. Children from different linguistic groups and backgrounds have varied experiences. Appropriate tools are critical for examining what children know, and what they need to learn.

5. Assessment should help to inform parents and involve them in children's learning. When teachers and parents understand the abilities of their learners, they make better decisions on what new experiences should be offered to help them develop further, and they create better connections between home and school learning.

The Five Essential Early Literacy Practices

Oral and written language are really just two sides of the same coin. Every time we promote children's literacy development, we also promote their oral language development; similarly, every time we emphasize oral language, we promote literacy learning. Children's quest for knowledge can be addressed to promote both their oral and written language abilities.

What are the most effective strategies to promote oral and written language? Research confirms five key essential practices that are directly tied to children's early literacy development (Neuman & Roskos, 1998). Briefly, they are:

1. A SUPPORTIVE LEARNING ENVIRONMENT

Supportive learning environments engage children in language. They provide both a physical and psychological place for learning. The physical space refers to the way teachers arrange things in classrooms. The psychological space includes the mood, tone, and values that teachers promote in learning.

When teachers spend time on an activity, children get the message that it's a valuable pursuit. If you engage children in conversation, so will they. If you sit with a different group each day and start a discussion, you'll find that children will follow your lead. You'll hear one child say to the group, "Let's talk about everyone's favorite snack" or "What did everyone do after school yesterday?" In

Chapter 2, we'll focus on creating spaces where language is valued. We'll encourage you to organize your space to foster learning and listening.

2. SHARED BOOK READING

Shared book reading is the single most powerful way to promote children's vocabulary and understanding of a topic (Snow, Burns, & Griffin, 1998). When children interact with adults during read-alouds, they practice communicating about ideas and using words in books. Children learn the difference between "book language" and everyday language, and soon they learn to tell their own stories as well. They'll pretend to read a book using book language like "once upon a time" and make new versions of favorite stories in their own words. The knowledge and vocabulary that children gain from read-alouds during the preK years can help them comprehend new stories and understand the more complex text structures of content reading in the upper grades.

As you'll find in Chapter 3, informational books are a powerful way to introduce children to new concepts and new words. Often during a read-aloud, children are exposed to knowledge and language that they would not have the opportunity to encounter in their day-to-day lives. For example, when you read a book about rain forests, children learn exciting new vocabulary such as *rain forest, canopy, toucan,* or *leaf-cutter ant.* They'll see pictures of things that are not part of their daily experiences. And when we give children new language and new knowledge, we support their ability to acquire more knowledge as they build more-complex schemas in learning.

3. SONGS, RHYME, AND WORD PLAY

Singing, rhyming, and word play enable children to focus on the sounds of language. As you'll learn in Chapter 4, the more opportunities children have to play with language, the more they'll be able to hear its sounds. For example, nursery rhymes have been shown to be extraordinarily important in helping children build a repertoire of common rhymes and rhythms (Maclean, Bryant, & Bradley, 1987). These playful activities support children's ability to hear the sounds of language, or what we describe as "phonological awareness," which will become especially important when children begin to read and write.

Songs, rhymes, and word play are also helpful in teaching children new words. The more words children know, the better they will be at hearing the sounds of language. And the more intentionally you emphasize the sounds in words, the better prepared children will be when they enter kindergarten.

4. DEVELOPMENTAL WRITING

Alongside oral language, writing has its roots in young children's growing ability to represent ideas, thoughts, and sounds symbolically. As you'll see in Chapter 5, children begin to use letters to stand for a word, or somewhat later, a sound. In their developmental spelling (some call it "invented spelling"), they develop a rather systematic way to represent sounds in words they consider important. While these spellings might look rather unusual to adults, they are actually important indicators of children's increasing awareness of the relationships between sounds and letters. For example, a child might write *sn* for *sun* or *luv* for *love*. In doing so, children are actively constructing a writing system that as they gain more experience and knowledge, will be modified many times, resulting in a fair approximation of traditional spelling.

Although handwriting and correct spelling are skills that children must eventually master, these skills are *not* the focus when we engage children in writing. As you'll see in Chapter 5, developmental writing is a form of communication for children, and an important motivation for learning about literacy.

5. LITERACY-RELATED PLAY

Play is essential for early literacy development (Roskos & Christie, in press). When children play, they develop oral language skills, and at the same time, children's language helps them to embellish play. The interconnectedness of this relationship is one of the many reasons that early childhood educators advocate play time. When children interact in play situations, they practice the language they know by applying it to their play and by stretching their uses of words in challenging ways.

Children use language to organize their play: "I'm going to ride the red trike first." "You're it." "You be the cat and I'm the owner." Part of this organization requires using language for conflict resolution. As in any pursuit when there are multiple people involved, at some point there will be disagreement over what should occur: "No. I want to be the owner. You be the baby cat." Play allows children, perhaps with adult help at first, to learn to negotiate difference of opinion. Play enables children to use language to express ideas and suggestions, to acknowledge disagreement, and to discuss and discover solutions.

When children play, they try out new language that they have recently learned. Often, this is language they've heard in a story or while listening to adults speak. Perhaps, you'll hear children pretending to be characters from a story you've read or incorporating new information from a topic the class is studying. You may hear a child in the dramatic play area say, "I'm the conductor on the train. Ticket please!" or a child in the block area ask a friend, "Wanna build a skyscraper?" Imaginary play allows children to practice exciting words like *conductor* or *skyscraper* that they otherwise may not have opportunity to use in their day-to-day lives.

What Children Need to Learn to Be Successful Readers and Writers

Literacy practices alone, however, are not sufficient to create successful readers and writers. Children are goal directed; they actively seek information. They are, for instance, fascinated with science concepts—what "sinks" and what "floats," how sand and water feel, how animals sleep and thrive in the wild. It is these kinds of questions that drive their thirst for knowledge. They come to preschool with background knowledge, skills, beliefs, and emerging concepts that significantly influence what they're likely to notice about their environment and how they are likely to organize and interpret it. The child who has been exposed to many different everyday activities, like pumping gas with her dad, writing shopping lists, going grocery shopping, and visiting the library, is likely to come to school with an intuitive understanding of how numbers work, why it's important to write things down, how to recognize some environmental print, and the joys of storybook reading. These past experiences influence her abilities to remember, reason, solve problems, and acquire new knowledge.

Even in infancy, children are active learners. They want to figure out how things work. Research confirms that babies give precedence to certain kinds of incoming information: the language of their caregiver, movement of objects, and colors in their surroundings. Children construct new knowledge and understanding based on what they already know and believe.

What this means is that learning is enhanced when teachers pay attention to the knowledge and beliefs that children bring to their learning tasks. This is a way to engage them in gaining new knowledge. It is the connection to developing more-complex understandings and the ability to transfer what they have learned to new problems and settings.

To develop competence in any area of inquiry, children must develop a foundation of factual information. Experts, even little ones like Benjamin, draw on a richly structured information base. The ability to talk about something, give explanations, and plan are all closely intertwined with experiences that provide children with a great infusion of information.

Yet knowledge of a large set of disconnected facts, especially for young children, is not really learning. To develop competence in subject areas, children must have many opportunities to learn with understanding. Deep understanding of subject matter transforms basic facts into more usable knowledge.

Therefore, your task is to engage children actively and move them in the direction of greater expertise. This will require both a deepening of their knowledge base and the development of conceptual understandings for each subject area.

Making this happen is a major challenge. The emerging science of learning (Bransford et al., 2000) underscores the importance of focusing on what is taught and teaching it with sufficient depth to allow key concepts to be learned, while monitoring children's progress along the way. We've developed a strategy that will enable you to do this, and we present it in Chapters 7 through 11. First, we've adapted state standards to guide you in identifying what preschool children need to know and be able to do, along with useful benchmarks for 3- and 4-year-olds. Specifically, we focus on the following subject areas:

* **Mathematics:** Number sense and counting; measurement; statistics and probability, organizing, and analyzing data about different patterns and relationships
* **Science:** The physical properties of objects, living things, the earth, and the environment
* **Social Studies:** How people live, work, get along with others, shape and are shaped by their environment; geography in relation to other people and objects
* **The Arts:** Creative activity, music, dance, drawing, and visual arts
* **Physical Education:** Health and well-being, nutrition, and healthy lifestyles

We then apply the five essential literacy practices to these content areas in ways that respect children's development, emphasizing various materials that meet the developmental needs of young children *and* enhance children's content knowledge at the same time.

Throughout the book, you'll find examples of lesson plans, activities, and interesting topics of study to help children explore rich content in the disciplines. The goal of these lessons is to help children use their background knowledge to learn more about the topic and to build conceptual understandings that they can use to apply what they've learned in order to solve meaningful problems.

Play is essential for early literacy development. It enables children to express ideas, cooperate, acknowledge disagreement, and discuss and discover solutions.

Closing

As knowledge seekers, children show a remarkable interest in their world. They want to know what things are, how they work, and how they relate to one another. This desire for better and deeper understanding of their world begins in early childhood and continues through adulthood.

Let us use children's natural curiosity, interests, and developing abilities to enhance learning and communication. Literacy learning should not come at the expense of children's desire to learn in meaningful ways. Rather, early literacy should serve as a springboard to help children explore, interpret, and engage in learning experiences of sufficient depth and intellectual integrity, allowing them to take control of their own learning.

Implementing any curriculum requires that teachers make a commitment. For children to become true knowledge seekers, teachers must be familiar with the process of inquiry, the language of each discipline, and the concepts that help children organize information usefully. But equally important, teachers must have a grasp of children's growth and development and how they learn, in ways that respect what they bring, and what they seek to know.

CHAPTER 2

Supportive Learning Environment

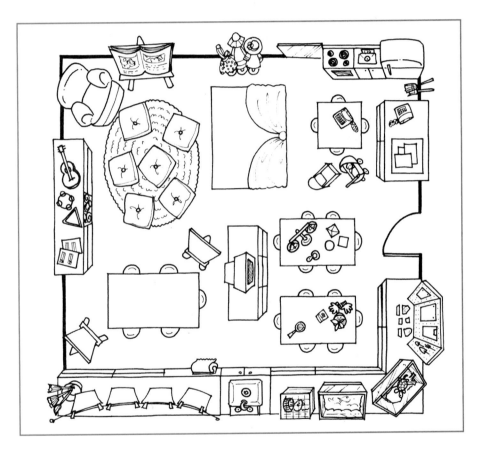

*T*his is a sketch of Shelley Johnson's preschool classroom. Right away we can spot the places for greeting and meeting, for reading and telling stories, for learning and sharing together. We notice the smaller spaces that offer opportunities for children to work well in small groups, to listen and be listened to, and to use language. We can imagine the situations that invite exploration and action in the activity and play areas. This is an engaging place for our eager young children. It sends the message, "Come in, come in! Play, learn, and have fun with your friends!"

In this chapter we invite you to "come in" and learn more about how to design supportive learning environments for young children. What we offer is a design guide for busy teachers, who often face difficult issues of limited space and materials and how to get the best use out of them. Not only research based, the guide that follows is also practical. It describes the basics of room design and how to architecturally plan a space that promotes social interaction, exploration, and learning. It explains how to incorporate print and educational content into the structure and arrangement of space, so that the environment can become another teacher in the classroom. It identifies some basic considerations for creating environments that are welcoming, accommodating of diversity, and flexible. We've included lots of charts, photos, and sketches in the guide to support your design skills and also to spark your creative genius. In the end, we want to inspire you as thoughtful designers of educational and caring environments for young readers and writers.

What the Research Says

Before getting into the details of design, be aware that good design is based on solid research, which is summarized in the box below.

Based on hundreds of studies, these critical design ideas converge on one important fact: environment matters. And for this important reason, you need to create well-designed indoor learning environments for your young children. The organization of a space, as well as its structures and materials, and the attractive ways in which these are set up, should give children a sense of well being and at the same time invite them to explore, learn, and communicate. Now let's go further into the creative world of room design for a close-up look at this essential practice.

SUMMARY OF RESEARCH ON SUPPORTIVE LEARNING ENVIRONMENTS

* The amount, arrangement, and organization of physical space influences human behavior (Greenman, 1988; Phyfe-Perkins, 1980). Where we are and with whom have an impact on what we think, do, and say.

* A print-rich physical environment stimulates literacy behaviors (Morrow, 2005; Neuman et al., 2001; Wolfersberger, Reutzel, Sudweeks, & Fawson, 2004). Children will eagerly explore print in their environment just as they do other things in the environment.

* Well-coordinated settings for activity (space, materials, purpose) support development and learning (Cohen, Raudenbush & Ball, 2002; Prescott & Jones, 1984; Tharp & Gallimore, 1988; Wachs, 1987). For example, book corners in a cozy space with ample books and opportunities for children to read together push along children's developing literacy ideas (Morrow, 2002; Neuman et al., 2001; Owocki, 2005; Schickedanz, 1999).

* The amount and quality of adult-child talk has a tremendous influence on children's language use and literacy concepts (Hart & Risley, 1995; Heath, 1983). Words children know and say can only come from those used by others around them and from the books adults lovingly share with them.

Close Up on Practice

PLANNING THE STRUCTURE AND ARRANGEMENT OF SPACE

Structuring and arranging your classroom space involves four steps: (1) measuring classroom space; (2) allocating space to meet educational goals; (3) locating activity areas in space; and (4) arranging space to clearly indicate activity areas.

Measuring Space

In the beginning of design work there is bare physical space. Before any planning can be done, you need to measure and know how much space you have to work with. The total amount of space—the square footage (i.e., length times width)—determines the possibilities for your classroom layout. Early childhood settings, as we know, vary tremendously in size, ranging from church basements to homes to specially built child care centers. Facilities standards recommend at least 950 square feet for pre-school classrooms (see www.edlawcenter.org). Some experts on child care design recommend 50 square feet per child to promote positive interactions (Olds, 2001). As a point of comparison, most kindergarten classrooms measure 1,200–1,500 square feet, averaging 60–75 square feet per child for a class of 20 children. Standard primary classrooms are somewhat smaller, approximately 900 square feet. This is 45 square feet per child for a class of 20.

How much space is just right for early childhood classrooms is not known. But evidence suggests that fewer than 25 square feet per child is too crowded for young children. They are more aggressive with one another, less social, and less involved with ongoing activities. Put simply, they are grouchy when crowded! Under these circumstances too little space can interfere with learning which needs to be immediately addressed. Use the handy chart in Figure 2.1 as a guide when you take this fundamental first step in planning your early learning environment.

But what if your classroom space is just too small? Under these conditions, you need to create a sense of space and use the space flexibly. You can do this by reducing clutter throughout, providing just enough indoor play areas (about four), limiting the number of children in play areas, and allowing enough space for whole-group activities. Use small-scale furniture and dividers that are easily movable to rearrange space for large- and small-group activities.

Allocating Space

Space needs to be allocated to fit the educational goals of your program, one of which is helping your young learners develop and grasp the early literacy skills they need for school. What this means in practical design terms is that you need to divide up the space you

CALCULATING CLASSROOM SPACE	
Physical classroom space for 20 children:	
1,500 square feet to allow	75 square feet per child
1,200 square feet to allow	60 square feet per child
900 square feet to allow	45 square feet per child
600 square feet to allow	30 square feet per child
TOO CROWDED	25 square feet per child

FIGURE 2.1

have into areas for work and play. Different architects suggest different ways of going about this. Anita Olds (1982), for example, suggests dividing the space into "neighborhoods," such as the Quiet, Relaxed Neighborhood, the Movement Neighborhood, the Wet and Messy Neighborhood, and so on. Architects Ann Taylor, Robert Aldrich, and George Vlastos (1988) recommend "zones," such as the research and library zone, the soft zone for privacy and quiet play, the technology zone, and the living things zone, where fish, crabs and small animals might reside.

Architects' approaches to layouts vary, but in general there are six common places you should think about when allocating classroom space:

* Entryway
* Play and project areas
* Large-group meeting area
* Library/book area
* Technology area
* Teacher area

Each of these areas includes possibilities for displays and storage systems. Each may include appealing ambient features, such as living things (plants, fish tank), light (from windows or lamps), and texture (wall hangings, cushions, carpeting). The entryway of the Diana School (in Reggio Emilia, Italy), for example, displays photos of the teachers and staff along with schedules and upcoming meetings high on the wall. Below, at children's eye level, are self-portraits and small pocket mirrors that open up for children to see themselves as they come in (and even make a funny face now and then).

Your decision on how much space to allocate to these different areas sends a message about the educational choices that form the basis of your program. Places with well-stocked play areas, attractive displays of children's art and projects, and a cozy corner library filled with books and playthings communicate the value placed on talking, reading, writing, and learning.

As you make design decisions, keep in mind the amount of space you have (from the measuring you did). Know that about 30 percent of the space is typically taken up by classroom furniture (chairs, tables, dividers, shelves). So this leaves about 70 percent of your space free for moving about, spreading out for play and work, and adding novel structures (e.g., a tent).

Locating Activity in Space

Activity areas need to be located in space. For these areas to function well, you need to be strategic about where you place each one. To get started, locate the area for large-group time first. This area will require about 6 square feet per child—that is 120 square feet for a class of 20 children.

Next, sort out the quieter areas from the noisier ones. For example, place the noisier areas, such as project work and block play, near one another and quieter areas, such as the cozy corner library and the computer station, close together.

Consider the pathways children will use to get from one area to another. Obviously, clear pathways are essential. Be mindful that different pathways encourage different kinds of behavior. Those that meander with forks and Ts encourage shopping and browsing for activities, as well as watching what others are doing. Straight paths help children make a direct beeline from point A to point B. Wide-open boulevard-like routes elicit in children a strong urge to run.

Pathways can also exercise motor skills by incorporating tunnels, objects to walk around (e.g., small towers), stepping-stones, and balance beams (on a rug) like railroad tracks along the way.

Arranging Space

How space is divided and marked is an essential aspect of good room design. It reveals the structure of interior space, which should be abundantly clear to children and adults. Dividers help to structure and define space whether they are real (e.g., walls) or improvised (e.g., a set of hanging plants). All kinds of dividers are possible as long as they are sturdy, stable, and safe. So let your creative juices flow. Use walls (solid and portable), panels (latticework, blinds, fabric), mini-dividers (pegboards and benches), lofts, and platforms to establish boundaries and borders and to create nooks and crannies. Consider less obvious means of defining space, such as hanging plants, artificial trees, low fences, and mobiles, to create the illusion of special places. Make the dividers multifunctional by building in busy boxes, attaching telephones, providing holes to peek through and poke through, adding mirrors, and including print and picture displays.

It is important to structure and define space clearly.

In addition to facilitating organization, the thoughtful arrangement of your space gives it an identity that helps children make connections. Different spaces encourage different kinds of thoughts, language, and action. And with the passage of time, these spaces evolve into stimulating places where wonderful ideas can come and go (just like the children who have them).

ORGANIZING MATERIALS AND TOOLS

The element that turns a physical space into a learning environment for children is what it contains, which we call its "resources." Major resources in learning environments include materials and tools, time, and—the richest of all—people. What makes everyday objects, toys, games, kits, books, play props, and tools educational, after all, is the quality of interactions their users have with them.

Literacy Materials and Tools

A well-stocked early learning environment contains an abundance of literacy items. Our recommendations are summarized in Figure 2.2. We vigorously promote provisioning the classroom with abundant print! But we also urge caution in not overstuffing the environment with print that serves no real purpose in your educational program. Too often we've seen the print-rich environment spill into a print-littered environment, where print quickly loses its meaning and real use for children.

We know that the sheer presence of books and other print materials stimulates children's exploration of print and motivates them to know more about it—how it works and what it can do. Print that is available, however, must also be accessible to young children's hands and minds. From a design perspective this entails the following:

* Locating print at the child's eye level to the extent possible
* Placing print materials throughout the classroom
* Ensuring print materials are developmentally suitable and age appropriate
* Creating places to explore and use print meaningfully

Some Content-Oriented Suggestions

Active preschoolers are not driven to learn print for print's sake. Rather, what motivates young learners is the need to explore their immediate environment and gather experiences firsthand. They want to handle objects and materials, observe things and happenings around them, compare one thing with another, question and argue about things, and test things out. They are driven to answer the big questions: What is it? How does it work?

It is in their response to these immediate urges that children acquire knowledge, increase vocabulary, and advance their communication skills. At the same time they develop an awareness of, and interest and concern for, the living and nonliving things of their world. Here are a few ways to organize materials and objects so that print supports the desire of young children to learn about their world and exposes them to basic ideas and terms in science, art, math, and social studies.

ESSENTIAL LITERACY MATERIALS FOR THE PRESCHOOL LITERACY ENVIRONMENT

Toys	Books	Print	Writing/ Communication Tools
⁎ Magnetic letters ⁎ Alphabet blocks and puzzles ⁎ Puppets ⁎ Dolls of both genders, representing a variety of cultures ⁎ Open-ended play materials, salvaged from "real life" (old kitchen tools, old cell phones, egg cartons, fabric, paper tubes, laundry baskets, boxes) ⁎ Wood blocks and Duplo blocks ⁎ Collections of props for dramatic play (grocery store: brown bags, food posters, sign with store hours, pretend food; restaurant: place mats, play money, open/closed signs, aprons, order pads; transportation play: luggage, travel brochures, tickets) ⁎ Dress-up clothes, play silks ⁎ Sorting and matching letter cards ⁎ Sequencing cards ⁎ Word making games, like Scrabble	⁎ ABC books ⁎ Big books ⁎ Books with predictable patterns ⁎ Rhyming books ⁎ Poetry ⁎ Nursery rhymes ⁎ Books with photographs ⁎ Fictional picture books ⁎ Informational books about science and nature ⁎ Picture dictionaries ⁎ Books stored in easily accessible bins, sorted by theme or genre, rotated frequently	⁎ Functional sign-up sheets (such as library checkouts) ⁎ Alphabet chart ⁎ Classroom schedules and charts ⁎ Shared writing pieces, including children's own dictated words ⁎ Labels on objects around the room (e.g., door, shelf, table, chair, toy bins, storage containers) ⁎ Children's names displayed on lists, charts, and cubbies ⁎ Collections of printed materials that supplement dramatic play props (e.g., old checkbooks, business cards, menus, receipt books, event tickets, No Smoking signs, maps, store advertisements, Work in Progress signs) ⁎ Posters that reflect children's interests (e.g., fine art posters labeled with title and artist's name) ⁎ Newspapers, magazines, catalogs, television guides ⁎ Song charts or cards	⁎ A variety of jumbo crayons, pencils, pens, markers ⁎ A variety of paper (different sizes, with lines, no lines, construction paper, index cards, etc.) ⁎ Rubber alphabet stamps and ink pads ⁎ Stationery, envelopes, address book ⁎ Blank notebooks or journals ⁎ Portable writing materials, such as small chalkboards and chalk or small dry erase boards and markers ⁎ Tape recorder and blank tapes to record children's stories or observations

FIGURE 2.2

* **Inventories.** Making an inventory of what an area contains is a fun and practical way to build vocabulary and counting skills. It also serves as a handy reference for checking when supplies are getting low and need to be replenished. Involving children in taking inventory and keeping track of supplies develops their sense of responsibility for maintaining the environment and also encourages them to link picture with print. Here's an example.

* **Mini-Museums.** Mini-museums are small spaces where collections of objects are kept and displayed. We really like mini-museums because they give children the opportunity to take a close and careful look at the everyday bits and pieces that surround them. At the same time, close scrutiny of the ordinary (rocks, seeds, buttons, etc.) lays the foundations for many of the big ideas in science and the arts. Take a look at the shells mini-museum as a model of the many different

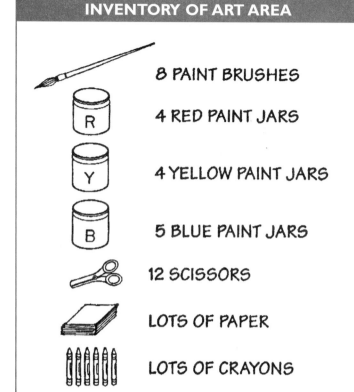

INVENTORY OF ART AREA

8 PAINT BRUSHES

4 RED PAINT JARS

4 YELLOW PAINT JARS

5 BLUE PAINT JARS

12 SCISSORS

LOTS OF PAPER

LOTS OF CRAYONS

MAKING A MINI-MUSEUM

Words You Can Use	Things You Will Need	What To Do
* museum * specimen * examine * observe * look * explore * collection * identify * label * name * discover	* Large, shallow cardboard box * 24 half-pint milk cartons * Collection of objects of interest to children, including: — rocks — fur — feathers — shells — seeds — bark — teeth — fabric	1. Remove tops of milk cartons and place in box. 2. Staple cartons together. 3. Fill cartons with specimens collected. 4. Label the specimens using print and pictures. 5. Talk about the items with the children. 6. Invite the children to explore the museum.

kinds of museums young children can make, label (with your help), and share with friends.

SHELLS MINI-MUSEUM

* **Collections.** Collections are more varied and less permanent than mini-museums. They may contain objects (like buttons) or amounts (like water). We know children are avid collectors of fascinating objects, or what some 4-year olds we know call "suspicious stuff" (in the sense of *intriguing*). Collections of shells, stones, seeds, toy animals, blocks, and so on offer many possibilities for sorting, comparing, weighing, and measuring. Different kinds of seeds, for example, introduce children to words like *wildflower seeds, ornamental gourd seeds, wheat, maize, barley,* and *oat seed.* Seed textures can be compared and described using different words: *rough, smooth, soft, hard, prickly.* Seeds can be measured—largest to smallest—and counted: *How many peas or beans does it take to fill a pudding cup?* All this talk about seeds builds background knowledge and also promotes children's phonological awareness, helps them to recognize letters and words, and draws their attention to the functions of print in naming and labeling. Here are some other ideas for building collections that reap learning benefits in different content domains.

1. Collect and sort buttons: large, small, two-hole, four-hole, plain, fancy.
2. Collect and compare amounts of rain.
3. Collect and display transparent things.
4. Collect and display shiny things.
5. Collect and sort things that float and sink. Be sure to label!

Storage

Storage systems in classrooms can do more than you think! Good storage maximizes the use of resources (because you can find them); builds up more resources (because you can store them); teaches children how things go together; extends and elaborates their play (because they can locate objects readily); teaches children to take responsibility for the upkeep of the classroom (because they know how to put objects away); and creates a sense of order and harmony (because everything has a place).

Storage can be open or closed, fixed or movable, multipurpose or specialized. An orderly classroom uses a balance of all three types. Following a few basic organizational techniques you can create "smart" storage systems that also teach.

* Locate storage units close to their point of use. For example, place manipulatives and supplies needed for an activity close at hand. Display books that relate to what is going on right in the area. This gives young children a chance to make choices, focus on what they plan to do, and follow through on their activities.

* Materials that are used together should be stored together in a logical way. Look at the storage system used for water play (Figure 2.3). The physical arrange-

"Smart" storage systems such as these also teach.

ment shows children how things go together as parts of a larger idea or network of ideas.

* The organization should be clear and understandable to its youngest users, 3- and 4-year-olds. It should be aesthetically pleasing. Simple, accurate language should be used to organize and label what is stored. Pictures and print should be bold and easy to read. High-quality graphics and labeling attract children's attention to print as a support for planning and interacting with what the space has to offer.

* The storage system should be safe. Avoid top-heavy shelving, base extenders that may cause tripping, and sharp corners or edges at children's eye level.

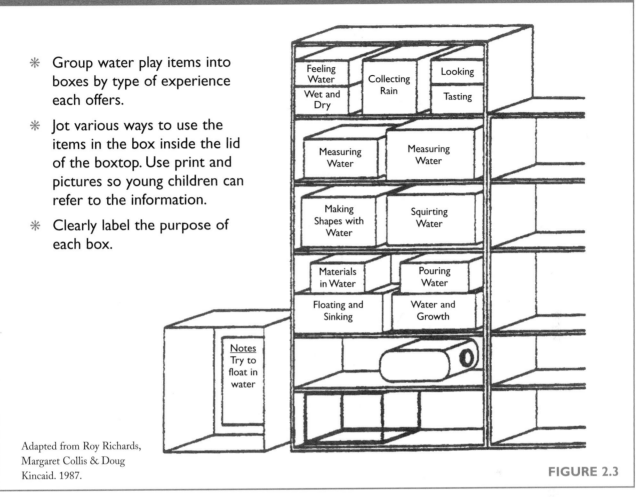

WATER PLAY STORAGE SYSTEM

* Group water play items into boxes by type of experience each offers.

* Jot various ways to use the items in the box inside the lid of the boxtop. Use print and pictures so young children can refer to the information.

* Clearly label the purpose of each box.

Feeling Water
Wet and Dry
Collecting Rain
Looking
Tasting
Measuring Water
Measuring Water
Making Shapes with Water
Squirting Water
Materials in Water
Pouring Water
Floating and Sinking
Water and Growth
Notes
Try to float in water

Adapted from Roy Richards, Margaret Collis & Doug Kincaid. 1987.

FIGURE 2.3

Signage

The purpose of signage (which we see all about us) and complementary graphics is to present information in ways that are easy to read, complete, and engaging. Following are some rules of thumb:

* Materials used for signs should be sturdy, with print in one color and the background in a second color.

* Print should be bold to attract and hold children's attention. To make print dynamic and bold, allow sufficient white space; use complementary images; use scale changes (small to large and large to small); make clear, crisp letters.

* Type style should be the same throughout an area or display, including the main topic, any graphics, and supplementary print information.

The learning environment should include signs with words children need to learn if they are to accomplish their play and work goals as well as your larger educational goals. But sometimes what signs mean is not abundantly clear. For example, the recently posted Wet Paint sign near the library door caused a flurry of questions (and ideas) among Shelley Johnson's preschoolers as they tried to discover what it meant. Signs should be arranged to develop children's visual and spatial perceptual skills, such as figure-ground discrimination, part-whole relationships, and shape recognition. Shelley's sign for blocks, for example, purposefully forms ideas of block size and shape.

Finally, signs should be strategically posted on walls and in corners, entryways, bathrooms, and window bays to invite children to learn (and study) words, the alphabet, numbers, color combinations, and print orientation.

SIGNAGE

Blocks

Putting Literacy Into Activity Settings in the Learning Environment

Up to this point, our design guide has dealt with how much, where, and in what ways classroom space is organized. Thoughtful design at this level starts to transform physical space into energetic learning environments rich in literacy experiences.

Another level of design focuses on activity settings. Elizabeth Prescott (1984) called activity settings "space-time units" that provide life to the program (p. 50). What she meant is that these places and the objects they contain stimulate thought and action and confront the child with the wonders and puzzles of the world. Well-designed activity settings put young children into the role of thinker and inquirer, budding reader and writer, awakening their curiosity and urging them to make sense of many experiences yet to come.

Features of Activity Settings

Every space we work or live in has activity settings—for example, the kitchen and living room at home, and the book corner and play area at school. Well-built activity settings in the classroom can be powerful promoters of language and literacy. It is helpful to imagine activity settings as three-dimensional spaces—more like small studios for work and play rather than subject-specific interest areas or centers (e.g., the science center). Here are a few design points to keep in mind when planning your activity settings.

* **Activity settings are places with boundaries and entries.** Make the boundaries abundantly clear so children know where the setting begins and ends. Recall our earlier discussion of dividers as a way to define space (see page 21). Use these to help establish a setting's boundaries. A well-bounded setting is often a well-used setting because it sends clear messages about its purpose.

* **Activity settings have size, shape, and height.** Size is a matter of getting it just right for the number and size of the users who will engage in an activity. A space that's too big can lead to too many children engaging in the activity (e.g., listening to audiobooks in the library corner). A space that's too small can make it difficult for children to accomplish an activity (e.g., bookmaking in the writing area). Shapes can vary, but remember that round and oddly angled areas are appealing to children. A feeling of height can be achieved by using hanging mobiles or signs, canopies, and cardboard facades on furniture.

* **Activity settings have personality.** The combined effects of a setting—its size, shape, height, furnishings, colors, surfaces, artwork—should create the feel of the place. Is it warm and cozy or businesslike and efficient? Is it calm and serene or kind of noisy and fun loving? Is it bright and cheery or sedate and reflective? Choice of activities, colors, textures, print, and graphics help to set the mood and tone.

* **Activity settings have rules.** Expectations are built into a setting through the arrangement of the furnishings, materials, and posted instructions. The placement of furnishings and materials can help children stay focused, remind them of what to do, and sustain activity. Instructions should be relevant, clear, and simple. A sign that says, No Hands Please, and a picture, as shown in the box below reminds our curious youngsters not to handle the precious snails in our terrarium.

* **Activity settings are aligned with program goals.** The essential point of an activity setting is to accomplish something, whether for play or more serious business. So in your classroom, you want activity settings to be in line with your program goals and philosophy. You want them to work together so well and so effectively that they become like another teacher in your room. To achieve this requires deliberate attention to the setup, the functional details, the materials, and the specific

"DON'T TOUCH" SIGN

No Hands Please

Activity settings should align with educational goals.

tasks of all your activity settings. Your goal is to organize content, language (vocabulary), and literacy into a coordinated set of learning experiences in each one. Further, you want most of these experiences to do the following:

- Develop children's thinking and reasoning skills
- Strengthen and expand what they know and can do
- Help them make connections to their everyday life
- Use language often and meaningfully
- Hold high expectations for children (thereby showing how much we value their capacity to learn)

This is challenging professional work but well worth the effort; thoughtful design builds the educational content in the environment and maximizes it as an opportunity for movement and interaction—the essentials of active learning (and teaching).

SITE VISITS

So now let's tour a few activity settings. We are going to take you to three popular early literacy activity settings in the early childhood classroom: the book area, the writing center, and the dramatic-play area. At each stop, we will point out the basic design elements, primary materials, an activity sampler, and architectural details that enhance the setting. As we go, keep in mind that activity settings vary in size, content, and architectural detail, depending on local conditions. There is no one "right" activity setting or collection of settings for all children.

BASICS

- Occupies approximately 10 percent of total classroom space
- Contains five to eight books per child (mixed genres)
- Has one open-faced bookshelf
- Contains traditional bookshelves, baskets for books
- Situated in a quiet location near computer
- Furnished with rug, pillows, rocking chair, stuffed animals

ACTIVITIES

- Book browsing
- Buddy reading
- Listening to stories
- "Reading" books on tape
- Puppet plays; felt board stories
- Playing library

MATERIALS

- Three to five new books each week (replacing older titles)
- Felt board and story characters
- Headsets and taped stories
- Story props (puppets) and text sets
- Electronic books and CD-ROMs (for computer)
- Writing tools and materials (e.g., pens, pencils, notebooks, index cards)

ARCHITECTURAL DETAILS

- Soft textures; muted colors
- Soft lighting; natural light
- Privacy corner
- Children's artwork; child-created books; photos of readers
- Book posters
- Displays of cultural items (e.g., photographs, decorations, artwork)

The Book Area. Book Areas in early childhood classrooms are not new. But what is new (and exciting) is the high-quality information we now have to design them. Take a look at the one in the photo above. Its physical layout, social opportunities, and symbolic features reflect what we know about effective book area design.

The Writing Center. We advocate including a distinct writing center in the early childhood classroom for several reasons. First, writing is a logical extension of drawing as a medium of expression and a critical pivot to reading (Both-de Vries, 2005; Ferriero & Teberosky, 1984; Vygotsky, 1978). Children need many opportunities to experiment with making marks to represent their ideas. Second, a writing center makes writing obvious in the environment. Like the art area, which highlights the value of artistic expression, the writing center highlights the value of written expression. And third, the writing center provides a central place to organize and arrange a wide assortment of

BASICS

- Contains a writing table and chairs
- Possesses sufficient space for three or four children
- Contains cubbies and trays to store writing supplies
- Has an alphabet chart at children's eye level
- Situated in a quiet location near computer
- Includes a bulletin board

ACTIVITIES

- Writing messages, letters, notes, stories
- Making books
- Forming letters and words
- Making lists
- Playing "school"
- Playing "office"

MATERIALS

- Writing tools: pencils, pens, markers, crayons
- Writing supplies: assorted paper, stationery, envelopes, index cards
- Bookmaking supplies: lined paper, construction paper, hole punch, brads
- References: picture dictionary, ABC books, informational books, storybooks, child-authored books, class name chart, concept books, calendar
- Stencils, letter stamps, letter forms, word cards, stickers
- Rulers, tape, sticky notes, large plastic clips

ARCHITECTURAL DETAILS

- Good lighting
- Bright colors; varied textures of materials (smooth, coarse, thick, thin)
- Displays of children's writing; word posters and charts
- Sample greeting cards, bookmarks, miniature books
- Posters of authors and illustrators
- Clear, brightly colored labels and directions

writing tools, paper supplies, and references. It serves as a supply depot for writing resources that children can use everywhere. Explore the writing center shown in the photo and the design features that make it a symbolic, functional, and motivating site in the classroom.

The Dramatic-Play Area. More-demanding early literacy expectations can push play to the edges of the early childhood learning environment. But we cannot let this happen because play is a powerful medium for early learning. In play, children stretch what they know and can do, as well as prac-

BASICS

- Has space for four or five children
- Possesses a clear entry-way into the space
- Feels room-like, with sense of sides and back
- Contains well-organized props appropriate to the setting
- Is adaptable
- Contains a sign with name of setting

ACTIVITIES

In the construction site:

- Reread, browse, and use related stories, songs, rhymes, information books
- Use construction-related words and phrases (e.g., hammer, tape measure, crane)
- Dress up and wear hard hats, goggles, tool belts
- Make plans and blueprints
- Post signs and warnings
- Construct buildings with cardboard

MATERIALS

- Theme-related props
- Handy writing tools and paper supplies
- Theme-related books (informational and stories)
- Environmental print
- Culturally relevant objects, books, and print
- Assorted authentic objects related to the setting

ARCHITECTURAL DETAILS

- Functional print to suggest and guide play activity
- Artificial greenery or trees and/or live plants
- Bright colors and fabrics
- Drawers, baskets, or cubbies for sorting props
- Photos of families, children, and community events
- Displays of children's artwork and writing

tice their emerging skills. The indoor environment should host inviting places to play, where children can use language and literacy frequently and meaningfully. Our tour ends here at this construction site play setting. It illustrates several important environment design principles: (1) a well-defined play space to guide children's interactions; (2) interrelated sets of theme-based materials that are appropriate, authentic, and functional; and (3) opportunities for variation and ownership of talk and activity in the setting.

Respecting Developmental Needs

Our guide would not be complete without a brief description of a few design considerations that accommodate children of different ages and levels of development in preschool. Three-year olds are different from 4-year-olds, and 4s are different from 5s. Moreover there is tremendous individual variation developmentally in the 3 to 5 age range. Young children really do grow by leaps and bounds, and their developmental prowess as well as their needs change rapidly. To ensure your physical space is appropriate for different ages and levels of development, keep these design points in mind as you plan.

1. The youngest children in your class will need more floor space for work and play, so plan the size of your play spaces and carpeted areas with your youngest learner in mind.

2. The oldest children in your class will need more challenging materials, books, and play objects, so stock the environment with resources that reflect a range of difficulty.

3. Special-needs children in your classroom may need space accommodations, as well as special materials, so consider how to make sensible adaptations that maintain a stimulating and active environment for all. A few are shown in Figure 2.4.

Establishing a Learning Environment

Our focus so far has been on designing physical space to create inviting places that say, *All young children welcome here!* We've talked about room layout, materials, and activity settings. We even went on a tour!

But there is still more to consider if the physical space in your room is to become an environment that guides and encourages learning. We will look at two more design concepts:

* Ensuring a certain level of predictability
* Creating a mood that fosters learning through interaction

PREDICTABILITY

Children like to feel in control of their environment, which in turn encourages them to explore and use what the environment has to offer. You can help children feel in control by building predictability into the environment.

One easy way to do so is to establish language and literacy routines that support the flow of activity across the day. Having children sign in is a good example of a literacy routine. Shelley Johnson explains: "Every day the children are given a piece of unlined paper with their first name already printed on it in forty-eight-point comic sans font. Papers are dated as a way of tracking the children's progress as they discover how to write their names throughout the year. Some children initially require adult guidance as to pencil grip, holding the paper still with their helping hand, which letter to start with, and so on. The daily exposure to and practice at forming their letters provides the children with a consistent activity that they can work on at their own level and progress at their own speed."

ADAPTATIONS FOR CHILDREN WITH SPECIAL NEEDS

In addition to the essential literacy materials listed on page 23, an environment for children with special needs should include these adaptations:

Toys	Books	Print	Writing/ Communication Tools
✳ Dress-up clothes with Velcro closures ✳ Washable cloth or vinyl alphabet letters ✳ Toys modified with suction cups, magnets or Velcro for stability ✳ Laminated game pieces and cards	✳ Large print books ✳ Books on slides or overhead projectors ✳ Books with symbols or pictures to indicate repeated lines ✳ Sturdy board books ✳ Scented books ✳ Tactile books ✳ Talking books ✳ Books with text labels (symbols or pictures); symbols to indicate repeated lines ✳ Page fluffers (small pieces of sponge glued to top right corner provides space between pages, making them easier to turn) ✳ Books with page tabs for easier turning ✳ Books in a three-ring binder (take books apart and place each page in a sheet protector, along with a piece of cardboard for reinforcement) ✳ Velcro on covers (a piece of rough, "male" Velcro on the covers helps the book stick to carpet, making the book stable while child is turning pages) ✳ Books on audiotape/video-tape/DVD ✳ Interactive storytelling software	✳ Tactile letters (sandpaper) ✳ Raised, colored, enlarged text (Wikki Sticks) ✳ Photos/pictures to accompany labels for toy bins and other storage containers ✳ Photos of children to accompany name labels ✳ Sign language boards and other communication displays	✳ Slant boards or book easels ✳ Jumbo pencil grips, weighted and/or tactile ✳ Flat-sided/ antiroll crayons and pencils ✳ Alphabet tracing templates or stencils ✳ Simple one-touch tape recorder ✳ Bulb-shaped finger crayons (with a hole to insert finger inside the crayon) ✳ Lap trays

FIGURE 2.4

Another way is to use charts. Charts are excellent reminders. Helpers, Weather, Question of the Day, Yes/No—these charts guide daily routines and should be displayed for children to see and read at their leisure. It's amazing how often children refer to them on their own. They even use them to remind us of what we are supposed to be doing!

MOOD

The mood or emotional qualities of a place help to foster in children a curiosity to understand. A number of room design features contribute to mood: organization of space, welcoming entries, sense of identity, homelike elements, and use of light and color. But nothing does more to establish mood than the opportunity for interaction that supports understanding. And to provide such opportunities you need to think small—small work and play spaces for small-group interactions, for forming relationships and attachments, for talking and explaining. You also need to have lots of small, informing conversations with children every chance you get. Here are five techniques you can use over and over again to create a prevailing emotional tone that sends the message *This is a place for being curious and for learning.*

1. **Clarify word meanings during conversations.** Teachers need to remember that young children are meeting many new words for the first time, and that even the meanings of commonly used words and phrases are often baffling to them. Even as it makes us smile, 4-year old Josie's comment that she has been waiting for "two whole whiles" should be a reminder to take the time to untangle children's confusions about word meanings. We might say, *Yes, Josie, you have been waiting for a long time. Look at my watch. You have been waiting from here* [9:30 a.m.] *to here* [10:00 a.m.]. *That's thirty minutes. That's a long while to wait for the bus to pick us up. It is a long time and the bus is very late!* Teachers need to take every opportunity to clarify what words mean during instructional times and in everyday conversations to build children's understandings.

2. **Use children's questions to help them make connections.** When children ask questions (even those with obvious answers, like "Do you love me?"), they are on a hunt for information, which they then use to build their knowledge of the world. Teachers are in an ideal position to support this knowledge-building process. When answering questions they can add information. (*Is it night for everybody? You know, when it's night here, it's day somewhere else. Isn't that amazing!*) They can provide on-the-spot explanations. (*Bet you wonder where the sun goes at night. It doesn't go to sleep like we do. It is always shining. Our earth spins and it moves around the sun, so sometimes we can't see the sun from where we are. It is night.*) And they can end an answer with another question that opens the door wider on children's thinking. (*So . . . when do you think we see the sun again each day?*)

3. **Wonder about the world together.** Teachers instill a sense of wonder in children when they frequently show their own wonder about things around them. They need to model being an active, curious learner who does not have all the answers just because he or she is grown-up.

How do teachers demonstrate an attitude of learning? One surefire way is to admit when they do not know something and show how to go about finding an answer. (*Now I'm not exactly sure how a moth is different from a butterfly. But we can find out in this nature book.*) They wonder aloud about intriguing and puzzling things. (*Well isn't it amazing how sticky that spider's web is! I wonder what makes it so doggone sticky.*) They demonstrate an openness to many possible solutions and answers to questions. (*I was thinking that we might do it that way, but here's another way we might arrange all these lovely buttons.*)

4. **Extend the topic and enrich children's understanding.** In order for this to happen, teachers must be deliberate, because the goal is to build up children's understanding of how the world works. Fundamentally the talk strategies of extending and enriching involve using language in decontextualized ways. What does this mean exactly? For starters, there needs to be a conversation going on between you and the child or a small group of children; otherwise there is no opportunity to extend and enrich children's thinking. On the occasion of conversation (of which there should be many), you need to intentionally talk about the past and future. (*Remember when we went to the apple orchard? We saw big tractors just like the ones we are going to read about in our story today.*) You need to discuss reasons and explanations. (*Oh! Our flowers wilted. They need water. You know why? It was hot in here and the water evaporated from the soil. It went into the air.*) You need to project into others' experiences and situations (*I bet Jenna was just delighted when we gave her that birthday cake.*) And you need to be imaginative and playful with language. (*You know what? I'm pretending I'm the best baker ever, and I'm making lip-smacking, tummy-pleasing, super-delicious, gooey, gooey snicker-doodles! Do you want to be my assistant?*) These uses of language go beyond the right there and invite children to think and search with words as well as by holding, poking, probing, and touching real things. More options for extending and enriching children's understanding are listed below, and we encourage you to use these strategies as often as you can.

5. **Tell children more of what's happening in the world.** In their immediate environment, children notice the smallest things—new water cups at the sink, a minor repair to the window sill, the Band-Aid on your finger, duct tape to hold down the carpet. It's useful to talk about these changes in a kind of running commentary on the ups and downs of everyday life.

- *We need to have our snack a little later today because we are having a visitor who will tell us about new babies at the zoo.*
- *You know what? Mr. Tyler, our custodian, got a bad cut on his finger and he's wearing a big Band-Aid.*
- *I bet you spied those new boxes in the corner, so we are in for a surprise.*

Comments like these provide children with information and supply them with words they can use later on in their own conversations.

Closing

*R*eflecting on the many delights of children's play, Maria Carmen recounted, "After about two months of lots of play in the housekeeping setting, I asked the children what they thought about making some changes. They were a bit hesitant because they really enjoyed 'playing babies,' and were especially fond of the stroller in which they had stacked books for reading to their 'babies.' But after some conversation (over a few days), we decided that a restaurant would be fun. We brainstormed all the things we would need—tables and chairs, menus, food, notepads and pencils, tablecloths, a sign (of course a sign!). We listed many possibilities for our restaurant. We all voted and chose *Chico's* as the best name for the restaurant."

No doubt about it, the environment is a powerful teacher! What it contains—the objects, materials, settings, and language—jump-start all kinds of social, emotional, and cognitive learning. When you consciously design appealing physical space and structures, you invite young children into a wide variety of language and literacy experiences, not to mention endless opportunities for interaction. Using basic design elements, such as those we have discussed here, you create a lively place that teaches, that promotes choices and activity, and that is full of talking, reading, and writing, and the real joy of learning.

CHAPTER 3

Shared Book Reading

*T*he early years are a time of joy and a period of great learning for young children. These are the years when children begin to interact with print and experience the delights of being read to. Today, a superabundance of wonderful books awaits them, due to the virtual explosion in publishing for the very young. But whether children benefit from this vast array of books depends entirely upon the adults in their lives. Why, how, and what you read to young children matters enormously in determining the role books will play in enriching children's lives and later school achievement.

The purpose of this chapter is to provide you with helpful information about reading aloud with children. We'll discuss the importance of books in children's lives as well as where and when to read, how to select books, and what children learn from different types of books. From our perspective, interacting with books should be the key way in which children experience print in the early childhood classroom.

What the Research Says

Aside from being just plain fun, research (Dickinson & Neuman, 2006; Neuman & Dickinson, 2001) suggests that shared book reading helps children develop many of the skills essential for eventual reading success.

* The amount of time spent reading aloud is related to children's reading achievement. Children who learned to read before entering first grade had been read to by parents, caregivers, and/or siblings.

* Children's language and vocabulary development is enriched by exposure to books. Reading books aloud creates a rich language environment that stimulates children's interactions with rare vocabulary or more sophisticated language than is ordinarily found in mere conversational exchanges. Children learn new words from books, especially when books are reread multiple times.

* Children's later educational achievement is related to early experiences with books. In one of the most convincing longitudinal studies on book reading, Gordon Wells (1986) found a significant relationship between reading and school achievement. Stories appear to help children make sense of life; they give meaning to observational events by making connections between them.

* Children build their understanding of stories from the stories they hear.

* Children who are frequently read to often pretend to "read" their favorite books all by themselves. For most children at this age, these reading routines include attending to pictures, and occasionally to salient print. A few may begin to attend to the print in the main body of the text, and a few may even make the transition into conversational reading with their favorite books. When you hear young children begin to tell a story with "once upon a time," and end with "the end," you know that they are conveying their initial understandings of how stories sound and are read. These narrative-like understandings eventually help them to become successful readers.

Books alone don't make a difference. There is no magic in reading to children. Instead, the magic comes about as you *engage* them in print. It's the engagement with print that helps children become good readers and writers. We know, for example, that reading to children in small groups enhances their comprehension and depth of understanding by allowing them to ask more questions and get more immediate answers than in whole-group settings. We also know that questioning strategies before, during, and after storybook reading, for example, strongly influence their vocabulary and comprehension development, and that reading a book several times will increase children's involvement in and comprehension of the story.

The benefits of book reading depend on *how* you read with children. Reading aloud to small groups, asking questions about the stories, pointing out interesting features, and providing critical background knowledge—these are the ways you can help young children learn about reading. We'll discuss these processes in depth in the rest of this chapter.

GENERAL TIPS FOR SUCCESSFUL READ-ALOUDS

There are a number of things you can do to promote successful read-alouds (Neuman et al., 2000). You'll want to consider your environment and how it supports good reading. You'll also want to think about how you read to children to encourage their attention, enthusiasm, and understanding of what you read. Following are some general tips.

Create comfortable spaces. Have areas in your room to read to the whole group, to small groups, and with individuals one-on-one. Use them consistently so that children learn to identify particular areas for reading and quiet activities (as opposed to, say, block building). It's also a good idea to create a relaxing space where children can "read" by themselves. Include a carpet, beanbags, or pillows (some teachers even put couches in their reading space) so that kids get nice and comfy when they read.

Keep read-alouds "short and sweet." Five to ten minutes of sitting is reasonable, especially in the beginning. More than this can really be too long for 3- and some 4-year-olds. If the whole group starts wiggling, that's the signal that you have gone a bit too long, and it's time to wrap it up!

Try again later. If the children just can't calm down enough to listen to a story at a particular time, simply try again later. Remember that for children, listening to a story should be fun. It should feel like play rather than work. In general, it's a good idea to plan read-alouds for first thing in the morning and/or after active play times, when the children are more able to sit and listen.

Expect that there will always be a few children who get distracted. Listening to stories in a group context can be difficult for some children. Young children may not be able to sit still for an entire story. You'll notice some may be looking out the window, twisting around, or playing with the Velcro on their shoes. That's okay. If most of the children are with you, keep going! Try to draw children's attention back to the book by changing your tone of voice or pointing out something new and exciting. But if this doesn't work, let it go. You might find that for certain children, listening to stories in a small group or one-on-one works better. And it's really important not to spend lots of time correcting behavior. Remember shared book reading is supposed to be enjoyable.

Provide lots of opportunities for children to read books independently.

Allow children to "crowd up" close to you and the book. If they're not close at first, you'll notice that they'll move toward you as you read. Being close helps to keep children engaged. Also, children want to be physically close to the book because they find it interesting and exciting, which is exactly what we want.

Show the pictures to the whole group at once. Children get disengaged if they can't see the pictures. They may move around to get a better view or stop attending altogether. You might be able to hold the book so that everyone can see and read the words at the same time. But if you can't, a better technique is to read a page with the book facing you and then, at the end of the page, turn it around and move the book slowly like a fan from one side of the group to the other. This way, everyone sees the picture at once and no one shouts, "I can't see!" while you're in the middle of reading a wonderful story.

Help children to understand what you're reading while you're reading. Always keep in mind that there is so much for young children to learn. Books are a place where they encounter many new words and many new ideas. Help children to understand by modeling, thinking aloud, telling, explaining, and questioning (see Figure 3.1).

WAYS TO HELP CHILDREN UNDERSTAND WHAT YOU ARE READING

* **Modeling** is demonstrating by your actions. You model how to turn the page every time you turn the page in front of children. It doesn't hurt to be explicit about what you're doing. *Now I'm going to turn the page.*

* **Thinking aloud** is talking about what you are thinking. This helps children to know how they should be thinking. *Wow! I notice that these words sound the same. Cat and hat sound the same at the end.*

* **Telling** is giving information. *Cows usually live on farms. They don't live in the jungle.*

* **Explaining** is clarifying something that might be confusing to children. *The caterpillar had a stomachache because he ate a lot of food. Sometimes our tummies hurt when we eat too much.*

* **Questioning** is asking questions to guide children's thinking in order to help them to better understand. *How do you think the boy might feel when he realizes that his snowball has melted?* Questioning helps steer children in the right direction so they can better comprehend a book. Questioning to assess whether children understand is something altogether different. We discuss this second type of questioning in a later part of this chapter (page 53).

FIGURE 3.1

Read books over and over again. You've probably heard it said that children need to try a new food many times before they get used to the new flavor. The same principle applies to books. The more times you read a book, the more children get to know the book. One time is not enough. Each time you read a book, children will attend to new information, especially if you draw their attention to different characteristics of the book with each reading. During one reading, children may simply focus on the pictures. During another reading, they may listen to the story. During another reading, they may notice the rhyming pattern. On still another occasion, they may grasp the meanings of new vocabulary words.

But repeated readings don't necessarily have to occur in one sitting or even in one week. You may read a book a few times in October and then pull it out again in January. The children will be older, and they'll know more about books; they'll love returning to an old favorite.

Provide opportunities for children to independently read books by themselves. Also, create times when children can choose books to "read" to one another. To help children choose books, the books should be placed face forward in a shelf or in a basket. There should be a reasonable number of books available, but not so many that choosing is overwhelming. Two to four books per child in the room are usually enough. The books should be at the children's height so that it is easy for them to make choices. Put new books out and put old ones away every few weeks. There may be a few favorites that the children don't want you to put away. You'll know because they'll notice immediately when these favorites are suddenly gone. Consider creating a special basket of classroom favorites that stay out at all times.

Schedule times to read to small groups of two or three children. If you can, try to make times to read to children in small groups or individually. It is particularly hard for young children to listen to stories in a large group. Reading with you individually or with only a few other kids will help them engage with the book. Children will sit right next to you so they can easily participate by pointing to interesting parts or turning pages. Also, children feel special when the teacher reads just with them.

Choosing Books for Young Children

Different types of books help children learn different things. Although this may sound obvious, it is worth keeping in mind because it will guide you in selecting books as well as deciding how you will read them. Each type or genre of book provides a specific opportunity for you to help children learn about literacy.

In the next section, we describe five types of books commonly found in preschool classrooms: alphabet books, rhyming books, information books, storybooks, and homemade books. For each type of book, we provide a description and some examples. We also answer two questions: (1) What do children learn from this type of book? and (2) what can you, the teacher, do to promote this learning?

FIVE REALLY GREAT ALPHABET BOOKS

Animalia by Graeme Base (Abrams Books, 1986)
You could spend hours poring over the extraordinary pictures that celebrate the animal kingdom accompanied by the challenging alliterative text.

On Market Street by Arnold Lobel (Greenwillow, 1981)
With Lobel's rhythmic opening and closing paragraphs, and illustrator Anita Lobel's imaginative paintings, a child will find this wonderful book thrilling to listen to again and again.

Chicka Chicka Boom Boom by Bill Martin Jr. and John Archambault (Simon & Schuster, 1989)
The joyous tempo of the simple story is enhanced by Lois Ehlert's clean, vibrant illustrations.

Dr. Seuss's ABCs by Dr. Seuss (Random House, 1996)
Combines rhythm, rhyme, repetition of letter sounds, and classic illustrations to reinforce several important prereading concepts: names of the alphabet letters, alphabetic order, phonics, and letter case.

Brian Wildsmith's ABC by Brian Wildsmith (Franklin Watts, 1962)
Alphabet books don't get much better than this: the left-hand pages feature the name of the depicted animal, person, or object in both lower- and uppercase, and the right-hand pages feature drawings with character and clarity.

ALPHABET BOOKS

Alphabet books offer many wonderful opportunities for reviewing the alphabet and savoring its sounds. These books come in a host of formats, and many feature advanced vocabulary words we want our children to hear and learn. From *Animalia* to *The Z Was Zapped,* these books are bound to capture your children's attention and fancy. Keep the reading playful and let children enjoy the pictures, letter shapes, and sounds, as well as the discovery of new words.

Alphabet books help children learn that the letters of the alphabet are special, interesting, and important, and that each letter has its own name. They also remind children that the letters in the alphabet have a consistent order. But perhaps most important, these books help children begin to associate each letter with objects or animals that start with that letter, which can be an important learning device. For example, they may start to associate *A* with a picture of an apple (Adams, 1990). And this strategy will help them learn that each letter can map onto a sound, an important principle that will be key to their learning to decode.

What Can You Do to Help Children Learn From Alphabet Books?

Children's experiences with alphabet books develop and deepen as children are exposed to the letters and as they learn to associate letters with their constituent sounds. For example, a 3-year-old may name the letters and pictures, but not see the connection between the two. A 4-year-old may be able to say all the letters and guess what letter comes next in a book, but will probably only know some of the letters and sounds that they make. A 5-year-old should be able to make connections between letters and sounds.

It's important to keep things lively and fun as you read alphabet books. You'll find that children learn their letters most easily not when they're drilled, but when they're taught in meaningful contexts. You can even make a game of it. Say something like, *This is a book that we know well. Now let's play a little game while we read. . . .*

Try reading alphabet books over and over again so that children get used to the order of the alphabet. Be sure to point to the letter as you name it, and invite children to point to the letter. Make sure children notice all of the pictures on each page. Name the pictures, accentuating the beginning letter (and sound) and invite children to repeat it. Say something like: *This is an* m. M *makes the mmm sound and I notice a picture of a man on this page. Do you see other pictures that start with the mmm sound?*

You might stop before turning the page. Invite children to guess which letter will be on the next page, helping them make the connection between the letter and the pictures by thinking aloud. *What letter comes after* m *and what animal might it be?*

How Can You Extend This Knowledge During Other Parts of Your Day?

There are many wonderful ways to extend children's learning after reading alphabet books. You might try the following:

* Get some magnetic letters. These letters are great for the housekeeping corner. Let children explore the letters or leave a message on the door of the refrigerator in the center.

* Help children to recognize the shapes of letters. Here are a few suggestions: (1) Use tape to make a giant letter on the floor. Let children walk, crawl, jump, or tiptoe the shape of the letter; (2) make letters in shaving cream or colored sand; (3) finger paint letter shapes; (4) make letters out of play dough.

* Make a class alphabet book. Children just love to see things in their everyday world connected to learning about letters. This reinforcement makes letters more personal to them, by tying their use into meaningful activities.

* Teach children the alphabet song. Even though many of them may first slur some letters together, like "elemeno" for "l, m, n, o," they will quickly learn their letters, especially if you slow it down and point to the individual letters.

RHYMING BOOKS

Being able to hear rhymes—to know that *cat* rhymes with *mat* (but not with *can*)—is an essential skill for learning how to read, because it means that children are able to distinguish among sounds. This in turn will help them make the association between written letters and sounds.

Nursery rhymes are an especially powerful tool for learning how to rhyme. Children who are familiar with nursery rhymes when they enter kindergarten often have an easier time learning to read. By the time children are about 3 or 4, they begin to identify rhyming words, and then, increas-

FIVE REALLY GREAT RHYMING BOOKS

Brown Bear, Brown Bear, What Do You See? by Bill Martin, Jr., and Eric Carle (Harcourt Brace, 1967)
Colors come alive through wonderful illustrations and rhyming text.

I Can't, Said the Ant by Polly Cameron (Coward-McCann, 1961)
With the help of an army of ants and some spiders, an ant helps repair a broken teapot with great rhythm and rhyme.

Down by the Bay by Raffi (Crown, 1987)
Song celebrates silly rhymes: "Did you ever see a whale with a polka-dot tail, Down by the bay?"

Horton Hears a Who by Dr. Seuss (Random House, 1954)
One of our very favorites, an elephant shows what it means to care as he tries to protect the tiny creatures on a speck of dust.

Green Eggs and Ham by Dr. Seuss (Random House, 1960)
A highly memorable rhyming book that will delight your young preschoolers and turn them on to poetry.

ingly, produce them on their own. Children who hear lots of rhymes through rhyming books are more likely to learn the concept, particularly if they are asked to participate by filling in missing words and phrases.

Children love to play with rhymes. Rhyming can help them strengthen their oral language skills and develop a greater sensitivity to sounds or phonological awareness (Maclean et al., 1987). It is the beginning, in many ways, of learning to unlock the relationship between sounds and words, and what a wonderful beginning.

What Can You Do to Help Children Learn From Rhyming Books?

Rhyming books are usually silly and can be delightful to read with children. Enjoy the fun. You'll want to read these books over and over again so that children begin to notice the rhyming patterns.

Especially for the first reading, try to read the book all the way through. Don't stop to ask questions. Stopping may actually disrupt children's ability to hear the rhymes and rhythms of the language. Rather, let children simply enjoy the sounds of the words. Remember, rhyming books don't necessarily make sense.

Here are some general tips for reading rhyming books:

* You can draw children's attention to the rhyming words by reading them slowly and deliberately.
* Allow children to join in with you as you read.
* Pause slightly and look at the children before reading a rhyming word, and give a nod or gesture of encouragement. When children know a rhyming book well, they will immediately

chime in with the next word. Give them a thumbs-up, a nod, and a smile when they get it, but don't stop reading. You want to maintain the rhythm of the book.

✳ After reading the book several times, you can help children to notice rhyming words by thinking aloud. Say something like: *See how* hop *and* pop *rhyme. They sound the same at the end.* You and the children can brainstorm additional rhyming words that are not in the book.

How Can You Extend This Knowledge During Other Parts of Your Day?

There are many ways to extend rhyming into other activities throughout the day. Try making up your own rhyming words to replace the words in a favorite rhyming book. Use sticky notes to put the new words into the book. This activity is very silly and can be lots of fun!

We also enjoy singing rhyming songs for transitions throughout the day. For example, you might make up a rhyming song for cleanup time, or for getting ready for snack. You might use rhymes to get the children's attention, saying, *One, two, three, eyes on me,* with the children responding, *One, two, eyes on you.* You can also play a rhyming game during transition times. *I'm thinking of a word that rhymes with* cat. *It's something you hit with a ball, and it begins with a* b. Most children love to rhyme, and will quickly join in the fun.

INFORMATION BOOKS

Young children absolutely love information books! Children are curious about the world and are eager to understand everything. Adults often choose storybooks to read because they think children naturally prefer fiction, but when given a choice, many children choose to read information books. For young knowledge seekers, there is nothing more interesting and enticing than to listen to and point to the interesting illustrations in information books.

Children are attracted to photographs in information books because they understand that the pictures show something "real" that is new or unusual. They are constantly trying to make sense of the world, and they'll learn with your careful tutelage and interesting selection of topics that information books hold a key to greater understanding. Often one child or a group of children will find an interesting information book with great pictures. They'll bring it to you to ask, "What is this?" or to confirm a guess, "Is this snake a cobra?" Helping them find answers to these and other questions through books is one of the most exciting ways that you can help young children's literacy development.

An explosion of research on the benefits of information books suggests that they are especially helpful in increasing children's background knowledge. This means that the more information books you read and discuss with a child, the more prepared that child will be for future books. Children also learn many new vocabulary words from them. Information books offer a great opportunity to encounter new words that a child probably wouldn't learn during daily conversation, like *seahorse* or *volcano*. And the more words a child knows, the more he or she will be able to understand and communicate.

FIVE REALLY GREAT INFORMATION BOOKS

I Read Signs by Tana Hoban (Scholastic, 1983)
Wonderful photos of 30 different signs that children are likely to encounter.

Nature Spy by Shelly Rotner (Atheneum, 1992)
Colorful photographs, some magnified, of objects such as seeds, feathers, and a spider's web help children explore the shapes and patterns found in plants and animals.

Wonderful Worms by Linda Glaser (Millbrook Press, 1994)
A book with simple, colorful illustrations that help children learn all about earthworms.

Biggest, Strongest, Fastest by Steve Jenkins (Houghton Mifflin, 1997)
Exciting animals facts supported by cut-paper collage illustrations.

How Kids Grow by Jean Marzollo (Scholastic 1998)
Photographs show how children grow from babies to six-year-olds.

What Can You Do to Help Children Learn From Information Books?

Information books are great vocabulary and conversation tools. Unlike storybooks, however, they don't always have to be read from beginning to end. Sometimes it is fine to read parts that answer a specific question, or to read the text that goes with a photograph that interests a group of children. Or you might only focus on a couple of pages that really intrigue them. You'll find that having information books on a variety of topics will serve as a reference in many of your ongoing projects.

Choose appropriate books for the age of your children. Be sure that the information is accurate and up-to-date. Try to find information books that present new ideas and new vocabulary in a way that is clear enough for young children to understand. And try to find books with illustrations that help children learn more about the concepts and information presented. Here are some other useful tips:

* Don't assume that children understand words. Things that are simple to us may be confusing to a child. Which part of a plant is the leaf? Which part is the stem? Point to pictures. Be clear and explicit.

* Define new words using clear categories. Say something like, *Bees and flies are both types of insects. Do you think a butterfly is also an insect? How about an elephant?*

* Draw attention to the connection between words and pictures. Point to the words that explain a picture. Say something like, *Let's learn more about the picture of the lion by reading these words.*

* Children frequently develop misconceptions about the new ideas they are learning. At snack time, for example, you might overhear a child say to a friend, "Orange juice comes from cows on a farm." This is a great time to read an information book about farm animals or how fruit grows. Often if you don't have an information book on a specific topic, your local

library will. And the librarian will be delighted to grab lots of books on a topic at a moment's notice.

How Can You Extend This Knowledge During Other Parts of Your Day?

Use information books to support topics that you are learning about in your classroom. Here are a few suggestions: (1) If there are earthworms on the science table, have books about earthworms available nearby; (2) in fall, have books about leaves, apples, and pumpkins; (3) put books about buildings in your block area; (4) put recipe books in your dramatic play area; (5) if you're going on a field trip, gather information from books before you go.

Make your own classroom information books. It's a good idea to choose topics that children know a lot about. You might make a book about children's favorite foods or how to take care of pets. You could also make a book about a field trip or create a recipe book of foods you've made for snack. The possibilities are endless!

Young children love information books about animals, dinosaurs, space, trains, trucks, or any other subject that captivates them. It's likely to be the pictures, not the words, that first draw them in, so dip in wherever children show interest. They will soon understand that the print offers even more interesting information than the pictures alone. The idea that you are trying to convey is that books provide information that will help children learn more about their world. And by always turning to a book for more information, you are demonstrating the purposes of reading and helping children read to learn.

STORYBOOKS

Narratives or stories are books that have predictable elements. All stories have settings (time and place), characters, and plots. Some may be very simple, like *The Little Red Hen* or *Runaway Bunny*, with settings that establish the tone of the story and simple characters. Others may be more complex, like the books about Curious George who gets into all sorts of mishaps. The action in plots usually begins with a problem to be solved, builds through a series of conflicts or dramatic incidents to the climactic resolution of the problem, and then wraps up after certain consequences are described. Understanding the elements of a story, even a very simple one, can help children know what to expect and how to compare different stories. It will also help them know how to plan their own stories later on.

Storybooks are a type of "make-believe" or "pretend." Children learn to imagine new worlds and new characters. In fact, children often pretend to be storybook characters in their dramatic play. They learn to make connections between their own lives and the lives of characters in a book. They also learn about abstract language that we sometimes refer to as "decontextualized language" (language that is not tied to the immediate context).

They also begin to get a sense of "story grammar," or the typical elements of a story. They learn that stories have: (1) a beginning, which includes the introduction of characters and the setting; (2) a conflict or problem, and (3) an ending that resolves the issue. Children don't need to understand terms like *setting* or *conflict* to know that these parts belong in a story.

FIVE REALLY GREAT STORYBOOKS (ALL FROM BOOK TIME)

Corduroy by Don Freeman (Viking Juvenile, 1968)
A toy-comes-alive story about a stuffed bear in a department store, hoping to find a home.

Swimmy by Leo Lionni (Knopf, 1963)
Swimmy, all alone, joins a school of fish even though he is a different color, and helps them scare off a bigger fish.

The Snowy Day by Ezra Jack Keats (Puffin, 1976)
The strikingly beautiful illustrations and simple story tell about a boy enjoying a snowy day.

Pancakes for Breakfast by Tomie dePaola (Voyager Books, 1978)
A wordless picture book about a little old woman who tries to make pancakes for breakfast.

On my Way to Buy Eggs by Chih-Yuan Chen (Kane/Miller, 2007)
A young girl's trip to the store to buy eggs turns into an adventure. Set in Taiwan.

Chrysanthemum by Kevin Henkes (Scholastic, 2005)
Chrysanthemum loves her special name, until she is teased about it at school. With support from her parents and a teacher, she learns to appreciate it once again.

And finally, they also learn about literary language, which is actually quite different from everyday spoken language. For example, you would likely never hear someone say in everyday speech, "Once upon a time" or "'Look,' said the boy," yet this is common in storybook language. Through many exposures to storybooks, children learn to distinguish this special storybook language from conversational language, and this helps them comprehend written language better.

What Can You Do to Help Children Learn From Storybooks?

✳ Read the book before you read it aloud. If you know the story, it will be much easier for you to help children understand it.

✳ Read favorite stories again and again. Children delight in the experience of rereading a favorite book.

✳ Read with enthusiasm. Read more quickly during an exciting part. Change to a whisper to create suspense. Create different voices for each character. The more you ham it up, the better the experience will be for the children.

✳ Help children to notice storybook language. Think aloud, *I wonder why so many stories say "happily ever after" at the end.*

✳ Guide children in making connections to their own lives. *In the beginning of the story, the child will not eat tomatoes. In the end, she changes her mind and decides she likes them. Do you like tomatoes? Did you ever change your mind when you tried something new?*

Nurturing Knowledge

* Encourage them to compare their favorite stories. *In what ways was "Three Billy Goats Gruff" like "The Three Little Pigs"?*

NOW IT'S YOUR TURN! MAKE YOUR OWN BOOKS

After reading so many wonderful stories and informational books to children, let them take a turn at becoming an author. Children will learn that the words they say correspond to written words. You'll also help them to become active participants in reading and writing rather than merely watching or listening while adults perform these activities. Just think how proud they will be to become an author and to learn how to savor precious memories of special or exciting events (field trips, a new class pet, a snowy day) in print.

What Can You Do to Help Children Learn From Homemade Books?

* Make sure that class books are bound well and covered in contact paper because homemade books are well loved and can fall apart quickly. You want to make the book strong enough for children to use it often.
* Write words down as children say them. Read the words back to the children, pointing to each word as you read it aloud. This helps children understand that the actual words they say are being put on a page. You can write or type a neat copy later.
* Include children's artwork as well as photographs to illustrate your book.
* Allow every child to be a part of book-making. Plan books so that each child can include a dictated or written idea and an illustration.
* Put homemade books in the library with the rest of the books. Make them easily accessible to children when they are choosing books.
* Make them often and read them often. This helps children to see that the books they create are very important.

Some General Tips on Making Homemade Books

Be sure to include every child in your class-room. There should be at least one piece of artwork and some dictated language from

Making books helps children see that the words they say correspond to written words.

each child. For example:

* If you are creating an alphabet book, each child can create the page for one or two letters. This may include drawing objects or animals that begin with that letter and labeling these drawings by dictating to an adult.
* If you are creating a rhyming book, help each child create a couplet.
* If you are creating an information book, help each child think of one fact.
* If you are creating a story, let each child add on a part of the story. Guide children to create a beginning, middle, or end. "Who should the story be about?" "What should happen to the prince?" "You're one of the last children to add to this story—how do you think the story should end?"

Also, remember that illustrations don't have to be crayon drawings. Illustrations are wonderful art projects. You can use collage (torn or cut paper), paint, finger paint, markers, colored pencils, charcoal, photographs, and crayon with a watercolor wash to make abstract pictures. It helps to glue children's artwork and words onto construction paper or other heavy paper before binding your book. This will help the book stand up to wear and tear.

Copy text over neatly or type it in a large font for the final version. Put the child's name under his writing so that all of the children can remember whose words are on the page. Staple or sew the book together. Then, discuss and create the title, class name, and a picture on the front cover. Wrap the book in contact paper for safekeeping, and read often!

HOW CAN YOU ASSESS CHILDREN'S LEARNING FROM BOOKS?

It's always important to assess children's learning. Teachers need to know if children are developing listening skills, phonological awareness, and letter knowledge so that they may learn how to read on their own.

Observe Children's Behavior

You can watch one or two children at a time during a specific activity. For example, you may choose to watch children as they select books and look at them independently. It's a good idea to write down behaviors that you notice so that you can remember them and think about them later. You may also choose to observe in general. Keep a notepad handy to quickly jot down behaviors as you see them or shortly afterward. What should you look for?

* Is the child attentive during read-alouds?
* Does the child respond verbally to the story by making comments or answering questions? Does the child respond nonverbally to the story (for example, by laughing or smiling at funny parts)?
* Can the child choose a book and look at it independently? If not, what seems to be the difficulty?
* When the child looks at a book independently, what does he do? Does he "read" the story to

himself from memory? Does he make up a story that goes with the pictures? Or does he simply pick up a book, open it for a few minutes, and discard it quickly?

✳ Does the child use characters, storylines, information, or language from books you have read during his dramatic play? Is a child saying the words from a rhyming book or singing the alphabet to himself as he colors?

Question to Assess Their Understanding

This can help you understand children's thinking. Such questions are different from the prompting or guiding questions that were mentioned earlier in the chapter. You can ask questions to see what children know. Ideally, you should ask open-ended questions. If a question simply has a yes or no answer, you won't get very much information. It is also important to ask questions in a gentle way. Make the questions seem like a natural part of storybook reading. Try to make sure that children don't feel uncomfortable or embarrassed when they don't know how to respond. There are some children who will regularly answer when you ask questions to the group. Others are more likely to answer if you are reading together in a one-on-one situation. As you get to know the children in your classroom, you'll learn the right way to ask questions to different children. Ask questions like:

✳ *What is this [point to a picture]? Do you know what this letter is [point to a letter in an alphabet book]?*

✳ *In this book,* hop *rhymes with . . . ?*

✳ *What is happening on this page [point to page]?*

✳ *What new things did we learn from this book?*

✳ *How did the story end?*

✳ *What was your favorite part of this book?*

Ask Children to Retell the Story

You'll get the most information if you do this one-on-one and if you use a storybook. Read the book, put it to the side, and then prompt the child by saying, *Now can you tell me everything you remember about what happened in the book we just read?* It's often a good idea to take notes on how the child responds. If the child is really struggling to talk about the story, let her look back at the pictures in the book. Here are a few suggestions about what to listen for as the child retells the story:

✳ Does the child's retelling indicate that she generally understood what happened in the story, or is she confused?

✳ Is the child telling the story in a logical sequence, or is she listing events out of order?

✳ Does the child include a beginning, a middle, and an end in her retelling?

✳ Does the child include a lot of detailed information or just a few events?

✳ Does the child use story language in her retelling, such as "once upon a time" or "happily ever after"?

✳ If you allow the child to look back at the pictures to aid in the retelling, does it help her? Does she use the pictures to remember what you read or does she just describe the pictures as if she's never heard the story before?

Closing

We enter a classroom right when children are finishing their snack, and find Elizabeth and her friend Maria playing "teacher."

"I'm going to be the teacher. You be the kid," Maria says.

"No, I want to be the teacher first," Elizabeth answers.

Elizabeth gets a book and brings it to the rug. She sits on the teacher chair.

"You sit on the floor over here," she tells Maria.

Elizabeth starts "reading" the story. "Once upon a time . . . ," she begins. After she "reads" the page, she shows the picture to Maria, moving the book slowly from one side to another as if she were reading to a whole group of children.

Elizabeth asks, "What was your favorite part of the story?" looking around as if she had an imaginary class. She calls on Maria. Maria answers, "This part," as she points to the picture.

Watching the play, we notice with delight that storybooks have clearly become an important element in these children's lives. These are children who want to read, who view books as pleasurable, rewarding, and worthy of imitation, who look toward print for information. And we give thanks to the supportive teacher who used the vast array of beautiful books to lead them onto the road to literacy.

...hymes, and ...d Play

Callslip Request   11/17/2014 8:44:52 PM
Request date:11/17/2014 04:18 AM
Request ID: 47426
Call Number:372.476 N4921
Item Barcode:

Author: Neuman, Susan B.
Title: Nurturing knowledge / Susan B. Neuman
Enumeration:Year:
Patron Name:Dinika Nicole Johnson
Patron Barcode:

Patron comment:

Request number:

Route to:
I-Share Library:
Library Pick Up Location:

Songs, rhymes, and word play are natural tools for learning about language. If you've ever played "Itsy-Bitsy Spider" or "This Little Piggy Went to Market," or if you've ever sung a children's song like "If You're Happy and You Know It," you've been preparing your children for learning to read—even if you might not have realized it at the time. These wonderful, old familiar songs and rhymes help to strengthen children's ability to hear the sounds of our language, a skill that will serve them well when they learn to map sounds onto letters (phonics) in kindergarten and first grade. Playing with songs and rhymes will tune children's ears to hearing differences and similarities in how words sound.

Researchers, early childhood educators, and literacy experts agree that children who have well-developed skills in phonological awareness and phonemic awareness have an easier time learning to read (National Reading Panel, 2000). In fact, research suggests that these skills are critical for children's success in reading. In this chapter, we'll first describe these terms, talk a bit about the research base, and then focus on our favorite songs and rhymes that support children's learning.

What the Research Says

"Phonological awareness" sounds like something very new and complicated, but in reality, many early childhood educators are already teaching phonological awareness to young children by singing, rhyming, and being silly with words.

Phonological awareness is the ability to hear, recognize, and play with the sounds in our language. It's the recognition that sounds in English can be broken into smaller and smaller parts: sentences, words, rimes (a rime is the ending of a word such as /at/ in the word *cat* or /ark/ in *park*) and syllables. It makes sense that children who can hear and notice the sounds in our language will be more comfortable when it is time to start reading and writing.

To learn how to read and write, children must shift their attention from the meanings of language to the explicit sounds of spoken words (Snow, 1998). This skill is considered "metalinguistic," meaning it involves helping children treat language as the object of thought, rather than merely as a tool for communication. For example, children will need to notice the features of words: their length, their similarities and differences, and their component sounds.

How can we enable children to do this? Experts (Ehri & Roberts, 2006) suggest that it happens in a rather predictable sequence, but *only* if children have good teaching to prompt and direct them. In others words, these skills don't emerge like magic. They must be taught.

Generally, we begin by teaching larger units of sounds such as rhymes and move to smaller units of sounds such as blends and segmented individual sounds. This progression helps children become more aware of the features of words, which will help them learn to read.

Here's the order in which it's most helpful to guide children's understanding of the features of spoken language (National Reading Panel, 2000).

Rhyming. Children need to become adept at noticing the ends of words, or rimes (easy to remember, because this is the part that rhymes). Some children seem to develop this understanding easily; others need much more practice. Children who hear lots of rhymes are likely to learn the concept, particularly if you ask them to participate in filling in the missing words and phrases.

> *I know an old lady who swallowed a fly. . .*
> *I don't know why*
> *She swallowed a _____ (let the children fill in fly)*
> *I guess she'll _____ (let the children fill in die)*

Alliteration. Once children seem to be comfortable noting the ends of words (rimes), we need to help them get the idea that the beginnings of words (onsets) can also sound alike. Lots of children's songs, like "Baa Baa Black Sheep" or "The Green Grass Grew," have examples of alliteration. You can help children hear the same sounds in words, especially if you accentuate the beginning sound as in *mmmoon . . . mmmmama . . . . mmmouse*. Tongue twisters like "She sells seashells by the seashore" are also a fun and silly way to work on alliteration.

Sentence Segmenting. You'll next want to help children learn that sentences contain separate words. Again, it's easiest to help them first "hear" words before teaching the convention of spacing between words. You can show children how to clap for each word, beginning with simple sentences with one syllable each, like *The cat is fat*, and then building up with longer, more elaborate sentences, like *I'm going on a bear hunt*.

Syllable Blending and Segmenting. The next step in phonological awareness is to help children hear syllables (parts of words) in familiar words like *fire-fight-er* and *kick-ball*. Try to say a word very slowly and pause between the separate syllables. Then ask children to guess what word you are saying. These segmenting and blending skills will lead into the more advanced skill of phonological awareness known as phonemic awareness.

Phonemic Awareness. This is one important aspect of phonological awareness. Children who are phonemically aware understand that spoken words are made up of separate sounds that can be broken up into component sounds, such as /c/ /a/ /t/. Many children will begin to develop this ability as they master other phonological awareness skills. But the more isolated sound aspects of phonemic awareness are better learned through developmental writing, described on page 76. Therefore, we believe that songs, rhymes, and word play are ideal for phonological awareness, whereas writing activities, combining letters and sounds are ideal for teaching phonemic awareness. (See box.)

All of these skills are essential for learning to read. Here's what the research says (National Reading Panel, 2000):

* Familiarity with nursery rhymes is related to readiness for reading.
* Phonemic awareness abilities improve reading skills.
* Phonemic awareness improves children's ability to spell.
* Phonological awareness and phonemic awareness are related to children's increases in vocabulary development.

> ## Phonological Awareness and Phonemic Awareness
>
> **Phonological Awareness** includes a whole range of abilities that have to do with focusing on oral language. A child who is phonologically aware is able to hear the rhythms and rhymes of our language and notice whether words have two syllables or three or whether they start with the same sound.
>
> **Phonemic Awareness** is one aspect of phonological awareness. A child who is phonemically aware understands that spoken words are made up of individual sounds, which can be broken up, such as /c/ /a/ /t/. Phonemic awareness involves breaking words up into smaller units of sound, and then combining them together to make a word, such as *cat*.

Teaching Phonological Awareness Through Songs, Rhymes, and Word Play

Let's now take each of the skills related to phonological awareness and highlight how to teach them. We'll discuss a variety of ways, so you'll need to think about which activities are right for the children you teach. Some children will be able to notice real sounds and rhyme; others may be able to hear alliteration. Preschoolers should be able to focus on syllables and words. At any age, help the children in your class to think of these activities as fun and playful language activities.

RHYMING

When two words rhyme, they sound the same at the end. Rhyming is an important phonological awareness task because it is entirely about listening to sounds. It is an oral language skill. For example, *fun* and *won* rhyme because they sound the same at the end, even though that sound is spelled differently. To determine whether two words rhyme, we separate the beginning sound, the onset, from the rest of the word, the rime. For example, *sun* and *fun* both end with /un/. /S/ and /f/ are considered onsets and /un/ is considered the matching rime for both words.

When we introduce children to rhyming, it is usually the first time that they are expected to specifically pay attention to a part of a word. This is not an easy task when the child has previously paid attention to whole words mostly with a focus on understanding their meaning. Although it can be challenging in the beginning, teaching children to rhyme is a significant first step toward being able to break words into smaller parts. Children who have experience breaking words into small parts will later be able to separate words into distinct sounds and then match these sounds with letters in order to read and write.

Nursery rhymes are especially powerful tools for helping children hear similarities at the end of words. They are short and memorable. They also contain the rhymes in rather close proximity, so that children can get attuned to their pattern more quickly. For example,

Jack and J*ill*
Went up the h*ill*
To fetch a pail of wa*ter*
Jack fell d*own*
And broke his cr*own*
And Jill came tumbling af*ter*

Children who are familiar with nursery rhymes when they enter kindergarten have an easier time learning to read. Of course, it could simply be that children who already know their nursery rhymes have been read to more often than those who don't, but it is probably also because these rhymes help children discover many common word "families" and notice how their sounds vary at the end of the words (e.g., *fall/wall* in "Humpty Dumpty"). The more familiar those patterns are to the ear, the more easily children will recognize them when they encounter these same word families in print.

Familiar word plays are especially great for transition times and active children. One of our favorites is "Five Little Monkeys." You might start by pointing out the rhymes specifically: *In "Five Little Monkeys," bed rhymes with head.* You can stress rhyming words by saying them intentionally— a little bit louder, or a little bit softer, almost in a whisper, or more slowly. Another effective strategy is to use an "oral cloze" technique. Stop and pause when it's time for a rhyming word, and let the children chime in:

> Five little monkeys jumping on the *bed*
>
> One fell off and bumped his _____ (let the children fill in *head*)
>
> Mama called the doctor and the doctor _____(let the children fill in *said*)
>
> No more monkeys jumping on the _____(let the children fill in *bed*)

"Five Little Monkeys" is an especially good example because each line provides an opportunity for children to hear the rhyme. The same thing is true for another favorite, "Fuzzy Wuzzy":

> *Fuzzy Wuzzy* was a *bear*
>
> *Fuzzy Wuzzy* had no *hair*
>
> *Fuzzy Wuzzy* wasn't *fuzzy*
>
> *Was he?*

Or:

> Monday's child is fair of *face,*
>
> Tuesday's child is full of *grace,*
>
> Wednesday's child is full of *woe,*
>
> Thursday's child has far to *go,*
>
> Friday's child is loving and *giving,*
>
> Saturday's child works hard for a *living,*
>
> But the child that's born on the Sabbath *day,*
>
> Is bonny, and blithe, and good, and *gay.*

Contrast these rhymes with another common favorite, "Row, Row, Row Your Boat," and you'll see that while "Row Your Boat" is a great song and lots of fun to sing, it doesn't provide nearly as many opportunities for children to hear the similarities in sounds:

> Row, row, row your boat
>
> Gently down the *stream*
>
> Merrily, merrily, merrily, merrily,
>
> Life is but a *dream.*

So especially, in the beginning, select rhymes that provide many opportunities to hear rhyming words:

Teddy Bear Teddy Bear

Turn *around*

Teddy Bear Teddy Bear

Touch the *ground*,

Then, graduate to longer rhymes, with hand motions:

Do your ears hang *low*?

Do they wobble to and *fro*?

Can you tie them in a knot?

Can you tie them in a *bow*?

Can you throw them over your *shoulder*?

Like a Continental *soldier*?

Do your ears hang *low?*

And, of course, rhyming activities involve oral language skills, and don't always translate easily to written form. You'll confuse children if they see that some words that rhyme, like *bear* and *hair*, don't have the same written endings.

As the children become more comfortable in hearing rhymes, encourage them to play with them. "Willoby Wallaby" is a favorite song with young children because they love anything to do with their own names. To help children rhyme, you can sing and let the children guess which child's

---

TEN REALLY GREAT RESOURCES FOR RHYMING

Using Children's Books in Reading/Language Arts Programs by Diane D. Canavan and Lavonne Hayes Sanborn (Neal-Schuman, 1992)

A Child's Treasury of Nursery Rhymes by Kady Macdonald Denton (Houghton Mifflin, 2004)

Tomie dePaola's Mother Goose by Tomie dePaola (Putnam, 1985)

Hush Little Baby: A Folk Song With Pictures by Marla Frazee (Harcourt Brace, 1999)

Animal Snackers by Betsy Lewin (Henry Holt, 1980)

The Random House Book of Mother Goose: A Treasury of 306 Timeless Nursery Rhymes by Arnold Lobel (Random House, 1986)

Inviting Children's Responses to Literature edited by Amy McClure and Janice Kristo (National Council for Teachers of English, 1994)

Read-Aloud Rhymes for the Very Young by Jack Prelutsky (Knopf, 1986)

It's Raining Pigs and Noodles by Jack Prelutsky (HarperCollins, 2000)

Nursery Rhyme Time by Ru Story-Huffman (Upstart Books, 1996)

name rhymes. You might sing, *Willoby Walloby waleb, an elephant sat on...* and then help the children to figure out that the missing name is *Caleb*.

You can also try a more advanced riddle game. *I'm thinking of a word that rhymes with* fat. *It's something you hit with a ball.* Or *I'm thinking of a word that rhymes with* fat, *and it begins with the /b/ sound.* This can be a real puzzler for preschoolers, and if the answers don't come easily, simply provide them cheerfully, and try again another day.

For more ideas on rhyming, check out the great resources in the box on page 60.

ALLITERATION

Alliteration is the technical term that we use to refer to words that start with the same sound. For example, *table, television,* and *tusk* are alliterative because they start with the same /t/ sound. While rhyming requires children to focus on the end part of a word, alliteration helps children to focus on the first sound in a word. Being able to distinguish the first sound in a word is a big step toward reading and writing that word. In fact, typically when children are first learning to write, they write down one letter for each word, and the letter they write almost always represents the first sound of the word.

Start helping your children hear the beginning sounds by orally stretching the words out. Imagine what a rubber band looks like when you pull it apart, and think about doing that to a word. Say the beginning sound slowly and distinctly so that children can listen specifically for that first sound. Rather than saying *dog*, say *dddd-dog*. In the beginning, you'll probably need to say the first sound separately to help children hear it. Rather than saying *cow*, carefully pronounce the word as *c . . . ow*. But you won't need to do this all the time. In fact, you don't want to artificially exaggerate the beginning sound so often that it gets to be a habit with children.

Like rhyming, start with simple alliterations that emphasize the beginning sounds clearly. Initially, it's best not to confuse the beginning sound and a beginning blend or digraph. For example, the word *sea* clearly makes the /s/ sound. The word *shells* begins with a digraph, which makes a unique /sh/ sound. To a young child's ear, these two uses of /s/ make two very different sounds. What this means, then, is that a verse like "She sells seashells on the seashore" is actually quite difficult, not only for children to say, but also to hear, the similarities of the beginning sounds in the words.

It's better to start with clear examples, like *Piggy in the Puddle*, a delightful book by Charlotte Pomerantz (1974), or *Buster Loves Buttons* by Fran Manushkin (1974). Draw children's attention to the beginning sounds and ask them to listen carefully as you say each verse. You'll find they catch on quickly. Once they do, you can introduce them to verses, and books that are a bit more complex. Your children will have great fun in a fascinating story rife with *f*'s at the same time as they learn lots of new words in *Four Famished Foxes and Fosdyke* by Pamela Duncan Edwards (1995).

Tongue twisters like "Peter Piper" are a fun and silly way to play with alliteration if they don't become overly frustrating to children. Certainly those children who have language delays or difficulties should not attempt them.

TEN REALLY GREAT RESOURCES FOR ALLITERATION AND WORD PLAY

Alligator Arrived With Apples: A Potluck Alphabet Feast by Crescent Dragonwagon (Macmillan, 1987)

Four Famished Foxes and Fosdyke by Pamela Duncan Edwards (Harper Collins, 1995)

Eating the Alphabet: Fruits and Vegetables from A to Z by Lois Ehlert (Harcourt Brace, 1989)

Six Sleepy Sheep by Jeffie Ross Gordon (Puffin, 1991)

Buster Loves Buttons by Fran Manushkin (Harper Collins, 1974)

"Fire! Fire!" Said Mrs. McGuire by Bill Martin Jr. and Richard Egielski (Harcourt Brace, 1971)

The Baby Uggs Are Hatching by Jack Prelutsky (Mulberry, 1982)

Rootabaga Stories by Carl Sandburg (Harcourt Brace, 1922)

Sheep in a Shop by Nancy E. Shaw and Margot Apple (Houghton Mifflin, 1986)

Falling Up by Shel Silverstein (Harper Collins, 1996)

You might write a verse like "Peter Piper" on a sheet of chart paper. Then, slowly read it aloud to the children and play with the alliterative language. You might ask children just to remember parts of the verse, like "pickled peppers," which is great fun to say. Invite them to join in as you come to this phrase:

> Peter Piper picked a peck of *pickled peppers*;
> A peck of *pickled peppers* Peter Piper picked.
> If Peter Piper picked a peck of *pickled peppers*,
> Where's the peck of *pickled peppers* Peter Piper picked?

You'll find other great resources for alliteration and other word play in the box above.

SENTENCE SEGMENTING

Sentence segmenting is really about helping children understand the concept of *word*. This may sound simple, but it's actually not. For young children, speech is a stream of spoken language. They might hear "Iwannagoplay" as a single chunk of meaning, one steady stream of speech, and so the printed word *want* may be quite incomprehensible to them. By slowing things down a bit, you can show children how to segment words in a sentence.

Generally we start with short sentences, like *It . . . is . . . hot.* You can encourage children to clap for each word. Another fun strategy is to use a big bouncing ball. Each time you say a word, bounce the ball. Once they have an example from you, they can do this with your instruction on their own.

You can help children build up to longer sentences, though initially make sure the words are one syllable only, like *We . . . will . . . go . . . out . . . for . . . play . . . now.* You might also write these words on chart paper, and then point to each word as you say it, helping children to focus on the structure of individual words.

Clapping and chanting games and readings can reinforce the idea of words. Challenge children to clap as you read Helen Oxenburg's *We're Going on a Bear Hunt* (1989), and to keep the rhythm going as you read. Also, verses that combine words with simple gestures, like "Hokey Pokey," slow down the words you say and may help children connect the words with actions.

Cumulative-pattern stories like "The House That Jack Built," in which one event builds on another, are wonderful resources for sentence segmenting. Because such stories are built on accumulated repetition, children begin to chant along as you read. They're highly interactive and helpful in getting children to add new words to stories.

You can further emphasize the concept of words by pointing out the white spaces between printed words, especially if these words are written in large print on chart paper. Explain that the spaces separate the words from each other, and that each word carries its own meaning. Don't expect young children to begin to track print word for word at this age. It's more important to give them some examples, and then move on to other fun things. See the box below for more ideas on sentence segmenting.

SYLLABLE BLENDING AND SEGMENTING

As we move to focus on syllable blending and segmenting, we are beginning the transition from phonological awareness to phonemic awareness. We are now training children's ears to hear the sounds

---

TEN REALLY GREAT RESOURCES FOR CHANTING AND CLAPPING GAMES

GREAT CUMULATIVE PATTERN STORIES

The World That Jack Built by Ruth Brown (Dutton, 1991)

Rooster's Off to See the World by Eric Carle (Aladdin, 1972)

Drummer Hoff by Barbara Emberley (Simon & Schuster, 1967)

Good-Night, Owl by Pat Hutchins (Simon & Schuster, 1972)

Root-a-Toot-Toot by Anne Rockwell (Simon & Schuster, 1991)

WORD PLAY

Wheel Away! by Dayle Ann Dodds (Harper & Row, 1989)

The Seals on the Bus by Lenny Hort (Henry Holt, 2000)

Hand, Hand, Fingers, Thumb by Al Perkins (Random House, 1969)

Chicka Chicka Boom Boom by Bill Martin Jr. and John Archambault (Simon & Schuster, 1989)

Down by the Bay by Raffi (Knopf, 1988)

---

within words, whereas before we were focusing on hearing the differences in sounds *between words*.

One of the easiest ways to begin is to help children clap out syllables in words. They don't need to understand that these parts of words are called syllables. But they do need to learn that words have parts and that you can plainly hear these different parts in words.

Start with simple compound words. Ask children to clap when they hear a different part of the word. *Say, I'm going to say a word fast. Then I'm going to say the word again, only this time, I will say it slow. Clap when you hear a part of a word.* Try the following:

birth day

cup cake

pop corn

see saw

day dream

Then try the game of syllable deletion. Say to them, *Say "ice cream." Now say it again without the "ice."* Notice that you are encouraging children to manipulate these sounds. And it's probably pretty easy for them to do, since these particular words represent rather large chunks of sound.

The next step is to move toward segmenting and blending syllables in words. One of our favorite songs for playing with syllables is "Supercalifragilisticexpialidocious." Children just love this silly *Mary Poppins* song, which challenges their capacity to identify sounds. But this song is certainly not one to begin with. Rather, you might want to start with the delightful verse of Dayle Ann Dodds's *Wheel Away* (1990) about a bicycle wheel which gets away and rolls, "ba-da-rump, pa-da-rump, pa-da-rump-pump-pump" through the noisy town.

These two skills—breaking words down into sounds (segmenting) and combining sounds into words (blending)—are essential skills for children to develop. At this point in children's development, you are introducing these skills. Young kindergarteners will probably become more proficient at putting sounds together than at taking them apart.

But it's not too soon to help children begin to play with stretching words out and by saying them slowly enough to hear their constituent parts. If they start now, they'll have plenty of time to develop and practice this skill when they begin to learn to read.

Songs lend themselves especially well to hearing parts in words and to blending words together. When you sing a song or recite a verse, you can accent the parts of words or pause to point them out. Just think of this favorite:

Twin-kle, twin-kle, lit-tle star,

How I won-der what you are.

Up a-bove the world so high,

Like a dia-mond in the sky.

Twin-kle, twin-kle, lit-tle star,

How I won-der what you are.

TEN REALLY GREAT RESOURCES TO SPARK SEGMENTING AND BLENDING

SONG BOOKS

The Mother Goose Songbook by Tom Glazer (Doubleday, 1990)

Shari Lewis Presents 101 Games by Shari Lewis (Random House, 1993)

Really Rosie by Maurice Sendak (Carole King recording, S. French, 1985)

Free to Be You and Me by Marlo Thomas (Running Press, 1994)

Jane Yolen's Songbook by Jane Yolen (Caroline House Boyds Mills Press, 1992)

CHILDREN'S BOOKS

Finger Rhymes by Marc Brown (Dutton, 1980)

Word Play: ABC by Heather Cahoon (Walker & Co., 1999)

Knock at the Door and Other Baby Action Rhymes by Kay Chorao (Dutton, 1999)

Don't Forget the Bacon! by Pat Hutchins (William Morrow, 1976)

There's an Ant in Anthony by Bernard Most (William Morrow, 1980)

Check out the selections in the box above for really great materials to spark segmenting and blending.

Children love to sing these familiar songs. With your help, they will begin to hear the parts of the words as they sing along. What you are doing is helping them use an activity they love in order to become more sensitive to the sounds of speech. And in doing so, you are preparing them to become readers and writers.

Successful Tips for Teaching Songs, Rhymes, and Word Play

Young children love to sing, clap, rhyme, and play with words. Your job is to help them use these fun activities with greater intentionality—that is, to help children notice the sounds they hear and are making.

Songs, rhymes, and word play are great ways to introduce children to many of the phonological awareness concepts mentioned above. And the skill of phonological awareness is easy to teach because it is so much fun for children. Almost all children's songs and nursery rhymes involve words that rhyme, and many have examples of alliteration. You can clap out the rhythm, the words, or the syllables in any children's song or nursery rhyme. You can also return to the same song or nursery rhyme several times during the course of a year to teach more and more advanced aspects of phonological awareness. Just think about all of the sounds that a child must notice in order to sing a song.

The child must recognize and remember the melody (tune), the rhythm (beat), the tempo (speed), and the order and pattern of words and verses. Usually, the best way to remember the order of the words is by paying attention to both the content and the way that words rhyme. Each new song differs from previously learned songs in all of these sound components. Therefore, it's not as easy as you might think for children to focus on all these components at the same time.

Whether you're selecting songs, rhymes, verses, or other word play activities, consider the following:

* **Your Purpose.** Are you trying to teach rhyming, alliteration, segmenting, or another skill? While all these activities are great fun for children, they serve different purposes and help tune children's ears in different ways. Try to draw children's attention to the skill you're attempting to teach—for instance to notice whether words have two syllables or three, whether they rhyme, or whether they start with the same sound. You may also want them to be conscious of rhythmic patterns, such as the beat of a song or a nursery rhyme. The more intentional you are in your purpose for teaching, the more you will help children begin to learn the skill.

* **The Difficulty Level.** Young children vary greatly in their sensitivity to rhyme and alliteration. Some are just naturals and seem to just get it. Others may seem as though they have a tin ear. It is better, then, to start with short, pithy rhymes before going on to more complicated ones. Remember that the purpose of these activities is for children to hear the sounds carefully. Slurring over words to get to the next set of phrases actually does more harm than good. Keeping it simple, especially in the beginning, helps children become more familiar with the patterns you're intending for them to hear.

* **How Easy It Is to Remember.** Songs, rhymes, and other word play are useful for teaching because they can be so memorable. In fact, we often call them mnemonic devices because they help children remember something that would be otherwise so much harder. You might recall "Conjunction Junction" and other *Schoolhouse Rock* favorites from the 1970s and 80s. What this series demonstrated is that clever animation and a catchy song could actually teach grammar.

  Select songs and other word plays that are likely to become favorites over time. You'll find that you return to them again and again.

* **First, Focus on the Whole.** It will help children if you introduce songs and nursery rhymes slowly and repeat them often. Begin by performing the song or nursery rhyme several times so that the children can hear and enjoy its sounds. It sometimes helps if you can make silly faces or add hand motions. Hearing the entire song or nursery rhyme will get children excited about learning something new.

  Then, begin to take it apart. Sing or say one line or even part of a line and then ask the children to repeat it. Always ask the children to sing everything they know from the very beginning before adding on a new section. The process of learning a new song or nursery rhyme may take several sessions.

* **The Vocabulary Words.** Vocabulary and phonological awareness are integrally related: When you teach vocabulary, children learn about the sounds of new words. And when they learn about sounds, they're actually learning to extend their vocabulary. Don't forget, then, to teach children about the meaning of the words in a song or nursery rhyme. This is a great way to introduce children to new vocabulary. Also, they won't understand why songs are silly or funny if they don't know the meaning of the words. What does it mean when a star "twinkles"? Is an "itsy bitsy" spider, a big spider or a small spider? In "Row, Row, Row Your Boat," what exactly is a "stream"? It is important for children to know the answers to these questions.

* **Hand Motions, Clapping, Marching to the Beat.** As you know, children use their bodies expressively when they learn. They love to sway to the music, dance, and clap their hands to the rhythm. You can draw children's attention to the rhythm of a song by clapping, or marching along, with the beat. You can also play along with musical instruments. It's fun to see your class marching around in a circle, using instruments and singing "Oh Susanna" or "Row, Row, Row Your Boat," but this silly scene is really about helping children to focus on sounds. It also helps to tell children to "sing the song in their heads."

But all this motion can also be distracting if you're not carefully monitoring the activity. The noise of banging on instruments may distract children from hearing the sounds clearly. Sometimes children can get so involved in the hand motions that they no longer recite the words.

One solution is for you to perform the hand motions and let them do the singing. Your hand motions will help them remember the words. And once they feel completely comfortable, they will join in and do both. You can also make other changes to help children pay attention to sound. You can ask children to chant a nursery rhyme or sing a song loudly and then softly or quickly and then slowly. Whatever strategy works, you are helping children attend to the sounds of our language.

Clapping, marching, or playing instruments encourages children to pay attention to sounds, rhythm, and words.

Closing

"Ready to sing for our guest today?" says Ms. Smith to her Head Start class. "Which song shall we sing?" What seems like a hundred hands pop up. It's so clear that the children are enthusiastic to perform before their visitor. After much deliberation and discussion among the children, they collectively select an old favorite, "John Jacob Jingleheimer Schmitt," singing with great gusto, playfully modulating their voices louder and softer as they come to the refrain.

Beyond the sheer enjoyment these songs offer, we see that it is a way to imbue children with the delights of language. Literacy is not just about skill development. It's also about grasping the various ways in which language supports playful interactions. In fact, it looks like play, and that is one way children start to learn about reading.

CHAPTER 5

Developmental Writing

Three 4-year-olds at the writing table:

COREY: We're makin' lines.

JAMES: Yeah, we're writin'. We're makin' lines.

MIRANDA: Lines is very easy.

When you are just 4 years old, writing seems pretty easy. But the developmental journey from making lines to writing real words is not so easy. In fact it is probably one of the hardest things young children ever do as emerging readers and writers. Learning to write (and spell) is hard because it requires children to use several physical and mental processes at once. Small hands must grasp and control a bulky writing tool. Active minds must focus attention on making marks that express ideas. But hardest of all, the marks must follow certain rules that make them readable later on and comprehensible to others. Managing all this physical and mental activity requires more than "makin' lines," although that's a good place to start when you are very young.

In this chapter we talk about what teachers can do to help young children begin to learn to write. Writing in preschool is a new big idea in early education, so we first provide the research foundations for it. Every day we learn more about how writing develops in young children, and we offer you the most current information on this amazing process. Our close-up on practice describes some techniques and strategies you can incorporate into your daily program. Early writing should be fun and exploratory for young children—and above all, meaningful. Name writing, shared writing, and play-based writing are the staples of practice that support early writing development.

What the Research Says

At a very young age, children show interest in writing and are tremendously curious about what writing is for and how it works (see Figure 5.1). From studies into early writing over the past few decades, we know the following:

* Before children enter school, they have some ideas about the purpose and content of writing (Ferriero & Teberosky, 1984; Mason, 1984; Teale & Sulzby, 1986).

* Social interactions between adults and children and among peers are important in helping young children learn to write (Dyson, 1993; Rowe, in press; Tomasello, 1999).

* Emergent young writers shift from *drawing* writing to *symbolic* writing, where the marks (letters) are understood to have meaning (Karmiloff-Smith, 1992; Levin & Bus, 2003; Treiman, Kessler, & Bourassa, 2001).

Used with permission of Elena Bodrova and Deborah Leong

FIGURE 5.1

Here Lora writes about her role as Sleeping Beauty in dramatic play.

Nurturing Knowledge

＊ Children's name writing is a stepping-stone to alphabet knowledge (Aram & Levin, 2004; Bloodgood, 1999; Dunsmuir & Blatchford, 2004; Ferriero & Teberosky, 1982; Both-de Vries, 2006; Read, 1971).

For all these reasons, writing should be a regular part of the preschooler's day. In these early years, children learn to write their name, and so become aware of the relationship between sound and symbol. They explore writing as a tool for making meaning and soon learn its power for expressing needs, wants, and emotions.

From Making Marks to Making Words

To become writers, children must learn that writing involves using alphabet letters (symbols) for spoken words and putting these marks (accurately) on paper. As we said earlier, this is no easy feat. So how do children get started with such a daunting task? Well, just like they do with most things: they watch others and try to do what they do. Children first learn about writing by watching adults, siblings, and friends write for a variety of purposes—grocery and to-do lists, birthday cards and bank checks, greeting cards and notes. Not to be left out, they too find reasons to write and often leave their marks on unintended places—walls, cupboards, chairs, and clothes.

At first, children use scribbles and drawings to communicate their ideas. Once they learn to write their own names, they discover letters and soon after that letter names and sounds. Children use the letters to write new words, and they make discoveries about the connection between letters, sounds, and meaning. They start to take a "grown-up" view of writing as a symbol system, and they try to spell words—which in the early stages can be just delightful (see Figure 5.2). When their writing is appreciated and encouraged, they begin to string random letters together. They learn to make more and more sound-symbol matches. They use beginning consonants to represent words and soon puzzle over combinations within words

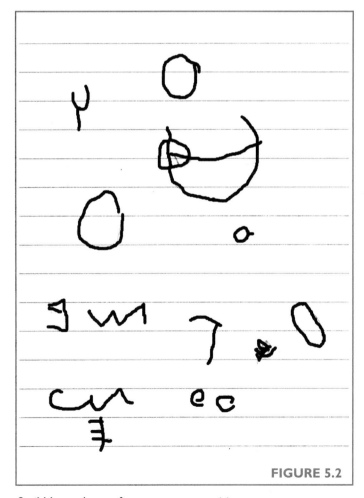

FIGURE 5.2

Scribble marks are first attempts at writing.

(e.g., *h-a-ch*) (see Figure 5.3).

But we are getting ahead of ourselves. For children to progress from making their first marks to writing real words takes a long, gradual journey. To appreciate this process, let's take a look at how writing develops over time—first with making marks, then drawing and writing, name writing, and finally, word writing. Your understanding of writing development will help you make decisions about how to help young children grow as emerging writers.

MAKING MARKS

Children's first attempts at writing are scribble-like marks that seem to go every which way, or "scribble-scrabble," as the children like to say. Although these random scribbles seem meaningless, they certainly are not. They are, in fact, the foundation of all writing and signal the onset of the learning-to-write process. The sheer pleasure of making them (and talking about them at the same time) motivates the child's desire and will to learn to use writing in a meaningful way. Take a look at 18-month-old Brian's use of crayons and pencil to create a message he just must write (Figure 5.4).

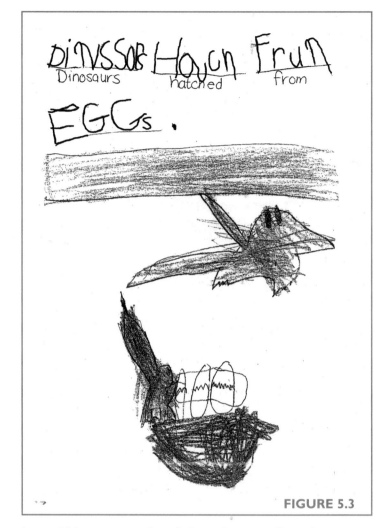

FIGURE 5.3

Later children use sound-symbol matches to spell words.

Notice how his markings are random, and that they're light, showing little control of the crayon. He is discovering that when he applies markers or crayons to paper (or other surfaces) they leave marks. Right now he enjoys scribbling and then looking at his marks. What power. This is a writing experience that will capture his attention for many months. But in the not so distant future he will begin to understand that marks should have meaning. They should "say" something, so he'll make scribble-like marks, point to them, and "say" what they mean (see Figure 5.5). As his writing experiences grow, he will pay more attention to the marks and become more deliberate in his writing actions. He starts to shift from scribbles to drawing and using letter-like forms that he has discovered in the environment and in his own name (see Figure 5.6).

FIGURE 5.4

At first, Brian's markings show little control.

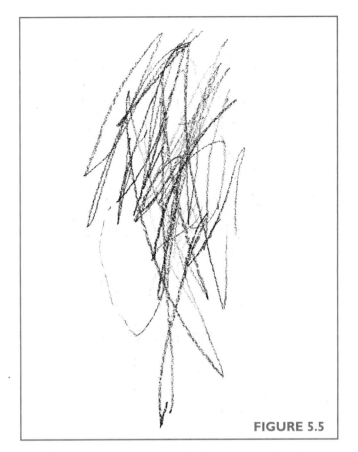

FIGURE 5.5

Soon he is making more controlled marks and tells what they mean.

FIGURE 5.6

This sample shows Brian's shift from scribbling to forming letters.

DRAWING AND WRITING

Before the age of 4, most children do not know the difference between drawing and writing. And in fact they mostly "draw" letters just like they draw pictures of the sun, their house, and their family. We can see this in their early compositions, which often contain combinations of letters, numbers, and objects. Look at the series of writing products in Figure 5.7. Here you can see how children include illustrations, or they create hybrid forms of drawing and writing, using color, forms, or numbers.

At around age 4 or so, children show signs of distinguishing their own writing from their drawings. You, too, can sort their drawing from their writing by looking at the pen motions. Smooth, circular motions indicate drawing while writing consists of shorter, smaller strokes. Children's writing, in other words, becomes recognizable as writing (not drawing). But the role of letters as the "true" meaning markers in writing can still befuddle children up to 6 years of age. Six-year-old Kalid, for example, wrote the word *roda* ("wheel" in Dutch) as the string *oa* four times when asked to write the phrase *four wheels* (Tolchinsky-Landsmann, 2003).

At some point in their early writing development children grasp (with adults' help) that drawing and writing are different ways of representing their ideas. In separating these two expressive modes, they make an evolutionary leap toward understanding the symbolic nature of writing. Children showing this awareness are on the cusp of understanding the connections between letters and meaning and well on their way to making the transition from drawing writing to symbolic writing. They actually redefine writing in their own minds and start to use letter combinations to express their ideas. Now they begin the next leg of their developmental journey as they search out just how speech maps to print. And on this trip, the richest source of information in the whole world is the child's own name (see Figure 5.8).

From Both-deVries, A. (2006). *It's all in the name. Early writing: from imitating to phonetic writing.*

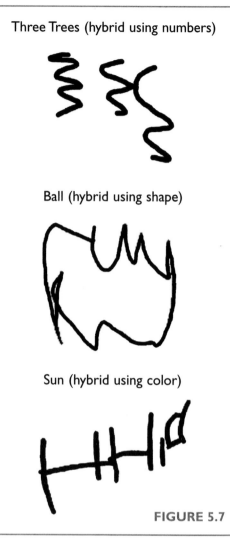

Three Trees (hybrid using numbers)

Ball (hybrid using shape)

Sun (hybrid using color)

FIGURE 5.7

These are examples of hybrid forms of drawing and writing.

FIGURE 5.8

Andrew writes his name.

NAME WRITING

Like so much of learning to write in general, learning to write one's own name is not simple—but it is always absolutely absorbing. Children start by memorizing the whole thing and then utilizing a helping hand (mother, father, sister, brother) to make the signature. The experience is thrilling and often repeated until whole-name recognition sets in. It continues then with a hard look at the individual letters and trying to make them (first a stick with a circle, then . . .) and to say them ("Paolo. P-a-o-l-o"). Later, letters in the name are used to spell other words. Notice how Emma, age 3, used letters found in her own name to take down the family's dinner order (see Figure 5.9).

Let's study this a bit. She clearly has the *a* figured out, but notice how her *E* has many lines, and some of her *m*-like letters have a few too many humps. She also has squiggly, letter-like forms and some drawings, such as the face in the bottom left corner. Emma knew that letters were needed to write the order. She

FIGURE 5.9

Here is Emma's dinner order.

had seen this modeled many times in restaurants, so she used letters she knew from her name to write. It is clear that she understood that a long order takes lots of letters, that letters can be used more than once, and that they can appear in different sequences ("AAMAAE, AMMM," etc.). She may also have a glimmer of the insight that combinations of letters carry meaning,

It is common for young children to use the letters of their name in their pretend writing. And once children begin to notice letters in their own names, they begin to see "their" letters everywhere. Mikalea sees the golden arches and cries out, "There's my letter!" So, the concept that "name" letters can be found in other places, too, begins to make sense.

But we need to ask: Does name writing help children learn alphabet letters and sounds? Does it push developmental writing forward? Well . . . *maybe*. There is some evidence that name writing helps children's phonological awareness and also their general ability to match sounds and letters. In other words, name writing primes children's abilities to decode and spell new words later on. But we have to be careful. Just because children can write their own name, there's no guarantee that they understand the alphabetic principle behind it—that is, sound-symbol matching. Children can recognize and even write their name yet have no idea about how the letters *spell* their name. For this they need to advance to word writing and a deeper understanding of the relationship between sounds and letters.

WORD WRITING

Families and teachers help young children learn to write their name. But they do a lot more when they name the letters and link sounds to letters, and in this way "teach" the basic skills involved in invented spelling of new words. Such support helps children gain letter knowledge and develop an emerging understanding of the alphabetic principle. Letters of their own name are used to spell new words.

The process begins with the first letter of the name, whatever it is, and spreads quickly to other name letters for invented spellings. Ahead of all the others, children know the sound of the first letter of their name, and being quick learners, they recognize it in other words and can correctly represent it in a new word. This rich bit of learning starts a cascade of letter-sound awareness that opens the door to invented spelling. The child's name becomes a kind of *decoder* used for spelling new words. Once discovered, invented spelling spreads out in all directions and the number of letter-sound matches proliferates.

The basic skills of word writing continue to develop through the primary grades. At first, children use one or two letters to represent an entire word (often the first letter, just as they did a while before in their own name) and usually represent the most prominent sound or sounds of a word. We refer to this developmental period as "early phonemic" because children are showing they know some letter-sound matches (see Figure 5.10).

Before long children start to "sound their way through a word" and identify a letter for each sound they hear. This period is frequently called "letter-name" as children make a one-to-one match between sound and letter. It shows that children can segment phonemes in the word and identify the correct letter for each one. It's amazing that now they can attend to and represent these tiny sound bits when just a few years before they could hardly control the marker to scribble.

Into second grade, children are starting to pay attention to the sound-letter matches and combinations within words. This initiates a long transitional period in spelling development when children explore and discover spelling patterns, syllables, and

Raccoons come out at night.

FIGURE 5.10

This is an example of early phonemic spelling. Note that the child copied the word *raccoon*.

morphemic structures, such as prefixes, suffixes, and root words (see Figure 5.11). What a long way children have come on their developmental writing journey! From making marks to writing words, they have grown and developed into writers who can draw on their mental dictionaries (and real ones, too) to express ideas, share stories, make reports, text-message, and in all ways take on the role of author (see Figure 5.12).

DOING LOTS OF WRITING

Your role in supporting and pulling forward children's developmental writing is key. The literacy routines, environment, and modeling you provide help children learn the basics of emergent writing. These include concepts and skills related to writing processes (e.g., writing for a purpose), writing applications (e.g., labeling) and writing conventions (e.g., spelling).

Here are four "must-do" instructional approaches we strongly recommend that you incorporate in your program: name writing, shared writing, scaffolded writing, and play-based writing. Each offers plenty of learning opportunities that help children acquire the knowledge, skills, and motivation (desire) essential for learning to write.

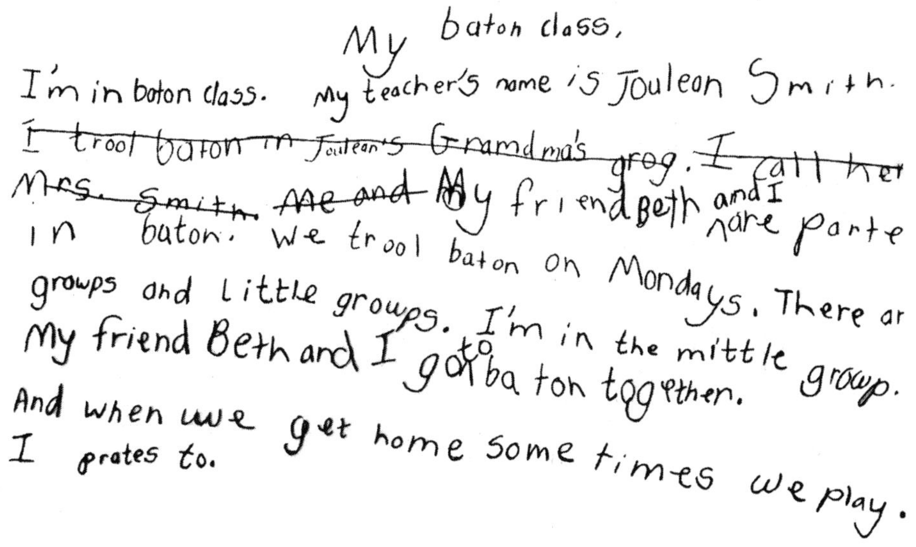

Name Writing
The first written word children recognize is usually their own name, and earlier in

FIGURE 5.11

This writer uses early transitional spelling.

FIGURE 5.12

This writing is an example of late transitional spelling.

the chapter we saw how children such as Emma use their name to write for different purposes. Name writing has lots of benefits for writing development at preschool. Here are a few:

* It's personal, so it's motivating.
* It draws attention to letter names and sounds.
* It provides a set of words for reading (one's own name and those of classmates).
* It can be a focus of instruction.
* It can help children organize their environment.

A preschool classroom should abound with name writing activities such as these.

Signing In. As adults the first thing we are often asked to do when we attend meetings, patronize walk-in businesses (such as hair salons and medical clinics), or enter government buildings is to sign in. Children often see adults signing in and out as they go about their daily routines. Many preschool teachers are adapting this idea to the classroom; the activity provides a quick, routine way for children to practice name writing within minutes of arrival.

While some teachers use standard clipboard sign-in sheets such as those found in offices, others have children sign in on chart paper, loose-leaf unlined paper (to be later put in a binder to show development over time), or on whiteboards. It doesn't matter how you have children go about this task. What matters is that children are routinely getting daily practice in letter formation.

Names as Labels. At the beginning of the year, when children are just beginning to learn to write their names, fill a pocket chart with computer-generated name labels. Each child has his or her own pocket with one of the labels on the front. Inside the pocket is a stack of name labels for the child to use to attach to artwork and writing samples as a way of independently labeling their work. Since identifying their name is difficult for some 3-year-olds, you might use a picture of an animal next to the name so that they can easily find their pocket. So, for example, there might be lion next to Lajita's name. This will help her to identify her name labels from everyone else's.

Class Photo Book. Attach the children's photos to blank name cards and then add first names. Next, bind these cards together in a book and place it in the Writing Center along with blank paper for copying and a set of uppercase and lowercase plastic letters for matching. Children love to practice writing their friends' names, and the books are very user-friendly. This activity fosters many skills, such as practicing left-to-right progression, letter formation, and horizontal letter placement, and meets each child at his or her individual level.

A Pretty Involved Name Game. Write children's first names on 4-inch strips of colored tagboard. For children with the same name, use their first name plus the first initial of their last name (e.g., James B.). Put the strips into a brightly colored gift bag. At circle time, show the children the bag and tell them that some very important words are in the bag. Encourage them to make guesses about what these very important words might be. After everyone has had a chance to guess, pull out a card strip and read the name (with gusto!). Invite the appropriate child forward to claim the name. Repeat for each child, using expression to read each name. Explain to children that everyone's name has alphabet letters, but that the letters are joined together differently for each name.

On another day, draw one name from the gift bag. Tell the children: *This is the Name of the Day.* (Continue until all children's names have a special day. Use the jingle *Higgledy, piggledy, dee/I wonder whose name it will be?* to select a name from the gift bag each time.)

Once a name is selected, take some time to talk about the letters in the name. *How many letters? Is it a long or short name? How does it sound at the beginning? What other words start like that?*

Write the name on a card strip as children "spell" the name. Cut apart the name into its separate letters. Ask the owner to put the name back together in a pocket chart.

As a final activity, invite the children to draw a picture of the child whose name is the Name of the Day and to put his or her name below it. Children should also include their own names as the artists. Assemble the pictures into a "my name book" for the child of the day to take home. The variety of pictures and name writing is a lot of fun to look at on a rainy day!

Sorting. To focus on letter-sound introduction, letter recognition, letter sounds in words, syllables, and the concept of words, class names can be displayed in a pocket chart where children can manipulate them. They can compare names and use them for sorting activities, such as sorting by number of letters, number of syllables, beginning or similar letters, boy names and girl names, alphabetical order, and names that rhyme/don't rhyme.

Letter Hunt. This activity helps children recognize letters in different font styles and to learn the uppercase and lowercase forms of each letter. Gather clean, empty boxes that the children might already be familiar with, such as cereal boxes, pizza boxes, and toothpaste boxes. Show them the boxes and remind them that letters go together in special ways to spell not just their names, but names of foods and other things. Explore a few boxes together and make discoveries, such as *The cereal* Kix *starts with the same letter as Kate's name. There's a z in* pizza *like in Zach's name.*

Hand out "magic glasses" (sunglasses) to each child. Put several boxes at each table and send the children to the tables with their name cards. Encourage them to look on the boxes to see if any of their letters appear on the box anywhere. After a few minutes, have the children switch tables so they can do more exploring with different boxes. Children can cut out words from boxes that have the same letters as their name.

Shared Writing

You need to offer plenty of opportunities for children to draw, scribble, talk, and write throughout the day, but you also need to accompany those opportunities with good models of writing. You can model many concepts of print, such as correct spacing, letter formation, punctuation, and directionality, through the shared writing experience. Shared writing also provides a way for you to think aloud as you model for children how to compose different kinds of messages (such as a letter to a principal or a sign advertising a performance) or listen for sounds and spell words—skills they will eventually incorporate into their own writing.

Begin:

* Engage the class in a discussion about the purpose of the task.

* Model thinking aloud about the task: *If I'm going to write a letter I should put "Dear Ms. Jackson" about here* [point to the spot on the paper].

Start writing:

* Write slowly, commenting on content and conventions. Make sure all of the children can see the print.

* Be explicit in your writing and comments. Point to words while reading and rereading sentences.

Have the children join in:

* Ask children to help with the writing and "share the pen" by having them add letters, words, or punctuation marks. They can even draw pictures in place of words or illustrate the text at the bottom of the page.

* Read the text chorally a few times.

* Post the text for rereading. Text created during the shared writing experience should be accessible to children at other times so that they can refer back to it and reread this familiar text.

You can encourage children to extend the shared writing experience by providing plenty of materials and opportunities to write. Every early childhood classroom needs to have a place for children to write, draw, and compose on their own. Since the same things do not motivate all children, it is important to provide a variety of writing materials. You can motivate children and create interest with different kinds of paper such as construction, lined, textured, and stationery. Envelopes, index cards, and old greeting cards inspire others. Add stencils, stamps, scissors, photos, and hole punches for scrapbooking and bookmaking. A computer is a great addition to any classroom, and some children are very motivated by old typewriters!

Shared writing is motivating for children.

Scaffolded Writing

Developed by Elena Bodrova and Deborah Leong (1996), scaffolded writing is an instructional technique that deliberately transitions children from dictated stories to their own independent writing. It consists of a scaffolded set of interactions in which the teacher progressively "hands over" the writing of a message to the child. First, the teacher models what to write, making lines and writing words on the lines. Next, the children make lines for each word, and the teacher writes the words. Finally, the children produce the lines and the letters on the lines for words in the message. Through these progressive interactions, children's attention is focused on making sound-letter matches and on the function of punctuation.

Here's a brief look at how scaffolded writing works in practice. Children need whiteboards to write on, markers, and sound maps that they can use later on to help them make sound-letter matches. A sound map is like an alphabet chart, but it is arranged differently. Letter clusters are arranged by how they are articulated. The letters *m* and *n* are clustered together because they are both nasal sounds. The letters *g*, *k*, and *h* are clustered together because they are all produced closer to the back of one's throat. The sound map is used in the Tools of the Mind program developed by Bodrova & Leong (1996). Children should be proficient at each step before progressing to the next one.

Get started:

* Substitute scaffolded writing for the traditional morning message.
* Tell the children, *Today's message is "We are going to run and jump in gym."* Have them repeat the message.
* Draw lines for each word in the message, as follows:

  ＿＿＿ ＿＿＿ ＿＿＿ ＿＿＿ ＿＿＿

  ＿＿＿ ＿＿＿ ＿＿＿ ＿＿＿.

* With the children's help write a word on each line. Show children how to use the sound map.

Up the ante:

* Provide a message that the children repeat. Use the same stem. "<u>We are going</u> to read about whales."
* Ask the children to draw the lines for each word.
* With the children's help, write a word on each line. Practice using the sound map.

Up the ante again:

* Provide a message that the children repeat. Continue to use the same stem. "<u>We are going</u> to visit the zoo tomorrow."
* Ask the children to draw lines for each word.
* Help the children write the words on the line the best they can. Accept all attempts (even scribble).

Once children are at this point, continue the sequence and encourage children to use their sound maps (and each other) to help them write the words. Figure 5.13 on the next page shows a few examples.

Here are four examples of play plans.

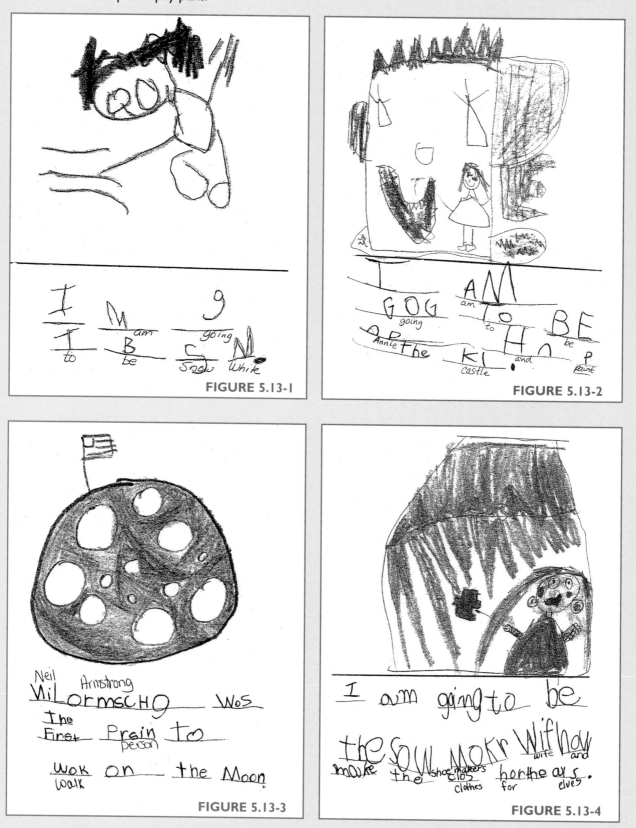

FIGURE 5.13-1

I M 9
I(to) M(am) 9(going)
I B S N
I(to) B(be) S(Snow) N(White)

FIGURE 5.13-2

I GOG AM TO BE
GOG(going) AM(am) TO(to) BE(be)
AP The KI and P
AP(Annie) The KI(castle) P(paint)

FIGURE 5.13-3

Neil Armstrong
NiLOrmscHg wos
The Prain To
First person(person)
wok on the Moon
Walk

FIGURE 5.13-4

I am going to be
the sow MoKr Wifhav
the(shoemakers) clos horthe ars.
make(make) clothes for(for) elves.

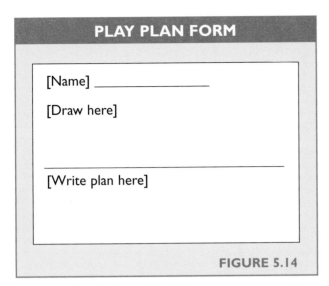

PLAY PLAN FORM

[Name] _____

[Draw here]

_____

[Write plan here]

FIGURE 5.14

Providing play plan forms for children encourages writing.

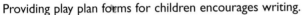

FIGURE 5.15

Saul writes about his plan to make a castle.

Scaffolded writing can also be used to help children make play plans, especially when play centers are organized around themes or story reenactments. See figure 5.14 for a blank play plan form and figure 5.15 for a completed plan.

Before going to the play center, children draw their plan and then write what they plan to do. The letters "P M N L SM" in the upper right-hand corner are for the teacher to make note of any assistance she provided. Did she help the child draw a *picture*? Decide on a *message*? Write his or her *name*? Make the *lines*? Use the *sound map*? Noting this, the teacher can gradually pull forward children's writing development to higher levels.

We've provided you with a very brief introduction to scaffolded writing, which is a rather complex early writing instructional technique. Before attempting it, we strongly encourage you to learn more about it and, if possible, participate in a training workshop. For more information on scaffolded writing, see Bodrova and Leong Tools of the Mind program.

Play-Based Writing

A lot of writing can go on in play, especially when play areas are well-stocked with writing supplies, such as markers, pencils, paper, templates, notepads, and the like. So, one of your main goals as a teacher is to make sure each and every play area has an adequate supply of writing tools and materials. To stimulate lots of writing, you can go one step further and link the writing materials at hand to the theme of the play area. In the blocks area, for example, you can add rulers, graph paper, and supplies for making signs. Liven up the traditional art area with assorted markers, sketch pads, and stationery-making ideas. The box on page 84 lists a few more ideas.

But how does play support children's writing development? Evidence points to at least three benefits. First, play gives children the opportunity to use writing for real reasons from their point of view. Do you recall Emma and her delight in writing a dinner order? Even though it's just pretend, it is a powerful lesson in the purpose of writing—in this instance to remember who gets what for dinner. When Steven grabs a paper strip and writes, "STOHAEOEHOLLLDEAS-DAGYAOE" (Stay out of here!), and tapes it at the entry to the block area, he uses writing to make his point—the area is off-limits. So, from a developmental point of view, play provides a learning opportunity wherein the function of writing becomes very clear to children. At play, children are focused on what writing can do and not so much on how words are formed. The insights they gain are critical because they fuel children's motivation to learn to write.

A second benefit of play is the sheer frequency with which it allows children to use writing tools (e.g., markers) and supplies to practice the physical work of writing. Take a look at the following exchange between Clifford and Leon. Notice how much fun they're having making *b*'s, *c*'s, and *d*'s, but also how much they're exercising their fine motor skills to form letters. Play can provide a pretty strenuous work out in handwriting for emerging writers!

> LEON: You did all of it, Clifford [*pointing to marks on the paper that Clifford has been very carefully making*].
>
> CLIFFORD: Lookee, dere, Leon, *b–b–c–l–2–d–l–3–c*. I just count all of 'em [*pointing to each mark he has made and naming each one*].
>
> I told you, Leon, a *b*, a *c* [*pointing to the marks*].
>
> LEON: You did good work, Clifford, . . . real good work.

A third benefit is the jumping-off place play provides for writing compositions. Many a good story has its origins in a good round of play. Take this one by Chucky, Jason, and (of course) Jeremy Michael Walton, for example (Figure 5.16). This kind of play-based writing, bubbling up out of play, prepares the ground for children's engagement in the writing process: choosing ideas

---

WRITING SUPPLIES

In science:
* Chart paper
* Small notebooks
* Markers
* Tape measure
* Sticky notes
* Graph paper

In mathematics:
* Shape templates
* Graph paper
* Protractor (child appropriate)
* Assorted rulers

In socio-dramatic play:
* Assorted forms for theme play (e.g., order pads)
* Pencils, markers
* Stationery/envelopes
* Assorted notepads
* Calendars
* Labels
* Postcards
* Stamps

Nurturing Knowledge

to share, determining a purpose for writing, considering audience, and producing a message for others. Play is a wonderful source of imaginative stories!

Indoor play is one place for play-based writing. But there are others. When going on a neighborhood walk or on a longer field trip, have the children pretend they are private investigators, scientists, or archeologists. Give them small notebooks to make drawings and to record facts and observations. Ben Mardell (1999), for example, encouraged his preschoolers to be "squirrel scientists." They took a squirrel census, marking down all the squirrels they noticed in the neighborhood. They recorded squirrel facts—"Gray squirrels eat acorns. Red squirrels eat pinecone seeds. They wrote down new questions— Do squirrels eat snakes? Do they live everywhere in the world?"

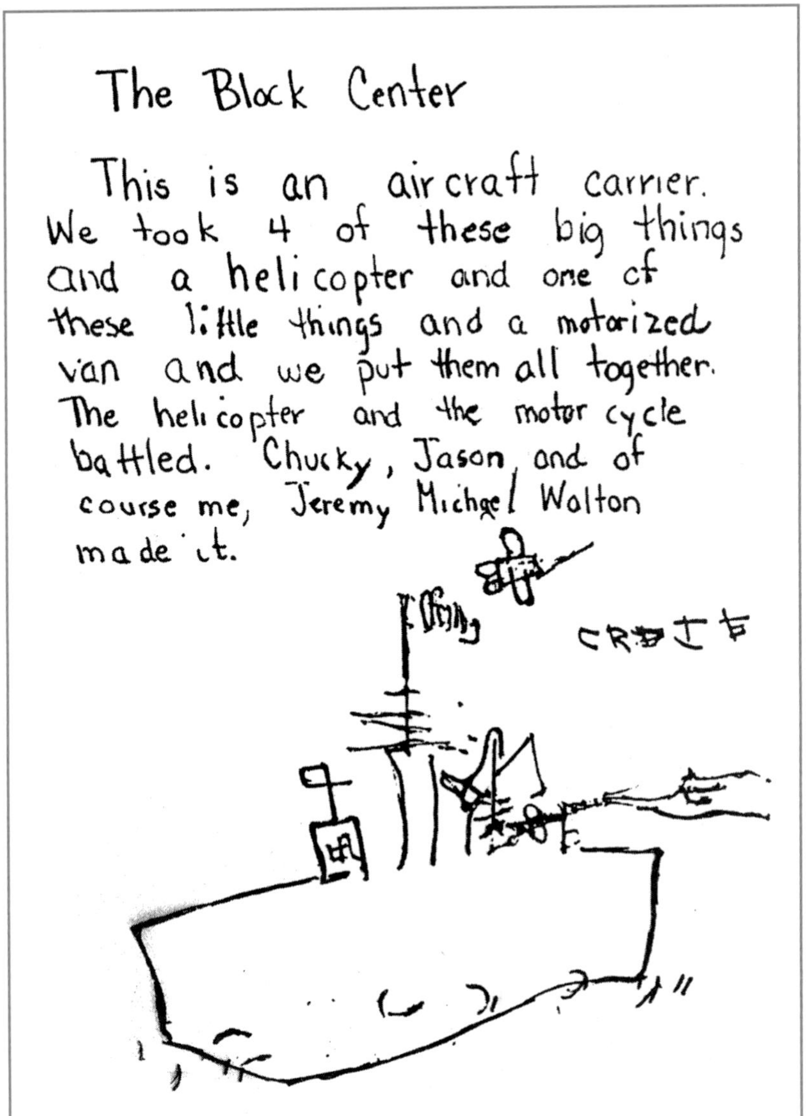

Encourage writing during outdoor play, too, by providing colored chalk, markers, and materials for signs and labels. Pretending to be park rangers, Joanna Austen's boys and girls made signs for their nature area, using blocks of wood and strips of bark to identify plants, trees, insect hiding places, and the always busy bird feeder. Labeling the outdoors for discovery and play, you see, can be as much fun as labeling the indoors.

The Black Center

This is an aircraft carrier. We took 4 of these big things and a helicopter and one of these little things and a motorized van and we put them all together. The helicopter and the motor cycle battled. Chucky, Jason, and of course me, Jeremy Michael Wolton made it.

FIGURE 5.16

This is a dictated play story from the Block Center.

Closing

*P*reschoolers Ericka and Jackie are deep in "doctor's office" play, and Jackie says, "One lady I know is comin' over. You know why? Her husband said she wanted . . . fifty-five pink and two purple. Write that down, Ericka, fifty-five pin-n-n-n-k and two . . . two pur-r-r- pl-l-l-l. Have you got that? Write her name on the medicine, too." So, Ericka writes on the "prescription" pad, referring to her name tag for letters now and then. "I writed it, and I'm waitin," she says.

It is in the preschool years that young children discover writing—and what it can do. Starting with their own names, they eagerly pursue making lines. In the process, they learn about letters—letter names, sounds, and how to make them, holding their pencil ever so tight. They discover the power of the written word: to claim what's theirs, to remember things, to tell ideas, and to express themselves.

"I will not taack off my new ckamoflag [camouflage jacket]," writes Deshona, "cus its my favrite culer pink and green. If it evr ript I will criy its my favrite I wir it to school. My mom bot it its speshol I will not take it off it speshol."

What a statement! And what a writing achievement! All young children love to write. They are budding authors, every one. And your preschool classroom should provide them with the writing tools, the time, the assistance, and the motivation they need to grow as writers.

Literacy and Play

The Players: Scott and David (the librarians) and Aaron (the visitor)

DAVID, to Aaron: Wanna buy books?

SCOTT: Write your name here. [*Aaron writes.*]

SCOTT, to others: They not buyin' 'em. This is a library. They rent 'em.

AARON: Could I rent this book, please? [*He signs card.*]

DAVID: You return it on this stack. You've got four days.

AARON: Does this mean four days? Wow! Neato, man! Hey! I bought this
scary book for four days.

*P*lay should be an essential part of any early literacy program. But play is in serious jeop-
ardy! Many preschools and kindergartens have reduced or even eliminated playtime from
their schedules in favor of more structured language and literacy lessons (Zigler & Bishop-Josef,

Chapter 6: Literacy and Play

87

2004). Play, the basic argument goes, is a waste of instructional time, especially in the areas of reading and literacy.

But this is a faulty argument (and a dangerous one). Considerable evidence, in fact, supports the critical role of play, and in particular pretend play, on children's language and emergent literacy in the preschool years (Zigler, Singer, & Bishop-Josef, 2004). According to Vygotsky (1966), pretend play is the leading activity of the preschool and kindergarten period because it *leads to* developmental accomplishments, such as imagination, higher-level thinking (e.g., problem solving), and self-regulation. Taking away playtime may actually stunt motivation and growth such that children gain less—not more—from instruction (Panksepp, 1998).

So, in this chapter we argue strongly for making play an integral part of your early literacy curriculum. We begin with a short review of the research on play and literacy connections. We want to you to be well informed and have key research-based points at your fingertips, so you can defend play in your program. We then describe a "blended" approach to the literacy-in-play practice—one that integrates direct forms of instruction with structured play activities that encourage practice of skills that have been taught. Using practical examples and procedures, we show how play works to support educational goals and content standards for early literacy learning in preschoolers. We also describe teaching techniques and facilitation strategies that support your role in play. Finally—because we want you to be a vigorous advocate for play in the literacy education of young children—we offer some suggestions for documenting literacy learning in play so you can help parents understand play's role in the early literacy curriculum, and so you can actively promote play in your community. Play, as 4-year-old Sheonna thoughtfully observed, "is what kids do so they know." We need to keep this insight squarely before us when planning and implementing the early literacy curriculum to ensure proper playtime for our emerging readers and writers.

What the Research Says

Play is necessary for young children to grow physically and mentally (Bruner, 1972; Piaget, 1969; Vygotsky, 1966). It is a prime opportunity to use symbolic thinking (using words to represent real objects and events) and problem-solving skills (using strategies to accomplish goals). Play's role in early literacy development is also very important and supported by research (see box on next page).

Children need to learn language, to hear sounds, to know the alphabet, to grasp basic print concepts, and to become interested in print. Play in early childhood supports this intellectual work. It provides a "zone" where children can practice established skills but also reach for new ones in flexible and enjoyable ways. They can stretch their thinking beyond the here and now. Play helps children practice self-regulation because good players play according to the roles and rules of the pretend, and thus cannot act any way they please; they must behave in a way that conforms to the play. And there's the fun!

RESEARCH ON PLAY AND EARLY LITERACY DEVELOPMENT

* Play develops children's oral language, oral language comprehension, and storytelling abilities (Bruner, 1983; Dickinson & Tabors, 2001; Eckler & Weininger, 1989; Sawyer et al., in press; Stone & Christie, 1996; Wells, 1986).

* Pretend play provides practice in early literacy processes (Bodrova & Leong, 1996; Bruner, 1984; Johnson, Christie, & Wardle, 2005; Roskos & Christie, 2004).

* Word play develops phonological awareness (sensitivity to sounds in words) (Cazden, 1976; Fernandez-Fein & Baker, 1997; Weir, 1976).

* Play in literacy-enriched settings increases literacy behaviors (Morrow, 1990; Neuman & Roskos, 1992; Vukelich, 1994).

* Play helps build background knowledge (Gmitrova & Gmitrova, 2003; Saltz, Dixson, & Johnson, 1977; Smilansky, 1968).

* Play makes reading and writing fun (Sonnenschein, Baker, Serpell, & Schmidt, 2000).

Literacy in Play: A "Blended" Approach

Play can further your goal of providing excellent early literacy instruction for all the children in your classroom when you blend instruction and related play activities. In other words, you deliberately mix or integrate the literacy content you are teaching with the indoor play activity you offer children. For example, in the block area you might help boys and girls create road signs. You can have them assist you with sounds in words, such as *stop* and *detour*, as you write and talk about the letters. This enables you to further teach early literacy concepts, strategies, and skills through an activity that is motivational for children. When playing with print, children are, in fact, learning "it" (written language) by doing "it."

A blended approach to literacy and play has several design features that put literacy-related play into the category of educational play, wherein educational goals, such as early learning standards, are combined with the characteristics of play—fun, choice, pretend, creativity, and personal meaning. According to Jim Christie and colleagues (Johnson et al., 2005), a blended approach includes the following:

* Large-group shared reading and writing to introduce children to new words, book language, and concepts of print

* Small-group instruction to teach specific strategies and skills, to provide guided practice, and to meet individual needs

* Content-rich language experiences to model, explain, and apply essential early literacy skills

* Theme-related dramatic play settings linked conceptually to language and literacy instruction

This blending of instruction and play does not need to apply to all your play settings, indoors and outdoors. Rather it should be used with a few, select dramatic play settings where language and literacy connections make sense and can be made obvious, monitored, and assessed. Here's an example.

Shelley Johnson's preschoolers are deeply involved in a theme on building and construction. They've already had several direct experiences with this theme. They went on a field trip to a construction site and visited a hardware store. A construction worker and an architect stopped by as classroom visitors and described their jobs. Everyone handled construction tools and blueprints—real objects of construction work.

During large-group time they sang songs and heard rhymes (see box at right). Shelley read a story about Builder Bob's toolbox mix-up, which the children thought was pretty funny. And later she read an informational book on how to build a doghouse, so the children were introduced to such words as *hammer*, *nails*, *saw*, and *level* and such phrases as *measure the boards*, *pound the nails*, *keep the boards straight*, and *raise the roof*. She showed them a medium-sized level and they all watched with fascination as the bubble went this way and that as she moved it up and down. Then the little bubble rested in the middle when she put it on the table. "Yes!" children exclaimed. "The table is level!"

In small groups of four to five children, Shelley helped the children make up a story using a wordless book about constructing buildings. She wrote it down on chart paper and, after reading it through together, the children signed their names. Each group posted their story in the library area for their friends to read. The next day, they sorted picture/word cards into three categories: tools for building (hammer, wrench, saw, level, tape measure); things to wear (hard hat, goggles, tool belt); construction vehicles (bulldozer, cement truck, crane, wrecking ball, lumberyard truck). Everybody thought goggles was a neat word with lots of /g/ sounds in it. The class agreed that the most fun was making signs for small buildings for Big Town, the model city they were working on in the block area. Spelling *hardware store* was kind of hard, they noted, and some kids even made a map of the town, which was really hard!

THEME RHYMES AND SONGS

Construction Song

(Sung to "So Early in the Morning")

This is the way we saw the wood,
saw the wood, saw the wood.
This is the way we saw the wood, so early in the morning. (*Make sawing motion.*)

This is the way we hammer the nails,
hammer the nails, hammer the nails.
This is the way we hammer the nails so early in the morning. (*Make hammering motion.*)

This is the way we . . .

   paint the room . . .

   turn the screw . . .

   drill a hole . . .

Construction Rhymes

"The Carpenter"
The carpenter's hammer goes knock, knock, knock,
And his saw goes see, saw, see,
He drills and measures,
He hammers and he saws
While he builds things for me.

or

"London Bridge"
London Bridge is falling down,
Falling down,
Falling down,
London Bridge is falling down,
My fair lady.

At playtime, children took turns in the construction site. They measured, planned, and built a cardboard box house. They designed other cardboard buildings, handled toy tools, and wore hard hats and goggles. They read signs Danger! Hard Hat Zone!, made many lists, and prepared blue-prints on lined graph paper. They took different roles and used lots of new words. After their play, they remembered what they did in their building and construction play books, and then displayed them on shelves by the entryway wall for everyone to browse and read (especially moms and dads). All agreed that the construction site was the best play area ever so far this year.

WHAT'S GOING ON HERE?

This is a delightful example of a blended approach that links early literacy instruction and play, but it is also one of serious pedagogy. Careful planning, monitoring, and managing ensure the coordinated flow of events that seem to so effortlessly move children along. For play to work in conjunction with your early literacy instruction, you need to make key pedagogic decisions before, during, and after playtime.

Before Play

Choose a theme or topic of study that is worthwhile, significant, and meaningful—one that will capture children's interest and lead to rich play that incorporates literacy activities. In practical terms, you should be able to demonstrate that your chosen theme meets the following criteria:

1. Provides world knowledge
2. Is relevant and appealing to children
3. Enables children to encounter important ideas and facts
4. Provides lots of opportunities for children to learn how to inquire

Themes such as fossils, color and light, and rain can stimulate rich dramatic play scenarios that involve new roles (archeologist, scientist, weather forecaster), new vocabulary (*sediment*, *transparent*, *downpour*), new behaviors (tracing, comparing, measuring), and literacy (recording, labeling, chart reading, word identification).

Tap and build children's background knowledge

MORE THEMES FOR RICH PLAY

Stormy Weather

Play examples:

- Weather forecaster predicting and monitoring weather
- Snowplow driver working during the storm to keep the roads clear

Building a Beautiful New Town

Play examples:

- Town planners planning and mapping the town
- Builders building the buildings
- Landscapers planting the trees and plants

In the Deep

Play examples:

- Marine biologist finding sea creatures
- Deep-sea diver searching for new marine life
- Artists drawing pictures of the deep

Starry, Starry Night

Play examples:

- Astronomers searching the night skies for a new planet
- Mapmakers drawing the constellations
- Planetarium builders designing an observatory

about the theme through direct experiences, such as field trips and shared reading. This helps children to remember what they know and to encounter new places, roles, ideas, and words they can use in their play. Without sufficient background, children have difficulty pretending and engaging in play sequences that stretch their language and behaviors.

Judiciously select content vocabulary (rare words) to encourage for use in dramatic play. These are words that children need to know for school subjects, that they cannot easily pick up in their everyday conversations, and that they do not yet likely know. Some examples for the construction theme are *architect*, *cement*, *porch*, and *shingles*. Recognize, though, that the words you select will vary with different groups of children at different times. Select a few key terms and introduce them deliberately in the context of shared reading and small-group activities.

Finally, collaborate with the children to establish some genuine purposes for play that are linked to the theme (which should be well aligned with your instructional goals). This helps young children to focus on their own play, to sort out what makes sense "to play" in the play setting, and to monitor their behaviors in play. You can easily do this by involving the children in planning for the dramatic-play area that will serve the theme. Shelley Johnson's preschoolers embraced this responsibility with enthusiasm by naming the area, helping to supply it, and identifying play roles. They even practiced saying words and phrases needed for fun play in the construction site.

During Play

One of the most important considerations (and maybe the most difficult) is to allow sufficient time for dramatic play in the theme-related setting. Three-year-olds need at least a full hour in a half-day program, and 4-year-olds no less than 45 minutes (Johnson et al., 2005). Less mature players will take longer to get started and will need more of your support for satisfying play experiences to occur.

To encourage meaningful play, assign children to small groups of three or four for each play area. For a class of 15 children, you will need to provide at least four play areas. Use a play center board to organize and manage children's playtime. The board might be a pocket chart with a picture of each play center and child name cards. Put each child's name next to his or her play center for the day. Once children are in their assigned play centers, coach their play for a few minutes to help them get started. Meet with small groups while children play.

Basically there are three roles adults can take in children's pretend play: onlooker, co-player, and play leader. (See continuum of roles in Figure 6.1.) Within any one play period, you may assume one or all of these roles depending on the maturity, goals, and pace of the players. When children are having a tough time getting going, you may need to jumpstart play by modeling certain play roles and action sequences. In this case, you are a play leader. Sometimes children need more players or

Managing Play Centers

- Assign groups—three to four children—in a play center at a time.
- Display a play center board for organizing children's play time.
- Have children rotate play centers systematically.
- Coach play to get it started.
- Meet with small groups while others are engaged in play.

invite you to play with them, and thus you assume a co-player role. Other times, children are in deep play and only need to sense that you are present for the play to flow.

The most challenging aspect of any role, however, is managing your use of language. When observing, you should make suggestions that encourage the play and talk to the children as if talking to the character they are role-playing. As a co-player, you assume a pretend role (such as a customer), using the actions and words relevant to that character, and also help to establish and broaden the play theme by making suggestions. When taking a leader or director role, you gently and playfully introduce a theme by naming it, take on a role to model it, assign roles, and guide the play forward by giving hints about what to do and say. Examples of facilitation strategies that accompany these three basic roles are further described in the next section.

After Play

You have prepared the children for theme-related play that supports your educational goals and they have played very, very well. Now you need to have them share with you and each other what happened. Such follow-through is critical because it creates a meaningful opportunity for children to talk and listen, and to use and hear new vocabulary again. It also provides you with a chance to assess what children comprehended (and enjoyed). You can handle after-play follow-through in these ways:

* Oral retellings during discussion in which children recount what happened. For example, after playtime Ella tells the teacher about what happened in the animal shelter center. "We fixed lots of animals," she says, "and made them feel lots better."

* Play logs or journals in which children use drawings and writing to document their play, as James did when he made a picture of his block structure, labeling it "The Fort."

* Language-experience charts on which you record play events of a selected play group. After the construction group has finished for the day, Mr. Lucas has the children tell him about their play experience. He records their recollections on chart paper: Who was who? What happened? How did the play time end? He posts this large chart in the play area for others to see and "read."

FACILITATING PLAY

How to interact with children during playtime is a major dilemma for many adults. Play by its very nature is child directed. When adults dominate the play, well, then, it isn't really play anymore. Yet when adults ignore play, it can remain at immature or even destructive levels, with its potential for positive learning untapped. Adults in early education roles need to develop strategies for facilitating play and guiding it to more mature levels of interaction that promote growth.

In the previous section we identified three basic roles that adults can use to support children's active learning through play: onlooker, co-player, and play leader. A more elaborated version of the onlooker role is the popular stage manager role, in which adults help to set the stage for play, but do not enter it. The full continuum of teacher roles in play is shown in Figure 6.1 (see page 94). Each is intended to support literacy in play. But what do they look like in everyday practice?

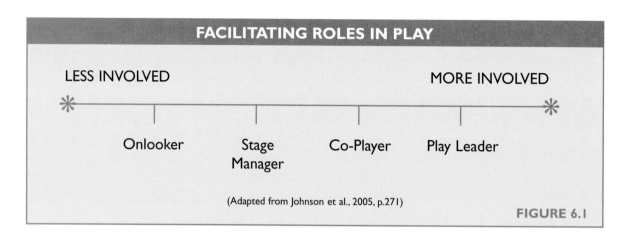

FACILITATING ROLES IN PLAY

LESS INVOLVED   MORE INVOLVED

Onlooker   Stage   Co-Player   Play Leader
                Manager

(Adapted from Johnson et al., 2005, p.271)

FIGURE 6.1

Here are some practical details that help to answer this question. We first present a short vignette of each role, then follow with a descriptive protocol that outlines its basic facilitation strategy. By protocol, we mean an organized sequence of teaching behaviors (talk and action) to help children learn. The key features of protocols for literacy-in-play roles include physical positioning (where you are located in relation to the play), level of participation (how involved you are), and attempts to engage children in play-related talk (the language you use) (Roskos & Neuman, 1993).

Onlooker Role

In this role, the teacher is physically present near the play setting, but does not enter into children's play in any sustained way. In the example below, the actions and talk of Betty W., a day-care teacher, illustrate this role in a day-care setting.

> Several children are playing in the book corner, leafing through books and talking about pictures in their books. Betty is sitting at a table nearby, watching the children with their books. She rests her chin in her hands, looking on with a smile. A girl from another area wanders over and gives Betty a hug. After returning the hug, Betty bends down and ties the girl's shoelaces. The child joins the other children in the book corner. Betty comments to the group, "You're having fun with your books. Aren't you having a good day?" The children look up at her momentarily, then continue to handle books, pointing at pictures.

The protocol for assuming this role is outlined in Figure 6.2. Although this role seems more concerned with child minding than literacy assisting, it is indeed literacy supporting because the adult serves as an appreciative audience for children's exploration and their "Watch what I can do" discoveries with reading and writing. Research shows that the mere presence of the adult within earshot of the play supports and sustains it (Bruner, 1983). Here Betty accepts the children's book browsing with positive regard, which in and of itself encourages the children to persist. Further, the role provides a golden opportunity for Betty to observe and assess children's play interests, language, and social interaction skills.

Stage Manager Role

A more active role than that of onlooker is that of stage manager. In this popular role, teachers help children prepare for play, respond to their requests for materials, help them construct props, and offer theme-related script suggestions to extend the play. Note in the following excerpt how Maria G., a preschool teacher, is supportive, but not otherwise engaged in the unfolding "toy store" play of several preschoolers.

> The children gathered toys they wanted to sell, and after they set them all up, I suggested that that they make a list of things for sale in the store. They liked this idea. They told me what to write and I wrote it down on a piece of chart paper. I said, "Okay I'm going to put the toy list right here." Joey started writing. "Look what I signed." He put his sign up [it read JKZFR] next to my list. And so I asked, "What's it say?" He replied, "It's closed forever." I chuckled and said, "Oh! Oh! Then we should make one that says the store is open. Can you make one of those, too? So we'd have a closed forever sign and an open sign." Just then Monica leaned through the store window and requested a hat. He told her: "Hey! This store is closed forever!"

The stage manager role extends the onlooker role, adding a few new steps to the basic protocol, as shown in Figure 6.2. Note how the teacher does not enter the play, but offers suggestions instead. The children are free to accept or disregard the teacher's assistance and ideas as clearly demonstrated by Joey. He chooses not to make an Open sign, quite taken with the power of his sign to close the store "forever." Still, in taking this role, the teacher provided a model (the toy list) that prompted Joey to make a sign of his own using invented spelling.

Co-Player Role

Assuming this role, the teacher becomes directly involved in the children's literacy-related play as a participant who contributes to the overall play activity. The goal is to "play along" and to follow the children's lead, as shown in the "making dinner" episode as on the next page. Note how Jessica F., the Head Start teacher, plays along.

GUIDING PLAY FROM OUTSIDE THE PLAY GROUP

Onlooker Role Protocol ●
Stage Manager Role Protocol ✳

POSITION
● Remain outside the play space

PARTICIPATION
● Act as an onlooker without taking a pretend role
● Nod, smile at, and encourage the children
✳ Help children prepare for play
✳ Provide props

TALK
● Make suggestions that encourage play
● Talk to the children as if talking to the character they are playing
● Compliment the children
✳ Respond to requests for props
✳ Offer suggestions to extend the play

FIGURE 6.2

Megan and Supraja want to play "making dinner" so I join them as a co-player. Megan decides we need more chairs, so she and Supraja scour the room to get chairs. They return with chairs in tow. I sit at the table and I ask, "What's for dinner?" Megan begins looking for a bottle for the baby. Then she says she has to vacuum before dinner and begins propelling the toy vacuum around the area. Meanwhile, Supraja says she is making dinner. She points to the back of a box, points with her finger and pretends to read. She says, "We need a mixing spoon," and begins stirring some food in a pot. I say, "Is that a good recipe? I hope so. I'm really hungry." She looks at the back of the box again as if reading and wags her head back and forth. "Yup. It's good." She gives me a plate and says, "It's macaroni and cheese and eggs." I say, "Thank you," and start to eat. But they say, "Stop! Stop! You have to wait until everyone has their food." So I wait.

The protocol for this role is described in Figure 6.3. You will note that it is more complex because the teacher is in the play space and a genuine player, so imposing adult logic (and status) must be held at bay. Yet this role lends tremendous support to children's literacy-related play, providing the teacher with opportunities to acknowledge literacy attempts, to model appropriate responses, to interject literacy information, to use new vocabulary, and to add significance to children's literacy uses in play, such as Supraja's pretend reading of the recipe on the back of the box. "Playing along" is demanding for adults but hugely rewarding for children. Their sense of efficacy and knowledge of literacy in practice are strengthened by adult involvement.

Leader Role

In this role, the adult deliberately uses play as an opportunity to teach a new play theme, simultaneously introducing literacy roles, objects, scripts, routines, and functional print into the play setting. It most often occurs in educational play. This more directive role aligns with the concept of play training, wherein the teacher directly models specific play behaviors to be adapted by the children in their own play efforts. The following account of the effort made by Sheena J., a day-care teacher, to teach "how to play McDonald's" is illustrative.

> I put up a McDonald's menu sign with golden arches, and I put cups and straws and the place mats on the table in the kitchen area with fish

---

GUIDING PLAY FROM INSIDE THE PLAY GROUP

Co-Player Role Protocol

POSITION
- Enter into the play space

PARTICIPATION
- Take on a pretend role in the established play theme
- Approach other players to stimulate play
- Help maintain the flow of the play theme

TALK
- Model language to imitate the pretend role
- Model language to establish the make-believe theme
- Model language to negotiate the play
- Broaden the make-believe into new possibilities

FIGURE 6.3

Nurturing Knowledge

fillet containers. I put the cash register right near them on the table. I set them out on Friday night, so Monday morning they would have them to play with. So on Monday I sat in there and I said to the kids, "I'm being a McDonald's person. I'm playing McDonald's restaurant." And I said that one of us needs to be the customer and come in and order something. They didn't want to be customers, so I said, "Okay. I'll be the customer. You take my order." So we did that a couple of times. I would read the words on the menu sign and give them pretend money. I pretended to count out the money. Then I said, "I'm going to be a McDonald's person and you kids be the customers. Read the sign to decide what you want, and count your money." Well . . . that went on for a long time, and they pretended pretty well.

The protocol for this role is more extensive and requires considerable practice to get the right balance of demonstrating and responding to children's play interests. (See Figure 6.4.) Leading play can easily slip into overdirecting it, which, as we know, can take all the fun out of it for children. In the vignette above, the teacher is careful: She yields to the children's unwillingness to be customers at first and demonstrates this role with some specificity. After a few rounds, she invites the children to try again, and this time they are willing to try this role. As they do (and for quite a long time), they practice certain early learning skills, such as "reading" the menu and "counting" money. In the play leader role, the adult shows children "how to play" by providing clear models, explicit directions, and lots of practice.

A Few Rules for Roles

We've described four roles, each with a protocol that outlines the specifics about your position, participation, and talk, all of which support and boost literacy in play. Realize, though, that in effectively facilitating the educational play of children in your program, you will need to switch between these roles often, even within a single play period. Your strategies should include the following:

* Being flexible, using a repertoire of literacy-assisting roles
* Meshing your roles with those children are taking in their play

---

GUIDING PLAY FROM INSIDE THE PLAY GROUP

Play Leader Role Protocol

POSITION
- Establish the play space
- Enter into the play space

PARTICIPATION
- Establish the play theme
- Assign the roles
- Lead the play forward
- Take on a pretend role

TALK
- State the play theme
- Model the language of the key roles
- Provide hints to help players stay in role
- Make suggestions to encourage interactions

FIGURE 6.4

* Responding to children's literacy play interests, skills, and needs
* Guiding children's literacy in play to higher levels of performance

Your goal, very often, is "to lead from behind" as Jerome Bruner (1983) describes it—observing children at play, setting the stage for literacy in play, playing along, and occasionally taking the lead to show children how to do more so as to pull their literacy learning (and playing) forward. Figure 6.5 shows a flexible role-taking model that you can use to guide your facilitation of children's early literacy in their play activity.

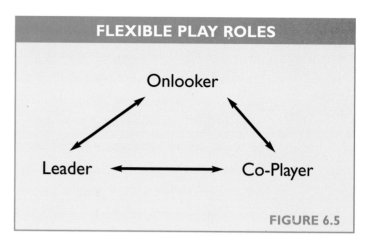

FIGURE 6.5

Documenting Literacy Learning in Play

Lev Vygotsky, the Russian child psychologist, argued that pretend play activity is essential in the preschool years because it leads development. By this he meant that the processes of pretend play helped children use language to guide their actions and to regulate their own behaviors. What motivates such play? The energy of social interaction (communicating, negotiating, and participating with others) can be immensely satisfying (and thus explains why children like to play). In play, children actually develop themselves further through self-instruction, a form of learning that is self-motivated or autotelic—*auto* meaning "self" and *telos* meaning "goal".

Theoretically this makes sense. But where's the evidence? Documenting the language and literacy learning that occurs through play is challenging. And there is good reason: Play can be guided, but not scripted; it can be organized, but not tightly structured; it can be educationally significant, but often indirectly. To systematically show what play can do requires some creative assessment approaches. Here are four we recommend.

* **Photo Documentation.** Systematically collect photos of play in target settings, such as a theme-related dramatic play area. Add short descriptions of what children are doing. For example, "Children are making a list of camping supplies. They're going to make 's-mores'! Yum!" Connect their playful activity to early learning standards. Display the photos with descriptions for colleagues and parents to look at as they enter and exit the school.
* **Play Plans and Logs.** Ask children to make oral plans about what they are going to do at a specific center. Next ask them to draw a picture of who they plan to be and what they will do. Then help them write their plan beneath the picture as best they can. After playtime, ask them to remember what they did and help them write it. Make play books with the plans and logs. Use these to document children's growth in planning, remembering, and writing.

Post for easy reading by adults and children. (See examples in Figure 6.6.)

* **Samples of Play Stories and Writing.** We strongly encourage after-play routines that serve as follow-up activities to reinforce children's retrieval of language. These routines also provide practice of essential skills and enrich the play experience with observations, reflections, and new thoughts. One follow-up activity that should be used frequently is capturing play experiences as play stories, as illustrated in Figure 6.7.

Another follow-up activity involves routinely collecting samples of children's writing samples that can be used to document children's emerging spelling and handwriting skills.

* **Play Maturity and Language-Use Checklist.** Movement from immature to more mature play in the early years is a strong marker of child growth and development. By the end of kindergarten, children's play should reflect the following (Bodrova & Leong, 1996):

1. Symbolic representations and symbolic actions (*Will you come with us? Let's go to Sea World!*)

2. Complex, interwoven themes (*We're following the treasure map to the scary mountain.*)

3. Complex, interwoven roles (*You can be the customers, and I'm the cash register guy. Jared's the waiter guy. Okay?*)

4. Extended time frames (over several days)

One way to document play maturity is to pay close attention to children's use of language before and during play activity. With the Pretend-Play Maturity Checklist (page 100) and the accompanying Language-Use Observation

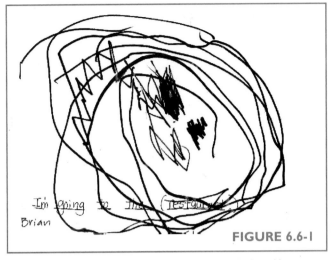

FIGURE 6.6-1

Above, Brian plans to play in the restaurant. Below, Kevin plans to play with a magnet in the science center.

FIGURE 6.6-2

Icky, Picky, and Oh So Yukky Cake
by Sheona and Sara

We made a icky, picky, yukky cake. First, we put syrup on it, because he hates syrup. Then we put sprinkles on it, because he hates sprinkles! And we put eggs in it. Then we put popcorn on it, because he hates popcorn! We put chocolate milk on it, because he hates chocolate milk. It's a icky and picky and yukky cake. And he won't like it. Not at all!

The End   FIGURE 6.7

Here is a dictated story from the Sand Table.

Pretend-Play Maturity Checklist

SIMPLE PRETEND PLAY (18 months–2 years)

____ Performs single actions (e.g., brushing doll's hair)

____ Performs same action on two different items (e.g., feeds self and doll)

____ Substitutes toy object for real thing if they have similar properties

____ Mimics adult actions (e.g., pretending to read)

SEQUENCED PRETEND PLAY AND ROLE TAKING (2–3 years)

____ Performs a sequence based on familiar to less familiar events

____ Assumes a familiar role (e.g., mother); may talk while plays

____ Substitutes dissimilar objects; creates imaginary props

____ Gives toys roles in play

PRETEND PLAY (3–5 years)

____ Develops imaginary themes

____ Takes on make-believe roles

____ Cooperates with others for an extended time period (at least 10 minutes)

____ Creates imaginary objects and places

____ Uses language to create make-believe

   ___ assigns roles

   ___ plans scenes

   ___ establishes identity of objects and places

   ___ substitutes talk for action

   ___ develops a story line

   ___ negotiates problems without adult help

Adapted from Bodrova & Leong, 2005; Weitzman & Greenberg, 2002, pp. 317–318.

Form (below), you can systematically monitor the play maturity of the children in your charge. Select three different months for making observations (e.g., October, February, May). In a class of 20 children, select 5 to observe during playtime each week of the month. Date and mark the checklist for each child's play maturity and language use before and during play. Summarize evidence to share with parents at scheduled conference times.

Language-Use Observation Form

ORAL LANGUAGE	DESCRIPTION
_____ No language	Repeats actions but does not talk
_____ Unrelated language	Makes sounds, but unrelated to play (e.g., humming, singing)
_____ Language comments on action	Describes actions with words or sounds (e.g., vroom…vroom as moves truck)
_____ Language directs another's role	Tells what to say/do to stay in role
_____ Language describes role as it occurs	Uses contextualized language (e.g., "I am feeding you. Yum! Yum!")
_____ Language describes own actions/role before it occurs	Uses decontextualized language (e.g., "I'm going to feed the baby, then go to the store.")
_____ Language describes own actions integrated with those of others	Uses language to plan cycles of action (e.g., "I'm going to feed my baby and the baby is going to get sick, so I take my baby to your hospital, and then you give him a shot.")
_____ Language describes a scenario and integrated roles over time	Uses decontextualized language to plan play

Adapted from Bodrova & Leong, 2005.

Nurturing Knowledge © 2007 by Susan B. Neuman and Kathleen Roskos, Scholastic Professional

Helping Families Understand Play's Role

An information society places new pressures on families to prepare their young children for the world. More emphasis is placed on academic achievement, and also on excellent musical and athletic performance. Parents worry that time for play is time lost for learning how to excel in these areas. Their worries translate into concerns about play-based curricula and the amount of time children spend playing in preschools. They ask (and often demand) that early educators spend more time on academic skills and less on play to prepare their children for school. Parents may believe that play is important for children to grow and learn. But acting on this belief in their children's education (at any level) is another matter.

Clearly, early education professionals have to do a better job of informing families about play's role in early learning and, more generally, in enjoying life. Decades of empirical research con-

It is important to share information with families about the benefits of play for children's cognitive, social, and physical development.

verge on the benefits of play for children's cognitive, social, and physical development (Roskos & Christie, 2000; Singer, Golinkoff, & Hirsh-Pasek, in press; Zigler et al., 2004). We need to share this information with families and show them how their deep-seated sense (and intuitions) about play's value can be put into twenty-first-century early literacy instructional practice. Some of this information can be embedded in the family involvement activities you already engage in. Some can be the topic of parent workshops, seminars, book clubs, and passing conversations as parents come and go. Some of it can be "pointed to" for families to learn more on their own. Following is an example of one way to become a more vigorous advocate for educational play in your program.

Interactive Workshops

Early childhood educators at Cuyahoga Community College offer a Super Saturday Workshop series devoted to helping caregivers develop knowledge and skills about early literacy development and learning. A popular workshop is entitled Connecting Play, Talking, Reading, and Writing. Its primary goal is to develop caregivers' understanding of the importance of play in early literacy learning. Through a variety of large and small group activities, participants identify key ideas that connect play and literacy development. They describe features of a play environment that would support lan-

PARENT RESOURCES

WEB RESOURCES

Parents can find educational materials that promote literacy in play at these Web sites.

www.specialkidszone.com
Achievement Products for Children
P.O. Box 9033, Canton, OH 44711
800-373-4699
Achievement Products carries many adaptive and modified materials including Wikki Sticks, pencil grips and weights, finger crayons, slant boards, tactile letters, modified toys, and classroom tools.

www.dragonflytoys.com
Dragonfly Toy Company
291 Yale Ave., Winnipeg, MB R3M 0L4, Canada
800-308-2208
Dragonfly stocks a wide range of adaptive toys, books, software, communication devices, and other equipment for children with special needs. The company specializes in identifying products matched specifically to the needs of each individual customer.

www.lakeshorelearning.com
Lakeshore Learning Materials
2695 E. Dominguez St., Carson, CA 90895
800-428-4414
With more than three thousand items in its early childhood catalog, Lakeshore features an impressive collection of materials for block play and dramatic play, as well as virtually any other materials needed in a preschool or home childcare setting.

www.novanatural.com
Nova Natural Toys and Crafts
140 Webster Rd., Shelburne, VT 05482
877-668-2111
Nova Natural Toys & Crafts has many unique wood toys and imaginative play materials. The company also carries beautiful play silks and cloths, as well as natural fiber dolls.

READ-ABOUTS

Parents can read more about literacy-play links from these articles and parent-friendly Web sites.

"Playing to Learn"
http://www.scholastic.com/earlylearner/age4/learning/playplan.htm

"You Are Your Child's First Teacher" (Learning starts with play)
http://www.familytlc.net/toddlers_articles.html

"The Beginnings of Literacy" (Play: making connections with reading and writing)
http://www.zerotothree.org/site/PageServer?pagename=ter_key_language_beginnings

"Rethinking Children's Play"
http://www.fun.familyeducation.com/outdoor-games/play/35262.html

Includes many family play suggestions and articles, searchable by child's age:
http://www.familytlc.net/

Milestones in listening, talking, reading, and writing for preschoolers. Includes some suggestions for play:
http://www.pbs.org/parents/readinglanguage/preschooler/main.html

guage development and discuss key roles an adult might assume in the child's play environment. After a pretty full day of listening and sharing, participants have a deeper appreciation of play as an opportunity for young children to encounter and practice early literacy skills. Other Super Saturday

Workshops with a play focus that are offered include: Play With Sounds, Play With the Alphabet, and Cooing and Connecting With Infants and Toddlers. The entire Super Saturday Workshop series, developed by Cuyahoga Community College faculty, is always packed with parents and other caregivers who want to know more (and still more) about early literacy development (O'Brien, 2005). Useful parent resources are listed on page 103.

Closing

Sheona says, "We're going on a picnic. Okay? At the beach, Adam, but don't bring your cat along! We need lots of stuff for a picnic." (She scribbles on a shopping list.) Adam agrees to go to the beach and goes along with the no-cat rule. "We need plenty of cups," she says. "One, two, three cups 'cause you wouldn't wanna wash 'em at the beach, 'cause that's where we're gonna swim, huh Adam?" She continues, "You should always bring potato salad, Adam. Always bring potato salad. It's an important thing to do."

Play is fun! Play is exciting! And it is filled with the building blocks of literacy: language, pretend reading, pretend writing, and imagination. This is why play needs to be an integral part of any early childhood program. Children need play experiences to feel good about what they know and can do, and to use language as a means of communication. Moreover they need lots of play experiences that include an abundance of literacy opportunities. Adults help when they create the conditions for rich play experiences—when they prepare generous, vibrant play environments, take different roles, and lead children into new play adventures. In all our efforts to help children learn, play, we must remember, is the wellspring of *joy in learning* that stirs children and keeps them going on the long literacy journey ahead.

CHAPTER 7

Linking Literacy and Mathematics

TEACHER: What size blocks do we need?

CHILD: Very long ones.

TEACHER: So, you're going to match these with these [*long ones with long ones*]?

How many do you think you will need to build it as high as the chair?

CHILD: Four.

TEACHER: How do you know that it'll be four?

CHILD: I can see.

*C*hildren have an intuitive interest and understanding of mathematical concepts long before they enter school. They explore their worlds, sorting, classifying, comparing, and contrasting objects through playful and daily activities. They wonder: *How many petals are on a flower? How much is one half? How long is five seconds? How big am I?* Puzzling over answers to real questions, preschoolers use their everyday experiences to begin to explore the relationships among many objects in their world.

Mathematics learning is not about rote procedures for getting right answers. Or memorizing facts, or responding to flash cards. At the heart of mathematics is the search for sense and meaning, patterns and relationships, order and predictability. It is tied to children's developing capabilities, the diverse strategies they use in problem solving and reasoning, and the sets of attitudes and beliefs that support their learning.

This chapter focuses on how to use the five essential literacy practices to promote mathematics learning. We'll first describe the components of mathematics and highlight the research on what children need to learn in preschool. We'll then describe how you can support children's learning through math-motivating activities that are targeted toward helping children learn these key ideas.

What Children Need to Learn in Mathematics

What are the important mathematical ideas for preschoolers? The National Standards in Mathematics (National Council of Teachers of Mathematics [NCTM], 2000) describe what children should know and be able to do. The key categories include:

* Numbers and operations
* Patterns and relationships
* Measurement
* Data collection and data analysis

Numbers and Operations

Number and quantitative ideas are the most fundamental concepts in the early years. Numbers and operations include counting, comparing, grouping, partitioning, and composing. Some infants, even younger than 6 months of age, appear to show basic understanding of addition and subtraction, suggesting that children might have intuitive and informal capabilities in these areas.

Counting is not simply reciting numbers from memory (as with the ABCs). Research (Clements, Sarama, & DiBiase, 2004) suggests the following:

* Children develop number concepts by working with real things.
* They need many opportunities to develop one-to-one correspondence, linking one and only one number with each item in a set of objects.
* Number names are often difficult for children to learn, especially after the number ten. Modeling or explicit instruction helps children keep track of what they are counting by saying the name of the number.

Preschoolers demonstrate understanding of number sense and operations in early learning standards when they do the following:

Number	Count to ten in the context of play or activities
	Demonstrate understanding of one-to-one correspondence
	Develop increasing ability to combine, separate, and name "how many" concrete objects
	Use the names for numbers and associate number words with collections or sets of objects counted, including zero
	Use numbers and counting as a means for solving problems

Patterns and Relationships

Children need to be able to recognize, create, and interpret patterns—all aspects of algebraic thinking. Stringing beads by alternating large beads and small ones, for example, helps children begin to understand the concept of a pattern. Asking them to place all the red beads in one area and all the green in another begins to build relationships among common objects. You'll need to help them use their understandings of patterns as tools for solving problems and making predictions. It will ultimately help them build categories of knowledge and develop inferencing skills as they attempt to solve problems.

Patterns can be experienced in a variety of ways, not only in numbers but in motions, as when children play Simon Says or Hokey Pokey; in designs and arrangements, such as gathering leaves that are similar and different; and in recurring events, such as the seasons of the year and the days of the week.

Research (Kilpatrick, Swafford, & Findell, 2001) clearly indicates the following:

* Children's understanding of basic geometric reasoning—their informal knowledge about shapes and forms—begins early on, before the preschool years.
* Children by age 4 can identify some shapes (e.g., square, circle), focusing first on global appearances of these forms, to be followed later on by a variety of attributes to describe them.
* Activities that help children learn to recognize, compare, and order objects, to judge whether two objects are the same size or not, and to use the language associated with these attributes (e.g., smaller, larger) improve the likelihood that children will develop greater proficiency in elementary grades.

Preschoolers demonstrate understanding of patterns and relationships in early learning standards when they do the following:

Algebra	Sort and classify objects
	Predict what comes next when patterns are extended
	Recognize, duplicate, and extend simple patterns

Geometry	Recognize shapes
	Describe how shapes are alike and different
	Match and sort shapes
	Use words that identify where things are in space
	Use positional words to describe the location of objects

Measurement

For young children, measuring things is a way to look for relationships in the real world. *How tall am I? How much bigger am I than my baby sister? How much can I buy at the candy store?* Children will often find ways of comparing things with one another and create measurement tools even if none are available.

Using the materials you provide, children will learn concepts and words associated with smaller, bigger, lighter, heavier, and so on. They will begin to use their intuitive understanding of measurement to gauge how large or small things are. They may use a long string to pretend to measure a table or measure the length of the rug on the floor by counting with their feet. In their desire to count and measure their own way, children are trying to figure out basic comparisons between objects.

An accumulation of research (Kilpatrick et al., 2001) now indicates the following:

* Young children come to school with a basic understanding of measurement, such as mass, length, and weight; however, they do not know how to reason about them.
* The traditional view of stagelike sequences of development, traditionally associated with Piaget, may not be accurate. Rather, studies (Clements et al., 2004) suggest that given appropriate activities and sufficient opportunities, young children can move to more advanced levels of reasoning.

Preschoolers demonstrate understanding of measurement in early learning standards when they do the following:

Measurement	Experience, compare, and use language related to time
	Use terms to compare the attributes of objects (bigger, smaller, lighter)
	Order a set of objects according to size, weight, and length
	Use tools to measure objects

Data Collection and Analysis

Clustering objects, such as favorite rocks or beautifully colored leaves, is a way of searching for patterns and organization. We describe these activities as data collection. Once children have collected objects, they often seek to compare them or find ways of classifying, organizing, and representing them in a way that can be easily understood. For example, children can sort objects and depict their findings in a graphic display. They can compare what they've studied by describing various items and drawing conclusions about them. However, research in these two domains is far less extensive than in the other areas, especially with respect to the early years.

What is known, however, is the following:

* Children use a variety of strategies to engage in day-to-day problem solving. They may try one technique, such as organizing a pattern by colors, and then try another, such as organizing by size. It is the ability to try many different strategies that relates to later mathematical proficiency (Clements, 2004).

* Children need opportunities to develop multiple strategies for solving problems (Kilpatrick et al., 2001). Creative play materials and lots of time for play helps children generate new ideas about how to use, manipulate, and try out new things. In some circumstances, the sheer number of different strategies children can show to solve problems predicts their later learning.

* Engaging children in these learning opportunities, according to a recent consensus report (National Association For the Education of Young People [NAEYC]/NCTM, 2002), should complement the attention traditionally given to numbers and operations in the early years (see Neuman & Roskos, 2005, for a review of the research).

Preschoolers demonstrate an understanding of collecting and analyzing data when they do the following:

Data Analysis/ Collection	Collect, organize, and describe data
	Use terms to compare the attributes of objects (bigger, smaller, lighter)
	Order a set of objects according to size, weight, or length
	Solve problems that involve collecting and analyzing data

Essential Literacy Practices in Mathematics

Linking literacy and mathematics will help young learners express their thinking in talking about, writing about, and playing with mathematical concepts. In the remainder of this chapter, we show how you can apply the five essential literacy practices to further children's mathematics knowledge and skills.

We'll first set the stage by describing a supportive learning environment, which is the foundation of effective instruction in all areas of preschool learning. Here details are important, so we provide you with several sources of information on creating a mathematics-motivating environment:

1. A sketch with specifications of what a mathematics-motivating area might look like
2. A list of material resources in mathematics, such as books, toys, and computer software

3. Ideas for mathematics conversations and talk

4. Three sample lesson plans that link literacy and mathematics

Then, we'll focus on the four other essential literacy practices, showing how each can promote mathematics thinking and doing—shared book reading; songs, rhymes and word play; developmental writing; and content-rich play. By the chapter's end you should have a good grasp of how essential literacy practices can support the development of children's mathematical thinking.

SUPPORTIVE LEARNING ENVIRONMENT

Curious preschoolers are active explorers of their environment. They're constantly busy observing, comparing, questioning, and testing things out. You can stimulate their mathematical thinking and also introduce new mathematical ideas by creating an environment that supports literacy and mathematics. Here are several environmental design ideas, beginning with an environmental sketch, followed by a materials list, suggestions for mathematics talk, and lesson plans.

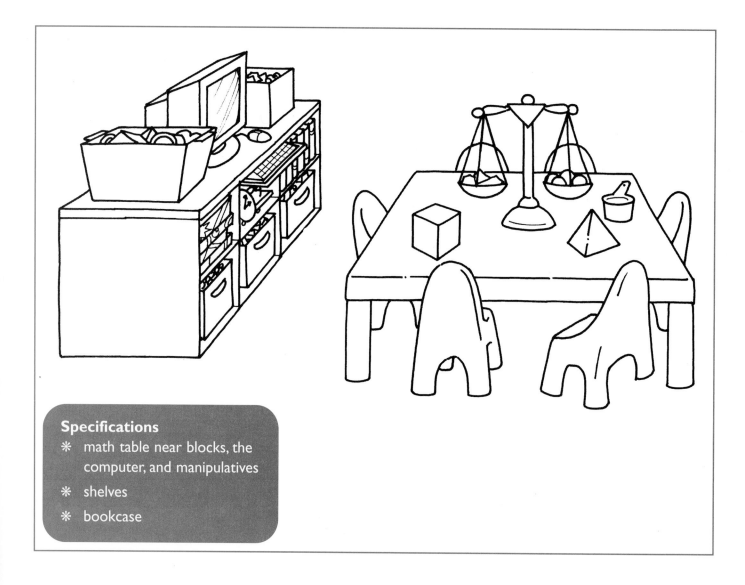

Specifications
* math table near blocks, the computer, and manipulatives
* shelves
* bookcase

BOOKS

One Lonely Sea Horse by Saxton Freymann and Joost Elffers (Arthur A. Levine, 2000)
From the authors of *How Are You Peeling?* this counting book is bright, friendly, and sure to please young children.

Benny's Pennies by Pat Brisson (Doubleday, 1993)
Benny has five new pennies and wants to spend them but cannot decide what to buy. He ends up spending the pennies on his pets and family.

My Granny Went to Market: A-Round-the-World Counting Rhyme by Stella Blackstone (Barefoot Books, 1998)
In this rhyming story, a grandmother buys a magic carpet in Istanbul and travels around the world to purchase local items from each country. As she makes purchases, she states the number of objects she is buying.

Inch by Inch by Leo Lionni (Astor-Honor, 1962)
The inchworm in this story saves his own life by offering to measure the birds that want to eat him, which eventually leads to his freedom.

How Many Bugs in a Box? by David A. Carter (Simon & Schuster, 1988) and *More Bugs in Boxes* (Simon & Schuster, 1990)
These pop-up books are full of surprises. Children can open the boxes and find colorful bugs inside to count.

Other books about counting, numbers, shapes, sizes, basic concepts (size, shape, space), patterns

CD-ROMS

Curious George Preschool Learning Games (Simon & Schuster Interactive)
This CD has games and activities for children related to patterns, shapes, colors, puzzle making, and letter identification.

School Zone Preschool (School Zone)
Comparing, problem solving, thinking skills, following directions, similarities and differences, sorting

Huggly Saves the Turtles (Scholastic)
Logic and reasoning, numbers and counting, pattern recognition, problem solving, creativity

How Many Bugs in a Box? (Simon & Schuster)
This CD is full of games, puzzles and music. The games are multileveled and include numbers, counting, rhyming, and a read-along digitized book.

"Flo": Return of the Water Beetles (Digital Praise)
Children learn about sorting, matching, sequencing, and social skills in a series of interactive activities. They can match flowers, count cookies, and create a concert in a musical garden.

TOYS
* cash register
* number magnets and/or groups of similar magnets that children can count (e.g., have a set of ten flower magnets of different colors to sort and count)
* groups of toys that are similar, yet different (e.g., a box of plastic frogs or cars or insects that have similarities and differences, to sort and count)
* building blocks and Legos for exploring spatial relationships
* puzzles for problem solving and exploring spatial relationships
* measuring tools to practice measuring (e.g., tape measures and measuring cups and spoons)
* beads and rope to practice making patterns

MANIPULATIVES
Number
* magnetic numbers (*numeral recognition*)
* counters—teddy bear counters, bean counters, bug counters (*one-to-one correspondence*)
* Unifix Cubes (*one-to-one correspondence, more, less, combining*)
* math games: Uno (*recognizing numerals*); dominoes (*counting and matching*)
* board games that use dice rather than spinners (*one-to-one correspondence*)
* playing cards (*counting, matching, and pairing*)

Algebra and Geometry
* geoboards and rubber bands (*shapes*)
* foam shapes (*shapes*)
* attribute shapes (*sorting and categorization*)
* buttons (*sorting and categorization*)
* puzzles (*shapes and problem solving*)
* wooden blocks (*shapes and problem solving*)
* pattern blocks (*shapes and creating or extending patterns*)
* Unifix Cubes (*creating or extending patterns*)
* beads, lace, pattern cards (*creating or extending patterns*)

Measurement and Data Analysis
* Unifix Cubes (*nonstandard measurement—length*)
* math links also called Link 'n Learn Links (*nonstandard measurement—length*)
* measuring cups, measuring spoons (*volume*)
* balance (*nonstandard measurement—weight*)

Talking About Mathematics

✳ **Use the language of mathematics.** In the lessons you teach and in your everyday talk, use math terms to provide information and to explain what is happening. Use words and phrases like *longer, shorter, fewer, less than, more than, taller, shorter* to compare and contrast things. Provide details using mathematical ideas. For example: *The circle has a curved line. It is round. It looks like a sphere or a ball.* Explain patterns and outcomes that show mathematical relationships. For example: *This is a pattern because it has squares that are repeating themselves.*

✳ **Wonder aloud.** As you go about your daily routines, think aloud when using math skills. *Let's see. There are one, two, three . . . twelve children here today. We have fifteen children in our class so—oh, my goodness —three children are not here today. That's more children absent than usual.* Wonder and speculate about what might or could happen *if . . .* as in: *If we don't measure exactly how much sugar to put in, our cookies could be too sweet or too bitter. We need exactly one-half cup. See?*

✳ **Support play conversations.** Seize opportunities in play to build on children's ideas by inserting math words and ideas. *Yes, your tower is taller, but let's look. Jared's is wider. See? His has one, two, three, four, five blocks on the bottom, but yours has only one, two, three.*

✳ **Take a pretend role that shows mathematical thinking.** For example: *I'm the baker and I'm going to use these measuring cups to make a cake.* In a role you can also pose math questions, like *How many blocks do you think we will need to build the castle?*

✳ **Ask "puzzler" questions.** These are a lot of fun because young children are always up to the challenge. *Do taller children have bigger feet? How much is a dozen? How many sunflower seeds does it take to cover your name? Can you go to sea in a sieve?* Puzzler questions are stimulating. They can lead to big mathematical investigations that provide many opportunities for children to count, sort, measure, and solve problems using numbers.

THREE SAMPLE LESSON PLANS

Lesson 1: Learning About Shapes

Learning Objective: To identify shapes and describe how they may be alike or different

Whole Group: Learn together

✳ Gather the children together in a circle. Show them a collection of objects (lids, picture frames, pennants, blocks). "Let me show you a square. It has four equal sides. Now look at this object. It is a circle, and completely round." Tell the children that they're going to hear a story about shapes.

✳ Read *Round Trip* by Ann Jonas (1983). The book provides a delightful adventure about shapes.

✳ Now play with some of the words from the story. Try the show-and-tell routine to learn each new word. Here's how it goes. The teacher says to the children, *I'll show you a rectangle. Now you tell me something about it.* The children respond, *It has four sides.* Encourage children to select objects from around the room to show to the rest of the class or a buddy for a simple description.

Small Group: Explore together and check

At their tables, have children . . .

* Match tiles (or other objects such as small blocks or tangrams) by shape. Ask children to point to and name the different shapes they matched, such as circle and square.
* Sort other small objects by shape. Ask children to describe their sorting. Have them point out and describe the features of circles and squares.

Lesson 2: Counting and Sorting

Learning Objective: To count and sort items

Whole Group: Learn together

* Using the felt board, tell the story of "Jack and the Beanstalk." Talk to children about the beans: *Jack's beans were magic beans, but what other kinds of beans are there?*
* Ask them to name the beans they know (lima, pinto, kidney, etc.). Create a graphic organizer.

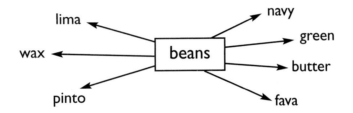

Small Group: Explore together and check

* Have a large container with a mixture of different kinds of dried beans in it (pinto, wax, kidney, fava, green, soy).
* Give each child a muffin tin for sorting. Ask children to sort the beans by color, by size, and by shape.

Lesson 3: Measuring Objects

Learning Objective: To use tools to measure objects.

Whole Group: Learn together

* Have children listen to the sound recording of *Curious George Visits the Zoo* (1985).
* After listening, tell children the class is going to make their own "zoo food" for snack time today. In the story George eats the bananas the zookeeper was going to feed to the animals. This recipe has bananas, too.
* Bring in a variety of measuring tools. Show children a few basic measuring tools such as a cup, 1/2 cup, or teaspoon. Ask them to share when they've used measuring tools (baking with mom or dad, taking medicine, etc.).
* Ahead of time, create a chart that shows the recipe (see box). Use words and pictures to write the recipe so the children can follow the directions. Then show the chart to the class.

Go over the recipe, and show the children the different measuring tools they will be using. Remember to ask the children if any of them have food allergies.

Small Group: Explore together and check

❋ Allow each child to measure his or her own ingredients into the cone.

❋ Place the sound recording of *Curious George Visits the Zoo* in the listening center with copies of the book for children to listen to and follow along in small groups. Let them enjoy their zoo food as they listen to the story.

> **Zoo Food**
> (For each child)
> * I plain ice cream cone to hold the zoo food
> * I teaspoon raisins
> * 1/4 cup dried banana chips
> * 2 teaspoons goldfish crackers
> * I teaspoon sunflower seeds
> * I teaspoons M&Ms
> * I teaspoon dried cranberries

SHARED BOOK READING

There are many wonderful children's books that explore the mathematics concepts that preK children need to learn. (See box on page 115.) When you read a book with mathematics content, help children in the following ways:

❋ Make information that you want to teach explicit. Say, *Today we are going to read a book about counting. Can you help me count while I read?*

❋ Let children participate as you read. *What number is going to come next?*

❋ Use and teach math language. *What do you think this word* measuring *means? What is the inchworm doing?*

❋ Ask questions that encourage children to apply what they have learned from a book. *In this book, we talked about things that come in twos. Can you think of anything else that always comes in twos?*

❋ If possible, connect your read-aloud to a hands-on mathematics activity so that children can practice, apply, and process what they have learned. *Let's make our own pictures with black dots. Count and see how many black dots you use in your picture.*

Remember, you don't always need to read an informational book from cover to cover. Here are some examples of what you might say after reading *What Comes in 2's, 3's, and 4's?*:

We saw lots of things in our book that come in twos. Let's think about the parts of our body and think about what may come in twos.

TERRELL: I've got two eyes.

TEACHER: That's right Terrell, and what do you do with them?

CHILDREN, together: To see.

DEREK: And two ears and two arms.

TEACHER: And two noses

CHILDREN: Nooooo!

And they all laugh together.

FIVE FAVORITE MATH READ-ALOUDS

Ten Black Dots by Donald Crews (Harper & Row, 1968)
Practice counting and be creative! Think about all of the things that you could make with ten black dots.

Five Creatures by Emily Jenkins (Douglas & McIntyre, 2001)
Learn about sorting and categorizing as a young girl explains how the five creatures who live in her house (two parents, two cats, and the girl) are the same in some ways and different in others. How many members of the family have the same hair color? How many like to sing? How many like to drink milk?

What Comes in 2's, 3's, & 4's? by Suzanne Aker (Simon & Schuster, 1990)
Strengthen children's understanding of numbers as you read about everyday things that come in twos, threes, and fours.

The Legend of Spookley the Square Pumpkin by Joe Troiano (Greenwillow, 2003)
Learn about shapes as you read this delightful story of an unusual square pumpkin. The round pumpkins tease Spookley because he is square, but when a storm causes the other pumpkins to roll away, being different helps Spookley to save the day!

Inch by Inch by Leo Lionni (HarperCollins, 1995)
Introduce the concept of measuring as you read about a clever and courageous inchworm that measures to save himself from harm.

There are many more wonderful counting books, including *One, Two, Three to the Zoo* (Sandcastle Books, 1990) and *The Very Hungry Caterpillar* (Penguin, 1969) both by Eric Carle; *Ten, Nine, Eight* by Molly Bang (Greenwillow, 1991), and *Anno's Counting Book* by Mitsumasa Anno (HarperTrophy, 1986).

SONGS, RHYMES, AND WORD PLAY

Counting chants are an excellent way to incorporate phonological awareness activities into math. Children love to learn these silly songs and rhymes. They learn to listen to the sounds and rhythms of language, and they become comfortable counting up and down. After you have taught a counting song or chant, you can incorporate it throughout the day. Sing a counting chant at circle time, while children are lining up, as you clean up, or at any point that you have a few extra minutes. To help children learn as much as possible from counting rhymes and songs, try the following:

* Hold up fingers to help children connect the counting word to what it actually means. When children first count, they are simply reciting words, but your goal should be to help them understand what the word *four* actually represents. Holding up four fingers helps children make this connection. Remember that at this age, children need lots of practice connecting numbers to physical objects. If you want to get more creative, you and your class can make little finger puppets, drawings attached to craft sticks, or felt cutouts to use as counters for a particular song. For example, if you are singing "Roll Over," make a bed out of felt and use Velcro to put ten felt people on it. Let a child help by removing a person with each verse.

* Encourage children to hold up their fingers as well. This can be challenging for some children.

* Let children do the counting. Say (and demonstrate with your fingers), *Last time we sang about three green speckled frogs, but one went away, so this time, how many will there be?*

* Sing or chant the same rhyme over and over again. This helps children to internalize the sounds and the meaning of the language they are using.

As you sing these charming

FAVORITE MATH SONGS AND CHANTS

Raffi: The Singable Songs Collection (Rounder, 1997); This audio CD as well as *Raffi in Concert* (Rounder, 1996), and *Raffi: More Singable Songs* (Rounder, 1996) contain the following catchy math songs:

"1, 2 , 3 ,4 ,5 I caught a Fish Alive"
"Five Green Speckled Frogs"
"One Potato, Two Potato"
"One, Two Buckle My Shoe"
"Roll Over!"
"Six Little Ducks"
"Ten Green Bottles"
"This Old Man"

Ten Little Lady Bugs by Melanie Gerth (Piggy Toes Press, 2001)

Eight Silly Monkeys by Steve Haskamp (Intervisual Books, 2003)

Over in the Meadow by Ezra Jack Keats (Puffin, 1971)

The following is a wonderful Web site for children's songs and lesson plans: Teachers Guide to Children's Songs www.theteachersguide.com

---

songs and chants, be sure to emphasize the numbers or highlight them in some way. Children are just learning what these numbers actually mean, and the more examples you can provide, the better.

DEVELOPMENTAL WRITING

An effective way to connect math and writing is to make class books. You can go about this in two different ways. You can ask children a question, such as *Why were the monkeys jumping on the bed?* and record their language on a large piece of chart paper during circle time. Later you can ask children to illustrate one of the words from the chart paper. This shows the entire class that writing is a useful strategy for recording people's words so that we can remember them later. You can collect these papers and bind them to make a book. The drawback to this approach is that it can be difficult for children to wait while you slowly write down what each child has said. Another option is to record their words individually and let them work separately on artwork. Children still learn the importance of writing when you spend a few minutes with them individually, showing them that you are recording their words. Collect their artwork and bind it together using masking tape.

The following day, after the class book is assembled, you can read it to the entire group. This option can be more engaging for the class.

Above, there are a few suggestions for class book topics that incorporate mathematics concepts. Know that you can make your own class version of almost any mathematics picture book. After you

TOPICS FOR CLASS BOOKS THAT INCORPORATE MATH

* **Who Is in Our Families?** Ask children to draw (and label) a picture of the people in their family. Help the child to count the number of people. You can write the number on each page. Staple the pages together, and you have created a personal counting book.

* **Our Shape Hunt** Ask each child to search the classroom for something that is a square, a triangle, or a circle. Children can draw and label their objects. You can write the name of the shape or a brief sentence on each page. ("Our table is a circle.") Staple the pages together, and you have a class book about shapes.

* **Our Black Dots Book** Cut out black dots from construction paper or get black dot stickers. Let the children make pictures using the dots (not more than ten) and label their pictures. You can help the children count their dots and write the number on each child's page. Staple the children's work together in numerical order to create a counting book.

* **Measuring Our Hands and Feet** Let each child make a handprint and a footprint on a large piece of paper. Help children to use links or Unifix Cubes to figure out how long their hands and feet are. Write a sentence for each child. Sarah's hand is five links and her foot is eight links. Staple the book together and read it often!

read about things that come in twos, threes, and fours, let children draw and write about objects in their environment that come grouped in these ways. No matter what you are studying, such as family pets, community helpers, or seasons of the year, it is likely that you can find some way to count and measure it. For example, if you are learning about pets, make a book about counting the different pets that children have in their homes. Label the number of dogs, cats, and turtles they have. If you are learning about parts of the body, make a book about counting body parts. Children can draw and label one nose, two legs, or ten fingers. If you are going to bake cookies for snack, write and illustrate the recipe. Ask children to draw and label two cups of flour or one bag of chocolate chips.

PLAY

Children develop mathematical reasoning when they explore and interact with math manipulatives. At times, you will want to structure this play by encouraging children to complete a specific task. However, children also need unstructured time to explore with mathematics materials. This play encourages children to discover new things and to practice what they already know. Try the following to encourage children's mathematical play:

* Introduce children to mathematics materials recommended earlier in the chapter (page 111) that are available in your room. As the year progresses, highlight new materials. Model some of the ways that they can be used. Encourage children to use them in new and interesting ways.

* Store mathematics materials in clear bins at children's level. Let children know that these materials are a choice during free-play time.

* Put mathematics materials out on the floor or on tables at arrival and encourage children to play with these "toys" while they wait for the rest of the group to arrive.

* Strike a balance between participating and allowing children to explore independently. Although you can scaffold children's thinking when you ask guiding questions and try to understand what they are doing (e.g., noting *It looks like you're grouping things according to their color*), children also need time to play and explore without adult interference. You can learn a lot about what children know by quietly observing their play.

* Don't be surprised when children use mathematics materials in unconventional ways. Children may take bug counters and enclose them in compartments to make a "bug zoo" in the block area, or they may build towers out of Unifix Cubes. These seemingly strange uses of materials can quickly become math activities. When you say, *I wonder how you decided which bugs should live in which cage?* the children will soon be explaining their categorization. When you ask, *How can we tell which Unifix Cube tower is the longest?* you will be encouraging counting and measuring.

* Encourage children's ideas and excitement. If the children in your class regularly play with math links, at some point in the year, a group of children will decide to make a chain that goes all the way around or across the room. This will probably make a mess and will mean that you (hopefully with the children's help) will, eventually, have to take the enormous chain apart. But don't let these practicalities hamper children's learning. Say, *I wonder if we have enough links to go all the way around the room. I can't wait to find out! Let me know when you're finished and we can hang your chain around our room.*

* Structure children's play around a particular mathematics concept by discussing a "challenge." Explain that a challenge is something difficult that you can do if you keep practicing and trying. At circle time on Monday, announce the weekly challenge. *This week, we will have a block challenge. Let's see who can make the tallest tower using exactly ten blocks. If you'd like when you're in the block area this week, you can work on the challenge by yourself or with your friends who are also in that area.* Praise children who choose to work on this activity. Take photos of their buildings and hang them around the room. Make announcements about the progress of children who choose to participate. Although this is optional, soon the whole class will be interested in this game. See the box on page 119 for some suggestions for block challenges that have worked well—but be creative. You can create a challenge that applies to almost any mathematics concept that you are teaching.

* Build the tallest tower that you can build using exactly ten blocks. (You can change this to any number that you are studying. Also, leave the towers up over the week and encourage children to label their buildings by writing their names on pieces of paper and taping them to their work.)

* Build the most stable building that you can build using exactly 12 blocks.

* Make a tall building using only blocks that are triangles (or pyramids).

* Make a pattern using blocks.

Taking Stock

Observations about children's mathematical activities in action can provide powerful and reliable information to teachers. Ideally, schedule a time each day to focus on particular children and make brief logs or notes about their learning. You might take stock of these informal behaviors.

Does the child . . .

* seem to be able to count to 10 in the context of playing with objects?

* use number names past the number ten?

* begin to develop a one-to-one correspondence with objects?

* use language associated with mathematical concepts?

* order sets of materials according to size, weight, color, or some other characteristic?

Try to examine these behaviors during different times of the day, such as in one-to-one interactions, or during small-group discussions. Always try to focus on what children are actually doing as they engage in activities. You'll find that these informal notes will provide a rich source of data for understanding children's developing concepts in mathematical and literacy learning.

Closing

$\mathcal{J}$oyce Scott's preschool class just loves to count. In fact, they seem to use every opportunity to count—the number of children in school for the day, the number of children getting chocolate milk for lunch, and the number of steps it takes to walk to the morning circle. She finds that they even like to count on their own when they play in the housekeeping corner, or when they make their tall towers with blocks.

To informally assess the children's learning, she invites several children at a time to play a game with her using large dotted dice. Tanya has the first turn and rolls the dice. She looks at Joyce and asks, "Mmm . . . What dot do I count?" Her classmate Reggie replies, "Hey, you don't have to count. You can just look and see it's a four."

Reggie's transition from counting each object to subitizing—or knowing how many items lie within a group—is the result of all the rich opportunities that he and his classmates have had to search for sense and meaning, patterns, and relationships. And it comes about when we respect young children's ways of thinking and when we provide instructional experiences for learning and building a foundation for the future.

CHAPTER 8

Linking Literacy and Science

Pointing to the shells in the jar, 4-year old Joanna says, "These are shells. I study them."

*B*elieve it or not—children and scientists are a lot alike. Scientists seek to understand the world all around (and beyond). So do young children. Scientists ask questions, experiment, solve problems, and try out new ideas. So do young children. Scientists are curious and filled with wonder, constantly puzzling, testing, and probing things. And so are young children.

In doing what scientists typically do, young children are learning to investigate their world. Science in early childhood is not about memorizing definitions or abstract principles that may have little meaning for young children. Rather, it's dynamic, involving children in observing, asking questions, and figuring out what happens when something is changed. In the course of these natural experiments, children are developing knowledge, principles, and general strategies that they will use to explain phenomena. Consistent with the goals for literacy and for science, your role is to help them explore their world. Your conversations and interactions lay the groundwork for building critical understandings of scientific literacy.

In this chapter, we'll first describe what children need to know about science. Then, we'll show you how the five essential practices of early literacy help children develop knowledge, vocabulary, and skills in science. We'll help you to plan and prepare activities to enhance children's capacity to think scientifically and to communicate their growing understandings of science concepts.

What Children Need to Learn in Science

The American Association for the Advancement of Science (AAAS, 1993) suggests a framework for what children should learn in early childhood science. The goals and objectives include the following:

* Physical science
* Life science
* Earth science

Physical Science

Children's innate curiosity about the natural world makes the physical sciences a great starting point for developing the building blocks of scientific thinking. Which things are smoother or softer? What happens when you bend this, or tear it, or twist it? Why does this happen? The physical sciences focus on the physical properties of objects and things. Children may explore how things taste, feel, and smell. They will use their senses and powers of observation to detect changes in their world.

Although young children are not yet methodical in their investigations, research (Chaille & Britain, 1997) suggests the following:

* It is important to expose children to science terminology, like *classifying*, *hypothesis*, *experiment*, and *observation*.
* Young children should be able to identify similarities, differences, and changes in materials and phenomena.
* Young children should be able to record (at least in some rudimentary fashion) their observations and data.

Preschoolers demonstrate an understanding of ways to investigate the physical sciences when they do the following:

Physical Science Knowledge	
	Describe the properties of objects and things
	Explore how things move and change
	Show increased understanding of changes in materials and cause-effect relationships

	Use their senses and tools to gather information, investigate materials, and observe relationships
Physical Science Skills and Methods	Observe and discuss common properties, differences, and comparisons among objects and materials
	Participate in simple investigations to test observations, discuss, and draw conclusions and make generalizations
	Describe and discuss predictions, explanations, and generalizations based on past experiences

Life Science

Children love to learn about their living environment. How do plants and animals grow? Why do they change their shapes and features? Where do they sleep? These are all topics of tremendous interest and curiosity to young children. Preschoolers will spend hours digging for worms and willingly share their observations with their peers. They'll focus most on the surface characteristics of what they see, hear, and smell about things. They'll also share their understandings by recording them in pictures or graphs or journals.

Children want to learn how their own bodies work. They like to use real objects like stethoscopes to hear their heartbeats and see life-size models to understand how their arteries and veins work. They're fascinated with animals and the changes in their life cycles, as with butterflies or new chicks. In every way, they enjoy exploring living things, their life cycles, and habitats.

Benchmarks for scientific literacy, proposed by the AAAS in 1993, suggest the following:

✳ Children who have many interesting, direct experiences with science concepts will develop the cognitive skills necessary to make more abstract generalizations.

✳ Children need to be actively involved in controlling the science process, not just in the handling of the materials or objects.

✳ The longer the interval between the children's action and the results, the more assistance children will need to remember the initial action (for example, the time between planting seeds and seeing them germinate).

Preschoolers demonstrate an understanding of ways to investigate the life sciences when they do the following:

	Identify features of plants and animals that help them live in different habitats
Life Science Knowledge	Show an understanding that plants and animals need water and food
	Recognize that people have unique features, but are alike in many ways

Life Science Skills and Methods	Show respect for all living organisms, including themselves
	Begin to systematically compile, classify, and order information collected
	Participate in simple investigations to test observations, discuss, and draw conclusions and make generalizations
	Name, record, and share information with others either orally or in written form

Earth Science

Earth science is concerned with the natural environment. Collectors by nature, children learn to explore the properties of the world around them: the seasons of the year, the weather, and the changes in the amount of light each day. They enjoy figuring out why the moon looks a little different every day, and why chunks of rocks come in many sizes and shapes, and wondering how there are more stars in the sky than anyone could possibly count.

In all ways, a study of earth science is a study of change, whether it focuses on plants, the earth, or other forces of nature. The National Research Council (Beatty, 2005) makes these recommendations:

 * Have children engage in "hands-on, brains-on" activities that actively involve children in identifying and solving problems based on logic.
 * Broaden each child's procedural and thinking skills for investigating the world, solving problems, and making decisions.
 * Increase each child's knowledge of his or her geography (land, water, mountains, deserts, rivers, and fields).

Preschoolers demonstrate an understanding of ways to investigate the earth sciences when they do the following:

Earth Science Knowledge	Recognize that some events in nature have a repeating pattern (e.g., seasons of the year)
	Recognize that the sun warms the land, air, and water, which leads to different weather patterns
	Identify different ways things move, such as back and forth, fast and slow

Earth Science Skills and Methods	Show respect for the environment
	Show interest in investigating phenomena
	Show appreciation for the beauty, balance, and orderliness of the environment
	Readily share information with peers and appreciate the perspective of others

Essential Literacy Practices in Science

Science can happen anywhere—in sand and water play, in blocks, by the aquarium, and on the playground. Because these activities are so engaging for children, we sometimes lose sight of what great learning laboratories for literacy development they can also be. For example, a sand and water table provides a golden opportunity to ask open-ended questions that encourage children to explore water pressure, textures, and buoyancy. A discovery area with sensory-rich materials can spark conversations about what children touch, feel, taste, hear, and observe about living things. Outdoor play areas, where children care for living things and use journals to record their observations, provide just about everything you need to create a rich, fulfilling set of investigations that will link children's developing literacy and science learning.

To help you reap the benefits of science discoveries in your classroom, this chapter provides a description of how to apply essential literacy practices to promote robust science learning. First, we discuss the specifics of a supportive learning environment that motivates science exploration; as in the previous chapter, we include an environmental sketch, lists of materials, ways to talk about the subject, and lesson plans. Then we provide some suggestions for applying the essential literacy practices of shared reading, word play, developmental writing, and play that help children build new science concepts and skills. We hope you leave this chapter with a solid set of ideas of how to link literacy and science in your classroom.

SUPPORTIVE LEARNING ENVIRONMENT

While science exploration can happen anywhere in the preschool environment, a special place for science play should be provided in the classroom for a few good reasons:

1. A designated place highlights science as an important activity for preschoolers to do.
2. A science area makes science activity always available to children whenever they have time and the inclination to do it. It also accommodates long-term projects, like watching seeds sprout and grow.
3. A science area provides a place to display the fruits of scientific work—the diagram of a cricket, a graph of springtime rainfall, and the results of experiments (e.g., what floats and what sinks).
4. At the same time, the science area can display scientific tools (e.g., funnels, magnifiers, thermometers) and science books, and provide storage for scientific equipment (e.g., microscopes) and notebooks. Here children can make science projects to take home or engage in theme-related science explorations of insect life, bones, plants, magnets, and colors. The sketch on page 126 of a science area highlights basic materials you need for an inviting and motivating preschool science center.

In addition, you should include science-motivating materials throughout the learning environment. Consider, for example, placing an artificial tree in a corner. Children can discover real-life objects (e.g., a nest), toy animals, puppets of local animals, and plants in the tree and nearby baskets.

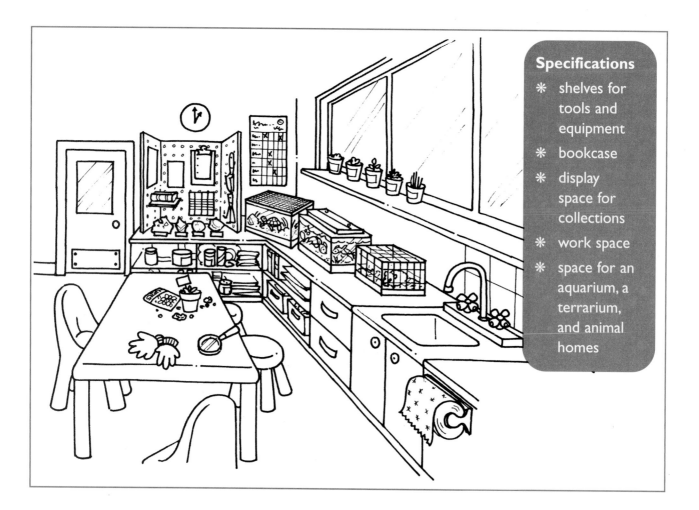

Specifications

* shelves for tools and equipment
* bookcase
* display space for collections
* work space
* space for an aquarium, a terrarium, and animal homes

Stock the shelves of a pretend store and encourage counting, weighing, and measuring food with scales, rulers, and calculators. Make sure the block area is complete with building sets, bricks, and tools for moving (rollers), lifting (a crane), and securing structures (braces).

Don't forget the outdoors, where children can plant, collect live specimens, make roads, build small bridges, and design miniature parks or zoos. Include supplies for gardening (gloves, spades, shovels, seed markers), collecting rain water (rain gauges), housing bugs and butterflies (small boxes), and constructing (small stones, sticks, plastic structures).

Finally think about displays you can create with children's help. How about a table that displays lots of shiny things, like utensils, pots and pans, ornaments, mirrors, jewelry, and even bubbles! Or build a collection of balancing things, such as a seesaw, a scale, balancing toys, a mobile, and objects to try to balance on your head, in your hand, on your feet, and on your very fingertip!

Talking About Science

* **Involve children in science talks.** Conduct weekly science talks with the whole class. Science talks can be linked to whatever open explorations or themes are underway in your classroom. For example, you might introduce children to exploring water. After giving them ample time to explore water at the water table area on their own, gather children together to reflect on their

BOOKS

Birds in Your Backyard by Barbara Herkert (Dawn Publications, 2001)
Describes the physical characteristics, habitats, and natural environment of various North American birds and provides tips for observing backyard birds.

Clever Chameleon by Alison Lodge (Barefoot Books, 2005)
Children will learn about how a variety of animals hide and disguise themselves in different surroundings.

Under One Rock: Bugs, Slugs and Other Ughs by Anthony D. Fredericks (Dawn Publications, 2001)
This book gives students an up-close look at the creatures they might find when looking under a rock.

Why Should I Protect Nature? by Jen Green (Barron's Educational Series, 2005)
The children in this book take a field trip to the countryside and begin breaking tree limbs, scattering trash, and doing what they want to the earth. Then they learn that if everyone did this, there would be no trees or birds. Similar books by this author include *Why Should I Save Water? Why Should I Save Energy?* and *Why Should I Recycle?*

Growing Vegetable Soup by Lois Ehlert (Harcourt, 1987)
This book has vibrant illustrations and describes the process of making vegetable soup, from planting the seeds to weeding to picking and washing vegetables to cooking and eating the soup. It is a great way to introduce the growing cycle and to help children gain a sense of appreciation for where their food comes from.

Sleep Is for Everyone by Paul Showers (HarperTrophy, 1997)
This book explores the concept of sleeping and what the body is telling us when we feel tired. It teaches that we all need sleep and cannot go without sleep for too long.

I Can Tell by Touching by Carolyn Otto (Trophy Press, 1994)
This book explains that the skin is very sensitive and that we can feel what we touch. It shows that we can learn about the world through touching. People can discover the texture, the shape, and the temperature of things.

The Very Hungry Caterpillar by Eric Carle (Philomel, 1969)
This book is a classic in many preschool classrooms because of its colorful illustrations and simple text. It shows the process a caterpillar goes through to become a butterfly. The caterpillar in this book eats many fruits and vegetables.

A Pill Bug's Life by John Himmelman (Children's Press, 1999)
This book is part of a series called Nature Up-close. In all of the books in the series, the story takes the reader up close into the world of a plant or insect. Some of the other books in this series study earthworms, dandelions, ladybugs, and spiders.

Let's-Read-and-Find-Out Science Series Level 1 (HarperTrophy)
This series provides a variety of children's books that explain how things in this world work. Level one is appropriate for preschoolers. The books include *My Five Senses, Snow Is Falling, How Many Teeth, Air Is All Around You,* and *From Tadpole to Frog.*

Other books about trees, flowers, animals, birds, butterflies, amphibians, snakes, shells, insects, clouds, sun, stars, rocks, water, air

TOYS

Gearation (Tomy)
Children can put gears on the flat surface of the toy. When they turn on the toy, gears begin to turn. Children can add gears as they go and control the speed at which the gears turn.

My First Chemistry Kit (Scientific Explorer, ages 4 and up)
Set includes microscope, prepared slide, blank slides, vials, handheld magnifier, citric acid, baking soda, measuring spoon, pipette, gelatin crystals, pH paper, plastic experiment tray, and instruction booklet with experiments.

Ladybug Land (Discovery)
This kit comes with a domed, see-through Ladybug Land habitat. The teacher can mail in a certificate that comes with the kit for ladybug larvae and food. It also comes with magnifying viewing lenses.

Best Ever Bug Jar (Insect Lore)
This plastic, shatterproof jar is a great place to display insects that you find on the playground. It has a unique airflow ventilated lid that allows the insects to breathe easily.

Critter Cabin (Toysmith)
This container is a great way to round up all kinds of insects. The mesh screen allows easy visibility for children and breathability for the bugs. Large enough to hold many insects.

continued on next page

Bug viewer—Choose from several different brands on the market or make your own. A bug viewer is a great way for children to study insects up close.

Planet Frog Habitat (Uncle Milton)
A lush, break-resistant, escape-proof pond environment that allows tadpoles and frogs to swim and explore—and children to watch them.

MATERIALS
For investigating
* stool magnifying glass
* hand magnifying glasses
* binoculars
* mirrors
* prism
* flashlights
* magnets

For measuring
* balance
* postage meter
* folding ruler
* tape measure
* wind-up rulers
* stopwatch
* twine
* yardstick
* hour glass

For containing and collecting
* cups, trays, jars, bottles
* boxes, egg cartons
* paper bags
* pouches, nets

For recording
* instant camera
* notebooks, pads, writing tools
* chart paper, graph paper
* tape, scissors

observations, experiences, questions, and ideas and build up excitement to learn more about water and its properties. Keep science talks short—about five minutes—and keep children engaged by using an object, photograph, or drawing to focus the talk. When engaging children in science talks, model descriptive vocabulary and help children refine their descriptions by asking questions. *How did the stream of water change? How much of the boat was underwater? How is this drop different from that one?*

* **Hold small group discussions.** During center time join children at a center where a science exploration is in progress (e.g., the water table). Ask children to tell you about what they are doing. Use follow-up questions like these to focus their attention on the "science" in the play. *What happened when you lifted the funnel up? What did it look like? What did you notice about what happened to the water? Did the same thing happen to anyone else? Did this happen before?*

* **Use drawing and telling.** Make sketches or take photographs of children's explorations. (You can also encourage children to make their own sketches.) Use sketches, photos, children's drawings, and notes to create a bulletin board that documents your investigations. Use the bulletin board to start conversations with individual children or during science talks with the whole group, and to talk with parents about children's science inquiries.

Here are some examples of questions you might ask: *What do you notice about how the water seems to be moving in this picture? Have you done anything like that with water? Look at how the illustrator drew the shape of water in this picture. Have you ever seen water look like that?*

Nurturing Knowledge

THREE SAMPLE LESSON PLANS

Lesson 1: Exploring Mighty Magnets

Learning Objectives

* To expand abilities to observe, describe, and discuss materials
* To participate in simple investigations to test observations, discuss, and draw conclusions

Whole Group: Learn together

* Give each child a craft stick with a piece of magnet tape on the stick. Before taking the children on a walk around the school to see what the magnet will stick to, ask them to make some predictions. *Do you think it will stick to the wall? A filing cabinet? A light fixture? Let's go find out!*

* Go on the walk. Be sure to plan for and include metal objects on your walk (kitchen refrigerator and countertops, metal cabinets, metal switch plates, etc.)

* When you are done exploring, check your predictions. Make a chart to record what you learned. Make two columns:

Attracted to *(Stuck to)*	Not Attracted to *(Did Not Stick to)*

Small Group: Explore together and check

* Have an assortment of magnets and objects such as paper, foil, coins, and paper clips for the children to experiment with.

* As you introduce each object, encourage predictions. *Do you think it's going to stick to the penny? Why?*

* Use content words such as *attract, magnetic,* and *pulling.* For example, you might say, *The magnet is attracted to the metal on the file cabinet.* Have the children describe what is happening using these content words. Make the point that magnets attract metallic objects, like paper clips, but they do not attract nonmetallic objects, like paper.

* Place magnets and objects in the science center for later exploration.

Lesson 2: Butterfly Investigations

Learning Objectives

* To participate in, observe, and describe simple science investigations
* To develop a growing understanding of science-related language

Whole Group: Learn together

* Ask children what they know about butterflies. *Do you know what the butterfly was before it was a butterfly? Do you know how the caterpillars got to be caterpillars? How do caterpillars turn into butterflies? Then what happens?*

* Read *The Very Hungry Caterpillar* by Eric Carle.

* Show picture cards depicting each stage of a butterfly with the word printed below the picture: *egg, caterpillar, chrysalis, butterfly.* With the children, put the word cards in order. (Refer back to the story if necessary.) Chant and clap the words *egg/caterpillar/chrysalis/butterfly;*

egg/caterpillar/chrysalis/butterfly.

✳ If you purchased a butterfly kit, show the children the small container with the tiny caterpillars in it. *What are they doing? (They're eating the food.) How did they get to be caterpillars? (They came from eggs.) What will happen next?*

✳ Put the container with the food and the caterpillars in the science area for observation. Each day, talk about the changes that are taking place with the caterpillars.

Small Group: Explore together and check

✳ Have children draw a picture in their lab book of what they saw each day and to describe what they noticed. Set up the lab book as pictured, right.

✳ Help the children to tell what they notice each day about how the caterpillar changes into a butterfly.

Name of Scientist _____
A picture of what I saw

Lesson 3: Growing Green Grass

Learning Objectives

✳ To observe, compare, and discuss differences

✳ To participate in simple science investigations, draw conclusions, and make generalizations

✳ To describe and discuss predictions

Whole Group: Learn together

✳ First sing (heartily), then read *Inch by Inch: The Garden Song* by David Mallet (1997). When finished, have the children recall what the plants in the garden needed to grow.

✳ Emphasize that *all* plants need sun, soil, and water.

✳ Tell them that during small-group time they will each have the opportunity to plant some grass to take care of and watch grow.

✳ Ask them to hypothesize: *What would happen if plants didn't get sunlight or got too much water?* Record their predictions on chart paper.

✳ Plant one pot of grass seed as the children watch. Water the seeds. Then explain: *We're going to be scientists and check our predictions. Let's put this flowerpot in the dark. Later you will plant grass in your very own flowerpots. We'll put those by the window in the sunlight. Let's observe (as scientists do) to see what happens.*

✳ Mark the planting day on the calendar. Check the flowerpots on the windowsill every day. Keep counting.

✳ When grass sprouts appear in the children's sundrenched flowerpots, check the flowerpot in the closet. Help the children make comparisons. Check predictions.

Small Group: Explore together and check

✳ Let the children paint small clay flowerpots with acrylic paints. Allow the pots to dry overnight.

✳ Help the children plant grass seed in their pots. Recall what plants need to grow: sun, soil, and water. Have the children water their grass regularly.

✳ Have copies of pages with a pot drawn on it. Have the children draw what they see each day as a way of recording observations.

SHARED BOOK READING

Children of this age are eager to understand their world, and science books provide answers to their many curious questions. Science read-alouds are critical for introducing new and sophisticated vocabulary to preschoolers. Books can help you infuse your classroom with the language of science. When you read a book with science content, help children in the following ways:

✳ Make information that you want to teach explicit. Say, *Today we are going to read a book that teaches us about how seeds grow into plants.*

✳ Ask and answer questions. Encourage children to ask questions when they are confused. Give them language to help them with this. Teach children to say, *What does that mean?* and *Can you explain what that means?* Also, ask questions to make sure that children comprehend the text.

✳ Teach word meanings. When you encounter a new or difficult word, make sure to explain its meaning to your class, even if the book makes it relatively clear. Reading about a bear in a cave, you might say, *A cave is like a hole in a mountain.* Children learn words when you state the meaning in simple language and provide lots of examples to help them understand.

✳ Use and teach science-related language, such as *predict* and *experiment,* and encourage children to think like scientists. Children feel especially bright and eager when you refer to them as scientists. *Okay scientists, can any of you predict what the caterpillar will become when it breaks out of its cocoon?* Respond to answers by prompting, *Very interesting. Why do you think that? Or* introduce activities by saying, *Scientists, today let's do an experiment.*

FIVE FAVORITE SCIENCE READ-ALOUDS

My Five Senses by Aliki (HarperCollins, 1989)
Learn about the five senses—how do they work and how do our senses help us? Also check out other science books by Aliki.

How a Seed Grows by Helen J. Jordon (HarperTrophy, 1992)
Investigate seeds and find out how they grow. Also, learn to do your own experiment growing a bean plant. Available in Spanish.

The Very Hungry Caterpillar by Eric Carle (Philomel, 1969)
Read this beloved book, which tells the story of a caterpillar who changes into a beautiful butterfly.

What Do You Do With a Tail Like This? by Steve Jenkins and Robin Page (Houghton Mifflin, 2003)
Guess which animal body part belongs to which animal. Turn the page to find out the answers and interesting facts about each animal.

Dinosaur Bones by Bob Barner (Chronicle Books, 2001)
Find out how scientists learn about dinosaurs by studying their bones in this wonderful rhyming book. Each page also includes detailed facts about dinosaurs.

* Demonstrate the ways that adult readers use informational books. You don't have to read a science book from start to finish. When a child asks an interesting question, and you say, *Let's look it up*, you are teaching your class an important lesson about reading for particular purposes. Adult readers often read nonfiction texts to learn specific information, and you can model this practice for your class.

* Connect books to hands-on or real life experiences. *We are going to take a trip to the museum to see the dinosaur bones like the ones we read about.* Or *Let's see if we can do the experiment in the book about growing bean plants. What should we do first?*

FIVE FAVORITE SCIENCE SONGS AND CHANTS

Library of Children's Song Classics by Amy Appleby (Amsco Publications, 1993)
"*The Seasons*"
"*Aiken Drum*" *(moon)*
"*Eensy, Weensy Spider*" *(insects)*
"*Farmer in the Dell*" *(farms)*
"*The Hokey Pokey*" *(human body)*
"*Oats, Peas, Beans, and Barley Grow*" *(healthy foods)*

Dem Bones (human body) by Bob Barner (Chronicle Books, 1996)

SONGS, RHYMES, AND WORD PLAY

There are many children's songs, poems, and rhymes (see box above) that address the topics you are studying in science in enjoyable ways. Include them where there is a sensible fit. Children benefit from the play with language and exposure to science-related topic words.

DEVELOPMENTAL WRITING

Writing fits naturally into most science explorations and activities. For example, when you go on a nature walk, bring along paper, pencils, and crayons for children to jot down their observations. Encourage lots of scribble notes that carefully describe how things look, smell, feel, and move. Ask children to make sketches in their notebooks and to label parts of things: *Where are the wings? Where are the legs? Did you show where the eyes are?* Remember that for preschoolers, drawing is a stepping-stone to writing. (You might want to refer to Chapter 5 for some tips on supporting children's journal writing.) When children are making science sketches, encourage them to look carefully at the object that they're trying to draw and to represent details. Preschoolers can "revise" their writing by adding to their drawings.

Consider "shoe box" science collections of objects (e.g., different kinds of leaves, different kinds of mirrors, different kinds of rocks) as writing opportunities. Have children work in pairs to look carefully at the contents of a collection and describe what they see. Encourage them to compare and discuss different sizes, shapes, colors, and so on. Then have them draw one object that they see and write about it. You can record what they say under their writing attempts.

Make class books, in which each child contributes a page, or, if an activity takes place over time, you can make individual books in which children add pages to their books every few days. Not every writing activity needs to become a book (although children *love* to make books). Children can do a "science drawing" and label it to hang on the wall or to take home.

TOPICS FOR CHILD-AUTHORED SCIENCE BOOKS

✳ **Growing a Plant** (individual books) If you are growing plants from seeds, let children make plant books. Each day (or every few days) children can look carefully at the plant and then draw the way it looks. Encourage children to label their pictures by writing a few "words" to go with their drawings. After a few weeks, each child will have made his or her own book that documents the progress of a seed as it develops into a plant.

✳ **Our Butterflies** (individual books) Order a butterfly hatching kit. As the larvae form cocoons and hatch, let children draw pictures of their progress every few days. When the butterflies hatch, children can draw them before they are released. Soon, each child will have his or her own butterfly book.

✳ **Our Trip to the Zoo** (class book) Bring paper and crayons with you to the zoo (or any other science-related field trip). Let children observe and draw a favorite animal. They can label their drawing or dictate a sentence to you. When you get back to the classroom, compile the drawings, and any photographs that you took, into a book about the animals that your class visited at the zoo.

✳ **Our Snowy Day** (class book) Create a class book about a particular type of weather. After a snowfall, take your class to play in the snow. (You may want to read Ezra Jack Keat's *The Snowy Day* (1962) for inspiration.) Take lots of photos. Bring some snow inside and watch what happens when you leave it in a bowl on the science table. Let children draw and write about their snowy day. Let children dictate what they learned from your "indoor snow" experiment. Compile the drawings, photos, and information about your experiment into a class book.

PLAY

Children need time for more structured science activities, when the teacher guides children toward completing a particular task (e.g., *Let's go outside and dig in the ground to see if we can find any worms*). But they also need plenty of time for self-guided and unstructured exploration, or free play, around science, such as building in the block area or playing at the water table. As you help children to develop their science knowledge and skills through play, consider the following:

✳ Give children the opportunity to play with science tools and explore science concepts every day.

✳ Include science books in play areas, and especially at the science table, for browsing and finding information. For example, if you have collected leaves, have books about trees and plants for children to look at and study.

✳ Adapt the dramatic-play area to specific science studies when appropriate. If you're studying animals, for example, dramatic play can become a farm or a zoo.

✳ Keep animals in the classroom. Even though they are a big effort, children benefit immensely from observing and playing with animals. Along with the usual bunny, guinea pig, or hamster, consider smaller and more manageable animals like hermit crabs, an earthworm farm, or frogs. Order larvae and watch them hatch into butterflies. Let children touch, feed, and take care of the animals in your classroom.

* Explore with science tools, such as magnifying glasses, plastic beakers, funnels of all types, microscopes, balances, and gauges (e.g., a rain gauge). Stored in the science area, these tools can be used across the classroom for science explorations.

Taking Stock

Conversations with children about their favorite science stories, TV programs, or activities in science can help you understand children's developing knowledge, motivation to learn, and interests in science. For example, after reading the book, *My Five Senses* by Aliki (1989), Anita's teacher asked her to share what she learned by asking these questions:

* How might she recognize that fall was coming?
* How might she identify a favorite fruit?
* How would she know that something was soft and fuzzy?

In one-to-one or small-group conversations, you can explore children's reasoning strategies and understandings, which can be used to develop more effective learning activities. These instructional conversations will help you informally assess whether or not, or to what extent, children are reaching the benchmarks identified in science standards for preschoolers.

Closing

Two children are at the science table. They are looking intently through magnifiers at pieces of wood. "There's spiders in there," they tell me. "Oh, really?" I say. "And how do you know that?" They each close one eye and peer closely through their magnifiers, pressing hard against the wood, and they say, "We can see their eyes."

Children at 3 and 4 years old are making emerging hypotheses and learning to share their observations with their peers. They are using their senses to try to figure out unfamiliar objects and events. It is this drive to make sense out of their surroundings that causes children to reach out, touch, and wonder, and it is this same curiosity that moves children to learn about science and communication. Children who have many interesting, direct experiences over time with these types of science concepts will come to understand the broader principles of science and literacy as they develop the skills to make more abstract generalizations.

CHAPTER 9

Linking Literacy and Social Studies

S ocial studies is an enormous and diverse content area. It includes geography, history, economics, and political science. Add in social science, social skills, and the study of people—the ways they act and interact with their environments—and you'll find a fascinating and multifaceted content area in which to engage young children in learning.

Studying people, of course, is nothing new to young children! They are keen observers of human actions and interactions from birth. They are captivated by questions like *Who am I? How do I work and play with others? Where do I live?* Children are interested in their own history and that of their families, and how people work together to form a sense of community.

As they explore their worlds, children discover how people affect their environment and are affected by it. They learn about how things change over time. They see themselves as members of a community and begin to work with others in creative problem solving activities.

Social studies is a study of people, places, and past events. You'll find many ways to integrate the social studies in your day-to-day literacy activities.

What Children Need to Learn in Social Studies

Social studies knowledge can be categorized in the following areas (for review, see Ravitch, 1995):

* History: learning about time
* Civics: learning about people
* Geography: learning about places

History: Learning About Time

Knowledge of history is essential. It is our common memory of where we began, of what our core values are, of what decisions in the past account for the present. But history for young children is not about memorizing facts or recalling dates. Rather, to understand history, children must develop a sense of the passage of time and the changes that occur in their lives and the lives of those in their community.

In finding out about themselves, children find out about others. They learn to accept others as individuals who are like them in many ways, but also different in background, appearance, feelings, and preferences. They learn about time in relation to themselves, including the sequence and order of their daily routines and schedule, what they did yesterday and what they will do tomorrow. "When I was baby," says 3-year-old Tanya, "I didn't knowed you weren't supposed to eat bugs. I eated a bug then . . . I did. I really did!" They learn their personal histories and treasure those photo albums and scrapbooks that chronicle their progress in the world. "Look, Vinnie—there I am at Disney World standing by Mickey Mouse. I was little then. See?"

Although history for young children is quite abstract, the research (Seefeldt, 1995) suggests the following:

* Providing children with compelling literature from many historical periods helps them bring historical times to life.
* Basing learning on firsthand experiences holds personal meaning for children; for example, connecting family life now and in the recent past with family life in various places long ago.
* Organizing daily routines in a predictable and dependable way helps children begin to develop a sense of time.
* Reflecting on the changes that occur in children's own lives, their school, and their community helps them begin to understand that change is continuous and ever present and affects people in different ways.

* Placing events into a chronology (retelling a story, recounting a field trip) introduces children to concepts of past, present, and future.

Preschoolers demonstrate understanding of history in early learning standards when they do the following:

History	Understand the difference in time—past, present, and future
	Begin to understand the relationship between cause and effect
	Begin to recount and analyze events

Civics: Learning About People

At the same time that children are learning history, they are also developing the dispositions and skills to interact with others. Children learn about roles and the rules of family life. *Keep quiet while people are sleeping. Make sure you close the door when you go outside. Share your toys with your little brother.* They listen to family stories and learn about their heritage and traditions. Family customs, they discover, can be lots of fun (like at weddings), but sometimes very serious, when all the family members gather round. As members of a family, children learn how to help, how to care for one another (and beloved pets), and how to have fun.

The demand for social knowledge escalates as children step outside the home and begin to work and play with others in their neighborhoods and classrooms. How to make friends, how to get along, and how to share become fertile ground for learning social concepts, such as fairness, cooperation, empathy, and social skills, such as turn taking, listening, and negotiating. Outside the home, children develop their first "sense of community"—and what it means to participate and contribute to that community. They learn to support one another, to understand how their choices affect others, to play by the rules, and to express their ideas, thoughts, and feelings so others get the message.

The research literature (see, Center on the Social and Emotional Foundations of Early Learning, 2006) on social and emotional development for young children highlights the dichotomy of socialization—the need for developing a strong sense of individuality while learning to put aside one's own needs and desires for the good of the group. The evidence suggests the following:

* Children feel valued and respected when they are treated with kindness and respect.
* Social-skill development doesn't just happen as if by magic. Teachers need to offer children explicit instruction to develop social skills and cognitive strategies for social participation. *Let's wait to begin our meal until every one has been served.*
* Teachers who respond openly to children's needs find that the children respond to one another in a similar manner.
* Children can be taught to resolve conflicts through language.

Preschoolers demonstrate understanding of civics in early learning standards when they do the following:

Civics	Cooperate with others and respect others' opinions
	Understand and follow basic rules
	Play well with other children
	Use language to resolve conflicts
	Recognize their own feelings and manage them appropriately

Geography: Learning About Places

Almost as pressing as the question *Who I am?* is the question *Where do I live in the world?* Children's geography includes their local community, their house, trips to the store and playground, visits to the homes of relatives and friends: this is the preschoolers' world. Their bed (and what's under it), the slide at the playground (and going down it), the rug and play centers in the classroom (across, beside, near, and far) are the landmarks of where children are and the locators of what they do. Directions to and from the playground, the bathroom, their favorite center, the library within the school are the first maps children can draw and paint, and the first ones they can use to find their way. Young learners can draw upon these places as a basis for exploring geographic concepts and skills.

Children's study of geography is like that of the social scientist (see Geography Education Standards Project, 1994). They dig in the sand, pour water, watch rain fall, and explore themselves in space. As they play, they use all the skills of the geographer. They ask questions like *What is this?* and *What is that smell?* and *Why is it shaped that way?* And although their world in spatial relationships is just forming, nevertheless children can begin to explore the physical characteristics of objects. Research (Brophy, 1990) suggests the following:

* The development of the abstract concepts of direction and space is best achieved through sensory motor experiences (encouraging children to climb, jump, run)—physically moving in space.

* Learning geography requires the sensitive interaction of an adult who gives children verbal labels, extending their information.

* Identifying and using words associated with the physical characteristics of objects (*hard, soft, rough, smooth, sandy, loamy, water, land*) helps children begin to learn and categorize the earth's surfaces.

Preschoolers demonstrate understanding of geography in early learning standards when they do the following:

Geography	Use language associated with space (*up, down, over, under*)
	Identify words associated with physical objects (*hard, soft, rough, smooth*)
	Identify different surfaces on earth (*ground, sky, water*)
	Identify basic direction-giving signs
	Begin to recognize environmental print

Essential Literacy Practices in
Social Studies

Your entire preschool room can be a content-rich workshop for social studies. Here children can study how people live, work, and solve problems together through their shared learning experiences. They can shape their surroundings and also observe how the environment shapes their own daily routines and activities. A sudden snowfall, for example, changes things—and we scurry to gather information about the condition of the roads, how to get home, who has a spare pair of mittens, and to find those books that tell us all about snow, snow, and more snow.

Dress-up and dramatic play are naturals for developing social studies concepts.

Helping your children create rules about getting along and cooperating with one another and writing them down is an example of linking literacy and social studies. Other examples are described in this chapter as we survey essential literacy practices applied to the development of children's social studies understandings and skills. We begin with the specifics of a supportive learning environment and then turn to the practices of shared book reading, word play, writing, and play that contribute to the social studies curriculum. Together the ideas for implementing these literacy practices offer a variety of ways for linking literacy and social studies concepts in your preschool classroom.

SUPPORTIVE LEARNING ENVIRONMENT

Infusing dramatic-play areas with props of community workers—post officers, police officers, firefighters—encourages children to use vocabulary associated with these activities in the community. The sketch on the next page highlights a motivating place for exploring the social studies concepts and skills embedded in these community roles.

Having a collectible table, where children are stimulated to talk about and categorize objects found in the city and country provides wonderful opportunities for linking literacy and social studies. You'll want to be sure to include these items in the play and learning environment:

* Posted agenda of the day
* Posted rules
* Direction-giving signs
* Maps of classroom, playground, neighborhoods

Resources for the social studies area are listed on page 141.

Specifications

* child-sized furniture for kitchen play
* full-length mirror
* baby's bed, high chair, doll buggy
* telephones
* corner storage for broom, mop, dustpan
* cooking utensils, plastic food
* signage

Talking About Social Studies

Children learn language with lots of help. They learn language skills from conversations with teachers who model and promote the use of language to solve problems, make plans, remember the past, and anticipate what will happen next. In the course of everyday conversations with children, and in more structured learning activities, you can help children learn and talk about the big ideas of social studies—ideas that are the building blocks of history, civics, and geography. Here are a few pointers.

* **Make references to time and place.** Ordinary conversation provides many opportunities to develop children's sense of time and place and the idea of change. Even very young children internalize a basic sense of day and night, breakfast, lunch, and dinner. Words like *yesterday*,

BOOKS

Words Are Not For Hurting by Elizabeth Verdick (Free Spirit Publishing, 2004)
This book stresses the importance and power of words. It helps children understand and take responsibility for what they say, as well as thinking before they speak. It encourages children to communicate in friendly ways.

My Many Colored Days by Dr. Seuss (Random House, 1996)
This book compares a variety of feelings with colors. Some days the child in the story feels sad, and these days are purple. Other days the child feels busy, and he thinks of yellow.

I Was So Mad by Mercer Mayer (Random House, 1985)
In this book, Little Critter is having a bad day, and it seems that nothing will go his way. Because of his bad day, Little Critter is feeling angry, and he tries different things to get out of his bad mood.

When Sophie Gets Angry—Really, Really, Angry . . . by Molly Bang (Blue Sky Press, 1999)
Sophie gets angry and learns how to cope with this feeling. The illustrations support the text by changing colors to reflect the emotion Sophie feels, such as red when she is angry and cooler colors when she is calm.

How Are You Peeling? Foods with Moods by Saxton Freymann and Joost Elffers (Arthur A. Levine, 1999)
The illustrations in this book are photographs of a variety of fruits and vegetables that are carved to look like they are showing emotions.

Glad Monster, Sad Monster by Ed Emberley and Anne Miranda (Little, Brown, 1997)
The monsters in this book are different colors and it explains what makes them feel different emotions. There are foldout masks and flaps that encourage the reader to discuss feelings.

Because Brian Hugged His Mother by David Rice (Dawn Publications, 1999)
Brian hugs his mother one morning, and this act starts a chain reaction of kindness and consideration that spreads throughout the whole town and eventually comes back to him.

Boys and Girls of the World: From One End . . . to the Other by Nuria Roca (Barron's Educational Series, 2005)
This book shows that everyone in the world has many similarities and differences. At the end of the book is a two-page section that offers guidelines and discussion points for parents and teachers.

Don't Call Me Special: A First Look at Disability by Pat Thomas (Barron's Educational Series, 2005)
This book, written by a psychotherapist, teaches children about individual disabilities, the special equipment that may be used to help a person who has a disability, and how all children can deal with disabilities to live a happy life. It also includes advice for parents and teachers.

Other books about the child's person (body, senses, body actions, clothes), house and home, people and family, food and eating, social life (birthdays, parties, trips), community environment, school, nature and pets

TOYS

Imaginext (Fisher Price)
All sets are compatible; plastic pieces snap together in a variety of ways, encouraging planning, creativity, and building skills. Various sets are available, such as castle and fire station.

Ready Set Learn! Paz's Fishing Set
This set can be used in your classroom water table. It helps children explore the role of fishing. The set includes: magnetic fishing pole, four magnetic fish, net, bucket, and a sturdy tackle box, which holds the fishing tools.

MATERIALS

* dress-up clothes and hats
* puppets and puppet theater
* any toys that help children explore roles and professions
* photo displays
* diversity puzzles showing other cultures
* miniature building sets of a farm, airport, train/bus station, town, seaport

today, tomorrow, especially when linked to real events (*After you clean up, we'll go outside for our walk*), help children develop a sense that time passes. The notions of "from long ago" and "from now on" are harder for young children to grasp. Pointing out clear examples of common things that are different from those in times past (e.g., clothing, transportation, work) in read-alouds or other structured activities can help children get a toehold on this complex idea. Words related to location (*here, there, near, far*), distance (*inches, feet, miles*), land features (*desert, mountains, lakes, ocean*), and landmarks (*bridges, towers, skyscrapers, statues*) should also be woven into conversations and book talks, so children develop a rudimentary sense of place.

* **Explain the actions and thinking of others.** Use conversation with children as an opportunity to talk about feelings and opinions. Explain feelings of sadness, anger, fear, frustration, excitement, happiness, friendliness, and delight. Show and talk about these emotions in real and storybook contexts, so children learn words they can use to describe their own feelings and think about those of others. Frequent language experiences of this nature cultivate children's empathy (considering thoughts and feelings other than one's own), and instill the language needed for perspective taking and future historical understanding. Also, don't be afraid to express opinions and impressions in a constructive way (*I think it is healthy to eat lots of fruits and vegetables*), showing children how to effectively voice their own opinions.

* **Explore causes for things.** Children really benefit from explanations about things. When you explain what is happening (*We need to wait for the bus driver because he got held up in traffic*), talk about outcomes (*Oh, boy! We forgot to order the milk, so we'll have to have juice today instead*), and justify opinions or preferences (*I don't like loud noise because it hurts my ears*), you are helping children explore the logic of situations. They learn to think and talk about conditions that help to explain why this or that happened. Developing these language skills builds children's readiness for the social studies, sharpening their abilities to understand history and community life.

* **Encourage storytelling.** Storytelling is a very important skill that takes time to develop. Children need to be able to tell stories in order to participate in conversations and play situations. The art of storytelling (and listening) is fundamental to understanding social studies in which the stories of different peoples are told. Your goal is to help children become better storytellers. Questions and comments are ways to get stories started and to keep them on track. Stories are best told in small-group or one-to-one situations. Provide children with opportunities to tell you stories in informal situations, and to be especially attentive to quieter, less verbal children, encouraging them to tell their stories. Listen—and be patient, so children can finish their stories. And, of course, remember to tell your own stories, so children can follow your lead.

THREE SAMPLE LESSON PLANS

Lesson 1: Feelings

Learning Objectives

✳ To think about feelings and the feelings of others

✳ To encourage children to express feelings

Whole Group: Learn together

✳ Invite children to sit in a circle with you. Ask the children to show you with their face how they feel when someone won't share a toy with them. Say, *What words would you use to describe this face?* (mad, angry, sad, hurt, etc.).

✳ Ask them to show you how they'd feel if these things happened:
  • Their grandma called and said she was taking them to get ice cream.
  • Their friend pushed them.
  • They just met someone new.
  • It was their birthday.

✳ Each time, follow up by asking for words to describe the feelings. *What's a word for how you would feel? Who should you tell how you feel or if something is wrong or you are upset?*

✳ Read *How Are You Peeling? Foods with Moods* by Saxton Freymann and Joost Elffers, a picture book that shows emotions using fruits and vegetables.

✳ Reread the book, taking time to discuss the faces and emotions portrayed on each page.

Small Group: Explore together and check

✳ Have children draw faces of their feelings on four different small paper plates. You might want to make several models in advance.

✳ Have them glue craft sticks to the bottom for handles.

✳ In the small group, encourage children to talk about the different faces and times when they have felt that feeling. *Ross, your face looks angry! Have you ever felt that way?*

Lesson 2: Community Workers

Learning Objective

✳ To develop an awareness of jobs and what is required to perform them

Whole Group: Learn together

✳ In preparation for a visit from a police officer to the school, talk with the children about questions they might have. *What do you wonder about police officers or their jobs?* Write the questions on chart paper.

✳ Allow the children to ask the police officer questions.

✳ Following the visit, review the initial list of questions listed. *What did we learn about police officers? What new questions do they have about police officers?*

✳ See page 144 for a song about calling 911 to teach to the class. Print the words to the song on chart paper and sing to the tune of "Bingo." As you teach the song, point to each word.

Small Group: Explore together and check

* In small groups, help children learn and memorize their street address and telephone number.

* Have a practice phone available so children can learn how to call 911. Ask, *When should you call 911? Should you call 911 if you hurt your toe? Should you call it if your house is on fire?*

911 Song

There is a number you can call when you need someone's help.

You call 911, you call 911, you call 911

And the policeman will help you

* Make a simple police officer hat and badge. Allow children to use it to dress up for dramatic play. Meet with children in small groups during dramatic play to encourage content talk about police officers and the role they play in the community: *I'm going on patrol now. I'll be back at the police department in a while.*

Lesson 3: People Are Alike and Different

Learning Objective

* To begin to understand similarities and differences among people

Whole Group: Learn together

* Gather the children in a circle.

* Wrap a shoe box (lid separately) so the children can't see a mirror glued inside.

* Prompt students to guess what is in the box. Say, *Everyone is going to see something different in the box. What do you think it could be? Take a peek in the box. What do you see?*

* Read *We Are All Alike . . . We Are All Different* (1991) a book written and illustrated by The Cheltenham Elementary School Kindergartners.

* After reading, ask the children how they are the same as their friends (they have some of the same toys, live in the same neighborhood, like the same foods, are both boys, etc.). Then have them share ways they are different (they have different houses, families, looks, ideas, etc.).

* Ask the children to look carefully at the person sitting next to them and tell you how they are like that person and how they are different. *I'm next to Chico. He has brown eyes just like me, and we are both boys.*

Small Group: Explore together and check

* Have the children draw a self-portrait, using the mirror to notice their uniqueness.

* Lead a discussion and encourage the children to discover that even though everyone is different, we also have similarities. *Lucy, you and Chantyiana are both girls, but you have light brown hair and Chantyiana's is dark brown. Can you think of a way you are the same?*

* Have each child dictate a sentence for you to write about his or her self-portrait.

SHARED BOOK READING

As you work with children to help them learn to interact with each other, you'll find that books provide useful examples. It's easier for young children to think about and discuss the way a character in a book is behaving than it is for them to reflect on their own behavior. When you start a new school year, many children feel anxious about meeting new children and making friends, but they may have difficulty articulating these concerns. Children don't always know how to join other children in play or how to invite another child to play. As you read Miriam Cohen's *Will I Have a Friend?* (1967), you can begin a conversation about these issues in a safe way that provides an example that is similar to the situation in your classroom. Books provide conversation starters for many of the social questions and issues that typically occur in preK classrooms over the course of the year, such as using words to solve problems and express emotions, friendship, sharing, and kindness. Keep books on these topics to read when the need arises, or introduce these topics systematically throughout the year.

Young children have particular difficulty learning language to articulate various emotions. They often have not mastered vocabulary to clearly express the range of feelings they experience. Many teachers help children by providing them with language to resolve a conflict or to solve a problem. Read-alouds are a fantastic time to introduce or review "feeling" words as a whole class or with a small group at a time when everyone is interested and calm. *How do you think* [the character] *is feeling right now?* is a difficult question for many preschoolers to answer, but it is an important question to ask on a regular basis. The children may respond simply with words like "happy" or "sad," but you can use the vivid examples from storybooks to share more specific and sophisticated language. *I think maybe the little boy is worried. Worried is when you are not sure if everything is going to be okay. You're just not sure, or maybe you're even a little bit scared. He is going to a new place and he feels worried. Have you ever felt worried?* The examples and language that books provide will carry over to the real-life situations that occur every day in your classroom, and you can encourage children to use "feeling" words that they've learned in books when the need arises.

You can also use read-alouds to provide children with interesting, new information. Although children learn a lot from field trips, walks, day-to-day interactions, and other experiential social studies lessons, it is often not possible for children to experience everything that you want them to learn and that they need to know about their world. Read-alouds of informational texts enable children to learn beyond their day-to-day experiences, and this becomes particularly valuable as you explore topics about the broader community. Whether you are studying the post office, food that people eat, or different types of homes, the information and the "real pictures" (photographs) in nonfiction texts will enhance children's understanding of the subject matter.

As part of the preschool social studies experience, children should be introduced to the notion that there are people all around the world who do things differently but participate in many of the same core human experiences. Children of this age are not yet ready to locate foreign countries on a map or to grasp concepts like nations and states, but this does not mean that they can't be exposed

FIVE FAVORITE SOCIAL STUDIES READ-ALOUDS

Will I Have a Friend? by Miriam Cohen (Simon & Schuster, 1967)
A reassuring answer is given to this familiar question in a book that has delighted children for 40 years.

Beyond the Ridge by Paul Goble (Bradbury, 1989)
With beauty and simplicity, Goble captures the spiritual journey of a Plains Indian grandmother.

Chrysanthemum by Kevin Henkes (Greenwillow, 1991)
Chrysanthemum loves her name, until she starts school and the other children make fun of it.

Take Turns, Penguin! by Jeanne Willis (Carolrhoda, 2000)
Penguin won't share the slide with others until Crocodile teaches him a lesson.

Don't Go by Jane Breskin Zalben (Clarion, 2001)
Daniel overcomes his nervousness as he plays in the sandbox, collects leaves, and bakes cookies.

to multicultural education in a way that is meaningful and appropriate to their developmental stage. Use nonfiction books to teach children that people around the world may look different and eat different foods, but all people are the same in important ways: grown-ups take care of children all over the world; children love to play games all over the world (you might wish to learn some games from other countries); people have homes all around the world; and people take care of their families, friends, and pets all around the world. It is never too early to teach children to respect and value people who are different from them. Read-alouds provide many opportunities for this important aspect of children's social studies education.

SONGS, RHYMES, AND WORD PLAY

In many preschool classrooms, songs are used throughout the day to facilitate routines and to create a sense of community. This starts in the morning when you sing a greeting song to begin circle time and ends when you sing a song to say good-bye. Many teachers use songs or chants to help children when it is time for a transition. For example, to get children's attention to clean up, you might sing the song below:

> (To the tune of "Twinkle, Twinkle, Little Star")
> It is time to clean up now.
> Clean up, clean up, we know how.
> We can clean up; you will see
> Just how clean our room can be.

Often, preschool teachers simply make up their own words to a familiar tune when they need a song to remind students about a particular routine:

Nurturing Knowledge

(To the tune of "If You're Happy and You Know It")
If you're ready and you know it, clap your hands.
If you're lined up and you know it, stamp your feet.
If you're sitting and you know it, wiggle your pinky.
If you'd like to have a turn, raise your hand.

FOUR SONGS ABOUT GETTING ALONG

In *A Treasury of Children's Songs: Forty Favorites to Sing and Play* by Dan Fox (Henry Holt, 2003)
"London Bridge"
"Amazing Grace"
"The Mulberry Bush"
"Old MacDonald"

Also, if you search the Internet, you can find hundreds of songs that teachers have shared for use at various times of the day. These songs and routines are not simply about making transitions run smoothly and making children feel safe and comfortable; they are part of creating a well-functioning classroom community. Adults have agreed upon ways of doing things that help our society to run smoothly (e.g., which car goes first at a four-way stop sign). When we create classroom rules and "traditions," we model the way societies function at a scale that is relevant and meaningful to young children.

There are also many songs about friendship, love, and getting along with others. As so much of preK social studies focuses on helping children to interact with one another, these songs are enjoyable to learn and also serve as reminders about the type of behavior that we are trying to encourage. Include these songs as part of your circle-time activities on a regular basis to keep children focused on getting along and being together.

DEVELOPMENTAL WRITING

As junior social scientists, preschool children learn to record and document the fascinating information that they discover. Writing is also a helpful tool for keeping a record of the agreed-upon rules and behaviors in your classroom community. Below you will find a few suggestions for incorporating writing into your social studies curriculum.

* Invite parents, friends, or other school personnel to your classroom to tell children about their jobs. Ask the guest to bring photographs of him- or herself at work and to bring objects or tools that he or she uses on the job. Ask the guest to explain how doing his or her job helps the community. Let children ask lots of questions. After the guest leaves (or the next day), let children retell what they have learned as you write their words down on a piece of chart paper. Have children draw pictures of the guest at work. Create a bulletin board to display what you have learned, or create a class big book about jobs that contains a page for each guest.

* Invite each child to bring one or two family members into the classroom to share a special family tradition or an activity that the family likes to do. Help each family to create a little project to do with the class. These projects may range from making the special pancakes that a family cooks every Saturday to learning to hula dance to learning about how a family celebrates a special holiday. After the project, help children to retell what they have learned.

Also, ask children to make pictures to go with their words. Make a book or a display. (Don't forget to help your class write thank-you cards when you have a special guest!)

* Take a field trip to learn more about your community. Visit a fire station, the supermarket, or the park. Learn about why these places are important. After the field trip, ask children to talk about their day, talk about a favorite part of the trip, or talk about something interesting they learned. Write down children's words and then let them create illustrations to go with their words.

* When you have a class discussion about social interactions or appropriate behavior, record children's words and suggestions. Whether you are discussing manners at snack time or words to use when a friend makes you upset, write it down. When you take notes on a large piece of chart paper, you model the ways that adults use writing to record important discussions and decisions. Also, when the situation arises again, you can bring children over to the chart and remind them of their previous suggestions. *Remember, our class decided that if a friend takes something we are still using, we don't try to grab it back. Look here, I wrote down the words that our class decided would help when that happens. We say, "Can you please give the crayon back, I was still using it." Why don't you go back and try to use those words.*

PLAY

The dramatic-play area is the part of the classroom that is most likely to encourage topical social studies play. As we've mentioned above, you can outfit your dramatic-play area with tools and objects that fit well with almost any social studies focus. If your class had a visit from a veterinarian as part of your study about pets, you'll notice that children will play "vet" and will use the toy stethoscope and syringe to examine stuffed animals. Or you may observe that one child is pretending to be a sick pet and another will be the owner who needs to take his pet to the vet. Children readily incorporate their newfound knowledge and vocabulary into their pretend play.

Although dramatic play is where we see children incorporating the content and vocabulary they have learned, social studies is really part of all play, as children learn to interact and grow in their ability to negotiate conflicts. Free play, both on the playground and in the classroom provides opportunities for children

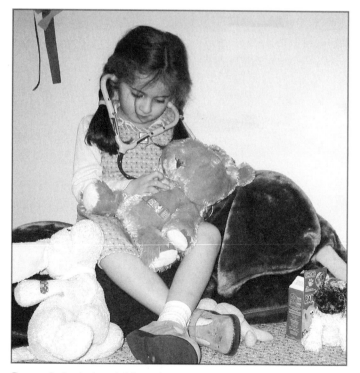

Pretend play helps children deepen conceptual understandings and develop vocabulary.

to develop their abilities to relate to peers. It is important for adults to provide the time and also the space for children to engage in play without active adult involvement. Often, this means observing patiently without interfering and making a judgment about when to intervene. This can be difficult to do, particularly when children have a disagreement that you could resolve easily by stepping in. It helps to keep in mind that our goal for children is that they learn to negotiate conflicts independently so that they are able to play and work cooperatively without constant adult intervention.

Try the following to help children learn to play cooperatively:

* Teach conflict resolution and language to be used when there are disagreements. Do this at circle time and during other parts of the day when everyone is calm. Play let's pretend. *Let's pretend that I am using a glue stick and Hannah also wants to use it. What could she do? What could she say?* After children give suggestions, let children practice by acting it out.

* Teach children that if they cannot solve a problem, it is a good idea to come and ask for your help. This may be particularly useful for children who tend to solve problems by grabbing, pushing, or hitting. Encourage children, *If you feel angry at a friend and you don't know what to do, come and ask me and I will help you to solve the problem.* (You may have to work with some children to teach the difference between asking for help and "telling on" friends.)

* Observe and monitor children as they play, but always try to let them resolve conflicts independently if they can. Again, this can be difficult to do when you see that there is a simple solution, and you know that you can easily prevent tears and frustration. Watch, listen, and wait. Give children a chance to solve problems by themselves. Often, they are able to do this, and play will resume without your help. If children cannot resolve their differences and continue playing or if they are becoming extremely angry or upset, step in and help them to express themselves.

* Take time to help children use language to negotiate a conflict and resolve the problem. Encourage each child to express his or her ideas and feelings. After each child has a chance to speak, ask the children if they can think of a way to solve the problem. If they can't do this, then you can make some suggestions. If you offer a solution immediately, you miss the opportunity to teach conflict resolution behaviors and language that can help children when the next disagreement occurs.

It helps to remember that kindness, cooperation, and verbal conflict resolution are some of the most important social studies concepts that children can learn, and taking time to address these ideas in preschool will help children in innumerable ways in the future.

Taking Stock

There is no better way to informally assess children's social skill development than by observing them during play. Use sticky notes to record children's involvement with others during group activities, outdoor play, and socio-dramatic activities. Here's what to look for:

* How well a child cooperates with others, and demonstrates respect for other opinions
* Whether the child uses language to resolve conflicts with others
* Whether the child is beginning to understand the relationship between cause and effect—recognizing that certain behaviors may have an influence on what happens next

Try to make regular entries for each child in various situations throughout your day. These anecdotal notes will help you document children's progress and shed light on what children are able to do, as well as the areas where they may need further support and assistance.

Closing

Sheena says that Sara fights over the tablecloth on the table in the house corner. "She keeps pulling it off the table 'cause she thinks that I have more and I don't."

"So, how do you fix that problem?" I ask.

"Well, we just take it off."

Sharing and respecting each other's feelings, Sheena and Sara are learning how to negotiate and solve problems. Without any coaching or assistance, they are demonstrating their ability to adjust to situations. And with these basic social skills, along with the understanding that others have perspectives that may differ from their own but that are just as valuable, children are developing a firm foundation for becoming productive citizens in a democracy.

CHAPTER 10

Linking Literacy and the Arts

"The child has a hundred languages," wrote Loris Malaguzzi, "a hundred hands, a hundred thoughts, a hundred ways of thinking" (1993, p. 3). Singing, dancing, drawing, playing—these, too, are languages that children use to participate ever more fully in this world. These are, in fact, universal languages that young children around the world use to communicate: *This is who I am, this is how I feel, this is what I dream, and this is what I think.*

As first languages, the creative arts—art, music, movement, and dramatic play come naturally to children. They are energetic modes of expression and bursting with promise (like all the young children who use them). We know the arts engage all the senses, involve different modalities (kinesthetic, auditory, and visual channels), spark imagination, and demand rigorous thinking (Gardner, 1980). Children's active participation in the arts may actually help to engage them in all sorts of future learning. But even more important for the learning child is that the creative arts are a source of joy, wonder, fun, and power.

Our focus in this chapter is on the arts—how to link the language arts (speaking, listening, reading, and writing) with the creative arts (art, music, movement, and drama) in the early childhood classroom. Specifically we want to show how the five essentials of early literacy practice go hand in hand with early learning through the arts. The arts, like four cornerstones, are a large part of the early childhood experience and easily support early literacy activities. We'll begin by describing arts standards—what we want children to know and be able to do—and focus on the research base in the arts. We'll then describe a creative arts play setting to spotlight a supportive learning environment that encourages early literacy and the creative arts in the early childhood classroom. Finally, we'll explore and develop children's knowledge about the arts through other essentials of literacy practices.

What Children Need to Learn in the Arts

Art

For many teachers of young children, art remains a mystery, something to be appreciated but not fully understood. But today, based on research (Dyson, 1982; Eisner, 1988), we know much more about the content of art education, and what children should know and be able to do:

* Although most art educators agree that children's own experience as creators of art should remain the central concern of early childhood art education, most also believe that children can and should become acquainted with works of art at an early age.

* Children need time to experiment with materials, to push and prod and examine and manipulate the art material that is provided for their use.

* Young children may recognize the qualities of expression in the works of other artists long before they recognize it in their own work.

* Art is nurtured by conversations that allow children to share the stories that may only be partially captured in visual forms.

* There is a close relationship between art and language in the early years that provides unlimited opportunities for visual and verbal storytelling.

Every young child is an artist! Crayons, markers, pens, and paintbrushes quickly become tools of self-expression. Whether it's painting at the easel, rolling "strips" of clay, or creating a collage, children explore (and learn) the elements of art: line, shape, color, and texture.

Scribbles, dabs, and blobs are the building blocks of art and the building blocks of writing. In making many of these scribbles, over and over, one on top of the other, children gain arm and hand control. They start to master the use of drawing objects (brushes, sticks, crayons, and pencils). Shapes begin to emerge in their creations: the rectangle, the oval, the triangle, the Greek cross (+), and the diagonal cross (X). And then out of an odd shape, an identifiable object appears in children's drawings: the sun! There it is, with its sticklike rays. Not long after, the human form evolves from this sun—the hair on top, the arms on either side, and the legs that come out the bottom. As Erika showed us, "See me. And that's mommy. And the baby. He's got no hair."

From ages 4 to 6, other recognizable objects appear in children's artwork, drawn from their mind's eye—houses, dogs, cars, trees. Children fill surfaces (boards, paper, cardboard pieces) with a repertoire of objects (not scribbles) that they like to tell you about. Their artistic expression at this point is a source of meaning that can be shared with others.

We know that children's activities in art change rapidly during these early childhood years, evolving from these first scribbles and random marks to more-complex representations of objects and events. But just as surely as children's art changes over the course of early childhood, we now know that it's not an automatic consequence of development and growth. As with all the other subject areas, children's learning about art develops as a result of an active process of learning that is facilitated by an adult. Children need assistance and support for their explorations of art from you as you listen to their plans, respond to their ideas, and provide opportunities for them to feel confident in exploring artistic activity. Preschool children demonstrate their knowledge of art when they do the following:

Art	Gain ability in using different art media and materials in ways that support creative expression and representation
	Develop growing abilities to plan, work independently, and demonstrate care and persistence in a variety of art projects
	Progress in their abilities to create drawings, paintings, and other art creations
	Begin to understand and share opinions about artistic products and experiences

Music

Not only do children love art and engaging with scribbles and shapes, they also enjoy humming, singing, tapping, and drumming. All of these activities involve music, and all contribute to children's developing phonological awareness—their ability to hear similarities and differences in tones, timbres, and tempos.

Music naturally delights children. It involves their bodies and minds in playing with sounds and language. Growing up with music, children learn about rhythm and melody. They learn to imitate sounds and make their very own music. They clap to the syllables in words, sing songs that are full of rhyme and rhythm, and expand their vocabularies through gestures and actions. Just as with art and writing, there is a natural integration between music and language.

Children's singing follows a sequence similar to their talking. Even infants are aware of music. Lullabies calm them down and lively music sets their feet to dancing (if not their whole bodies). They experiment with sounds—coos, gurgles, squeals, and babbles—and are attracted to rhythmic sounds, like "bibblety, bobblety, boo!" By the time they are toddlers, they are "swaying to the music," seeking out and making sounds they like, and may join in on favorite nursery rhymes and songs.

As preschoolers, children are quite the musicians, with better voice control, rhythmic responses, and mastery of song lyrics. They are active listeners of music and love to make up their own songs. Take a moment to enjoy this absurd song, "Science Andrew Science," composed by the Preschool Band in Ben Mardell's day care. It helps to know that it was sung "opera style."

> Cousin Andrew had been walking along
> He found an extra, extra, extra science book,
> Then he wanted to see a movie camera with a flashlight
> Then Cousin Andrew got eaten up by a shark
> Then he went home with a Band-Aid!

Investigations of music across the preschool years should expand children's vocabularies to include words such as *lyrics*, *chorus*, *verses*, *instrumentals*, and *solos*. Children should become careful, informed music listeners, paying attention to the instruments used and vocal qualities of different voices.

Music brings children together and is best explored in an interactive environment that is rich in manipulative objects, instruments, and materials. It's really not about memorizing song lyrics and performing in front of a group. Rather, it's about exposing children to music by hearing it, feeling it, and experimenting with it in their daily lives.

And the research evidence (Andress, 1995) confirms that music has a powerful influence on children's literacy development:

* Music can act as a mnemonic device to help children learn new vocabulary.
* Musical patterns such as clapping or using rhythm instruments promote phonological awareness and phonemic awareness.
* Children can learn how to segment and blend words using music rhythm and rhyme.
* Playing with instruments helps children hear similarities and differences in sounds.
* Singing, playing, and moving with music is highly motivating to young children.

Preschool children demonstrate their knowledge of music when they do the following:

Music	Gain ability in a variety of music activities that include listening, singing games, and performances
	Experiment with a variety of musical instruments

Movement

The origins of dramatic expression and acting are in movement. Children first learn to express themselves in action and dance. For young children, movement is at the center of their lives. As children develop their skills, they gain an increased awareness of their physical abilities. What an ego builder to feel in control of one's physical self and to show off!

Children often dance and use movement to convey meaning. They enjoy such activities as walking, rolling, running, sliding, creeping, hopping, crawling, and jumping.

All of these activities help to expand children's language and concepts of time (fast, slow, short, long), space (personal, common, shape) and energy (heavy, light). They begin to use language to describe their movements. In many cases, you'll want to incorporate movement in songs, poems, and word plays to accentuate rhymes and repetitions.

Children in the early years often use gestures and movement to convey meaning. They love to dance in different ways to music and to react to favorite stories. You'll find that singing, dancing, and word play all fit closely together.

Preschool children demonstrate their knowledge of movement when they do the following:

Movement	Express through movement and dancing what is felt and heard in various music tempos and styles
	Show growth in moving in time to different patterns of beat and rhythm in music

Dramatic Play

The preschool years are the "high season" of imaginative play, when simple pretending gives way to elaborate plots of make-believe. There are a number of good reasons for ensuring children have many opportunities to engage in collaborative socio-dramatic play. Here, we highlight its many relationships to literacy development and learning:

  * Considerable research links make-believe play to favorable outcomes in early childhood development. Children's engagement in play, for example, has been shown to improve the self-regulation skills so essential for attending to and gaining from instruction (see Roskos & Christie, in press).

  * Play builds up children's abilities to symbolically represent experiences from the real world, allowing children to move beyond the here and now to thinking about and using ideas in other times and places (Christie, 1991; Pellegrini & Galda, 1993).

  * Play exercises children's narrative competence as they create imaginary settings, take roles, and follow through on plots (e.g., treating, healing) (Christie & Enz, 1991). To be a "good" player, children must call on their story-making abilities to set the stage, stay in character, and follow through on the plot—otherwise, it just wouldn't be fun.

Preschool children demonstrate their understanding when they do the following:

Dramatic Play	Use extended conversations in dramatic-play settings
	Show growing creativity and imagination in using materials to represent objects
	Use tools for writing and drawing
	Use thinking skills to resolve conflicts
	Take on pretend roles

❋ Play encourages children to use language. Collaborative play demands that children *talk about* the play as well as *talk to* it. We call this "meta-play language," or "talk about the play"—language to explain, plan, and negotiate. This is a high-level use of language, to be sure, and stretches children's language abilities to new levels.

Across the early years, children's pretend play develops from simple forms, such as mimicking what they see (drinking from a pretend cup, for example), to highly complex play, involving elaborate story plots that may continue for days. The Pretend-Play Maturity Checklist in Chapter 6 (page 100) outlines the development of pretense in children's symbolic thinking and language use. It also details the skill sets that children should develop in the preschool years.

Essential Literacy Practices in the Arts

The whole early childhood environment should be an inviting place for drawing, singing, dancing, and playing. It needs to say, "Come here and tell me about yourself . . . what you can do, what you feel, your wonderful ideas, your song."

In the following sections we show you how to use essential literacy practices in ways that contribute to an inviting place for the arts. The arts thrive in a supportive learning environment, and so we provide a sketch showing what the arts areas might look like. We provide a sampler of materials to include, along with sample lesson plans to consider. Since conversation is at the heart of interaction, we also offer some suggestions for stimulating talk about the creative arts.

Displaying children's work is a powerful way to encourage artistic exploration.

SUPPORTIVE LEARNING ENVIRONMENT

How can early educators make classrooms into places alive with the creative arts? They can provide small, hands-on spaces for children to explore and experiment with a variety of materials, to display their work, and to perform their ideas. Like small studios or workshops, these spaces should be transformable to allow for change, expandability, and the different ages of children. Partitions, movable panels, and screens can be used to define and redefine space for flexible use.

A number of other particulars for motivating the creative arts should be kept in mind:

❋ Walls should permit extensive displays of two- and three-dimensional items (at children's eye level).

Nurturing Knowledge

* Other areas, such as classroom doors, entrances, hallways, and kitchens, can support communication and children's explorations (e.g., mirrors hung at children's height).

* Resources such as tape recorders, video cameras, instant cameras, and overhead projectors are essential for in-depth observation and documentation.

* Possibilities for looking from one space to another should be used to create a sense of transparency (translucent screens, mobiles, hangings).

* The environment should include a broad range of color shades in harmonious balance (not just primary colors of red, blue, yellow), with a preference for muted hues and medium shades.

* Natural elements (plants, flowers, wood, stones) should be available, adding texture and variety, as well as real references for creative explorations.

* Porous materials, open-work panels, bamboo grates and shades, plants, and textured materials can help to control noise yet support acoustic variety for exploring sounds.

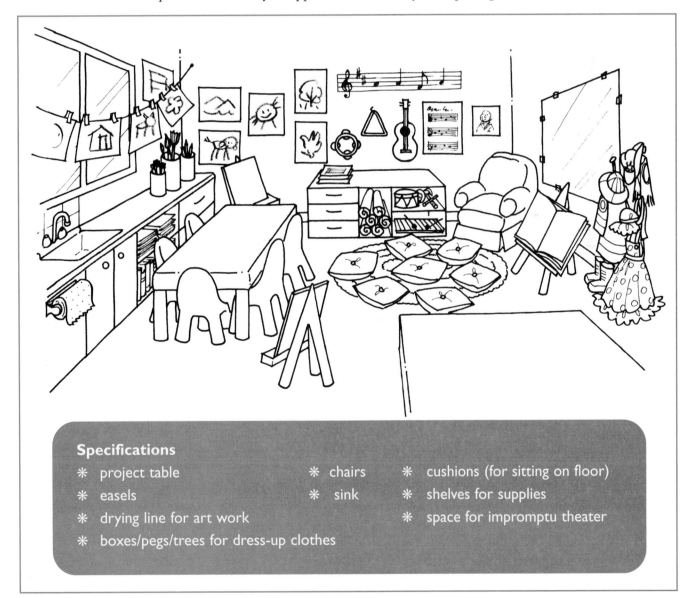

Specifications
* project table
* easels
* drying line for art work
* boxes/pegs/trees for dress-up clothes
* chairs
* sink
* cushions (for sitting on floor)
* shelves for supplies
* space for impromptu theater

BOOKS

Mouse Paint by Ellen Stoll Walsh (Harcourt, 1989)
Three white mice find three jars of paint and have fun mixing colors. It is a great story for those just learning about colors.

Polly Molly Woof Woof: A Book About Being Happy by David Lloyd (Candlewick Press, 2001)
This book is about a girl who takes her dog on a walk. The audience is encouraged to join in and act out different parts by acting like dogs. As Molly the dog meets new dog friends, the audience is encouraged to sniff and bark, just like the dogs.

Earth Dance by Joanne Ryder (Henry Holt, 1996)
This book has the children imagine that they are the earth. It encourages movement and dancing, such as spinning and dancing around the sun, wiggling shoulders as the mountains tremble and shake, and so on.

We All Sing With the Same Voice by J. Philip Miller (HarperCollins, 2000)
This book can be read or sung to music. Its illustrations portray children of different cultures and encourage children to see that everyone is different yet the same. The book comes with a CD that plays the song.

The Colors of Us by Karen Katz (Henry Holt, 1999)
This book is about a girl who paints people in her life. Everyone she paints has a different color of skin and she compares the colors to foods. It shows that no matter what color people are, they are beautiful.

In the Garden With Van Gogh by Julie Merberg and Suzanne Bober (Chronicle Books, 2002)
Set against the backdrop of the work of Henri Matisse, the rhyming text tells a story from the artwork of van Gogh. Also by these authors: *Dancing With Degas, A Picnic With Monet, Sunday With Seurat, Sharing With Renoir.*

Rockwell: A Boy and His Dog by Lauren Spiotta-DiMare (Barron's Educational Series, 2005)
This book describes real incidents from the life of Norman Rockwell. It also includes pictures of his artwork.

The Animal Boogie by Debbie Harter (Barefoot Books, 2000)
This book comes with a CD that includes a catchy tune that goes along with the text of the story. The song encourages children to guess which Indian jungle animal will appear next, and the lyrics encourage them to participate in the movement of the story.

We All Go Traveling by Sheena Roberts (Barefoot Books, 2003)
This book comes with an audio CD containing a song performed by Fred Penner. The book takes children through the town to see various landscapes and is an introduction to colors, modes of transportation, and music.

Creepy Crawly Calypso by Tony Langham (Barefoot Books, 2004)
This book includes an audio CD that contains a catchy song sung to a calypso beat. There is a counting theme throughout to help students practice counting skills.

What Is Music? by Nuria Roca (Barron's Educational Series, 2003)
This book teaches children about music through singing and dance. It also teaches about how each instrument has its own distinct sound. Children learn about the fundamentals of music and the difference between happy and sad music.

Other books about art, artists, color, crafts, musicians, sound, instruments, songs, dancing, stage plays

CD-ROMs

Kid Pix Deluxe 4 (ages 4 and up, Broderbund)
This program has animated stickers and stamps, wacky brushes, fun art tools, realistic paint effects, unique sound art, and digital photos that can be edited. Also includes project starters, templates and activity suggestions for teachers.

TOYS

Band in a Box (Melissa & Doug)
Durable musical instruments that are appropriate for preschool. The box includes maracas, a tambourine, finger cymbals, a triangle, and wooden sticks, among other instruments.

Mozart Magic Cube (Munchkin Embryonics)
An electronic toy that invites musical experimentation. Different instruments are pictured on the cube, and children can learn how the different instruments sound. Children can add and subtract instruments to songs.

Ready Set Learn! Jump and Dance Music Mat (Discovery)
This music floor mat offers two different ways to play. In the Tune Selector mode, the lights and sounds respond to children as they dance on the mat. In the Follow Me mode, the challenge is to follow the lights on the mat.

MUSIC CD'S

Playground Music by Putumayo Kids
African, French, Latin, Swing, and Reggae are just some of the diverse offerings from this company.

Raffi—He sings traditional songs from all around the world. Some of his songs also teach lessons and uses rhyming lyrics that help children develop phonemic awareness.

MATERIALS

Art

* crayons, paints, markers
* paper (various sizes, weight, colors)
* tissue paper
* pipe cleaners
* paper towel tubes
* old puzzle pieces
* clay
* bingo markers and dabbers
* ribbon and yarn

Music

* musical instruments
* CDs
* rhythm sticks
* tape recorder and cassettes

Movement

* stepping stones
* balance beam
* beanbags and balls
* cups for stacking

Drama

* dress-up clothes, hats, shoes
* theme-related props
* small-scale furniture
* dolls and doll buggy
* plastic food and cooking utensils
* baskets, boxes, bags, and purses
* puppets

Talking About the Creative Arts

* **Use the language of art, music, movement, and drama.** There are so many delicious words to use as children draw, sing, and play that it's hard to know where to begin. Color words, of course, should be used a lot—and in different ways, such as *dark, light, pastels* (lovely), or terms for warm colors, like *earth tones,* and for cold colors like *blues* and *greens* for the sea and sky;. Talk about light—how much light, daylight, transparent things, translucent things, and shadows on the wall. Touch is another area rich with word-learning opportunities. Look at all the vocabulary possibilities shown in this word map (Figure 10.2).

  Don't forget the words of sound: *loud, soft, sound wave,*

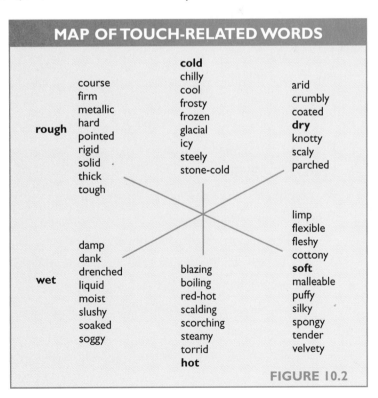

MAP OF TOUCH-RELATED WORDS

rough
course
firm
metallic
hard
pointed
rigid
solid
thick
tough

cold
chilly
cool
frosty
frozen
glacial
icy
steely
stone-cold

arid
crumbly
coated
dry
knotty
scaly
parched

wet
damp
dank
drenched
liquid
moist
slushy
soaked
soggy

blazing
boiling
red-hot
scalding
scorching
steamy
torrid
hot

limp
flexible
fleshy
cottony
soft
malleable
puffy
silky
spongy
tender
velvety

FIGURE 10.2

frequency, tone, melody, reverberation, acoustics (wow, what an interesting word). And of smell: *flowery, minty, musky, putrid* (yes, *putrid*), *pungent,* and even *smells like cotton candy.* Incorporate the language of drama into children's dramatic play and performances, such as *take a role, stick to the script, don't get stage fright, break a leg,* and *take a bow.*

Use every opportunity as children construct places (real and imaginary), create situations and landscapes, and explore the elements of color, light, sound, touch, and movement to expand and enrich their vocabulary for self-expression and self-learning.

✳ **Join in and add to creative dramatics.** Children use some of their most sophisticated language when engaged in the creative dramatics of pretend play, puppet play, pantomimes, and story theater. Here are some suggestions for supporting and even boosting children's language use in these creative contexts.

- Select poetry or stories that have a lot of action for "acting out" in different settings (e.g., puppet plays or story dramas). Fairy tales and other classics are a rich source.
- Use voice intonation and body language to share stories, plays, and poems with gusto.
- Pretend that you are part of what is happening in a story. Say, *Let's be . . .*
- Close your eyes and visualize scenes from stories. Think aloud and use lots of descriptive words.
- Act out a story scene or part for children. Use a prop (perhaps a hat or scarf) to add interest.
- Encourage spontaneity and originality.

One of the special joys of children is their spontaneity and the fresh view they bring to what has grown familiar to adults. Take every chance you get to support these precious childhood qualities of openness, wonder, and originality. It is our special privilege as adults to express awe at children's discoveries, applaud their achievements, and acknowledge (with delight) their newfound prowess. We smile widely, say thoughtful things, compliment children (often), build on and pass along their ideas, and speak very, very well of them in their presence. And so, we build their confidence and courage to express who they are and what they can do in a promising world.

THREE SAMPLE LESSON PLANS

Lesson 1: Expression through the Arts

Learning Objective

✳ To express oneself through music and dance

Whole Group: Learn together

- ✳ Play a jazz or instrumental music CD for the group.
- ✳ Ask the children to listen and think about what kind of animal or feeling the music makes them think of. Ask, *Is it like an elephant or a hummingbird? Does it make you feel happy?*
- ✳ Encourage children to use descriptive words to talk about the music, and write the words they say on chart paper.
- ✳ Next, ask them to move or dance the way they think the music sounds.

Small Group: Explore together and check

In small groups have the children do the following:

 * Make dancing streamers to use in the dramatic-play area. Cut out the center of yogurt containers or other small circular containers and use them as handles. Attach ribbon or yarn as streamers.

 * Put on a music tape or CD for dancing during playtime. Take pictures of the children dancing. Remind them of the descriptive words they used in whole-group time and capture pictures of them portraying these words. *Dante, you are dancing so lightly.*

Whole Group: Back together again

 * Create a dancing big book featuring photos of the children dancing.

 * Ask children to help you write a sentence for each page of the book. Use plenty of descriptive words.

 * Display the book for parents to see. Then place the book in the book corner for all to read.

Lesson 2: Building Language through Play

Learning Objectives

 * To use extended conversation in dramatic play
 * To show creativity and imagination in using materials to represent objects

Whole Group: Learn together

 * To build background knowledge, read *Jonathan Goes to the Post Office* by Susan K. Baggette (1998).

 * Tell the children that they are going to help set up a post office play setting, and you will need their help.

 * On chart paper, write "Post Office" and then have the children suggest things this play setting will need to work. *What will we need to mail letters? How will we write the address on the envelope?*

 * Write down the ideas. *Where will we get the envelopes? Does anyone have a hat we could use?* Discuss where you might get these items, and write the source next to the item on the chart.

 * As the items come in, check them off the list. With the children's help, set up the play center. To motivate the use of language and print around the theme ask, *How will I know the post office is open? How will I know how much a stamp costs?*

Small Group: Explore together and check

 * Meet with small groups in the dramatic-play area to scaffold the play and model higher levels of play by introducing new words, new roles, and new routines. *I'd like to send this doll to my granddaughter—how do I do that? How much postage do I need to send this letter?*

 * Observe the language the children are using and the writing samples they are producing in the play area.

Lesson 3: Patterns in Rhyme

Learning Objective

❋ To discover different patterns of beat and rhythm

Whole Group: Learn together

❋ With the words printed on a chart or in a big book, sing a familiar nursery rhyme to the children or play a recording of it.

❋ Clap, snap, or tongue-click the rhythms of the familiar rhymes.

❋ Listen for and point out the rhyming words in the nursery rhymes. For example, in Humpty Dumpty, *wall* and *fall*. List them on a chart. *What are other words you know that sound like wall and fall? Let's make a list of them.*

Small Group: Explore together and check

❋ Using nursery rhymes as a starting point, play a game with nonsense words and phrases to practice rhyming. *Okay, so* Humpty *was a word in the song.* Humpty *rhymes with* Dumpty *and also with* gumpty. *What other words can you make that rhyme with* Humpty, Dumpty, *and* gumpty?

❋ After you have played with rhyming words for a while, see if the children can play with language and put some of the nonsense words in real phrases so they sound like they have meaning. For example, a child might say, *Yesterday I walked my pet Gumpty down the street.*

SHARED BOOK READING

Ways to connect books and the creative arts abound. Here are a few suggestions:

❋ **Choose books with themes that relate to art, music, or movement.** Help preschoolers to connect their arts experiences to children's literature. As children explore paints and color mixing, read *Little Blue, Little Yellow* by Leo Lionni (1959) or *Mouse Paint* by Ellen Stoll Walsh (1989). Both books teach about mixing primary colors in the context of wonderful stories that preschool children appreciate. *A Color of His Own* by Leo Lionni (1975) and *Brown Bear, Brown Bear, What Do You See?* by Bill Martin Jr. and Eric Carle (1967) both highlight the wonderful colors of animals in nature (and some colors that animals could be if we use our imaginations). When you encourage children to dance and enjoy moving to the music, read *Giraffes Can't Dance* by Giles Andreae (2001), the story of an awkward giraffe who feels too uncomfortable to dance until he finds music that inspires him, and he realizes that he is in fact a fantastic dancer. Children will enjoy singing along as you read Pete Seeger's book *Abiyoyo* (1963), the story of a boy who uses his ukulele to defeat the giant Abiyoyo.

❋ **Act out stories.** Choose a favorite picture book and encourage children to act it out as you read. For preschool children, this activity may work better in a small group. Children may also need guidance to help them know what to do. Pause your reading when appropriate to encourage children. *Are you pretending that you're a very hungry caterpillar?* [Continue to read story.] *Now you're in your cocoon.* [Continue to read story.] *Okay everybody, let's see you push out of your cocoons and . . . wow! I see some beautiful butterflies flying around this classroom.* You can use this technique to connect dramatic experiences with almost any children's book.

✳ **Study picture book art and make your own.** Choose a picture book artist and learn about his or her art technique. A favorite artist to choose is Eric Carle (whose works include *The Very Hungry Caterpillar; The Very Clumsy Click Beetle; Brown Bear, Brown Bear, What Do You See?* and many other wonderful children's books). Eric Carle uses printing, finger painting, splatter painting, and any other techniques he can find to make his own unique collage paper. He then uses the paper to illustrate his books with appealing collages. Preschool children will be excited to get dirty making big sheets of brightly colored painted paper. Then cut (or tear) simple shapes and glue them down to make collaged pictures. Read lots of Eric Carle books for inspiration and even have children make up stories about their artwork! The goal of this project, and other projects like it, is for children to explore a new art technique. The purpose is not to produce art that looks exactly like Eric Carle's illustrations. (See his book *The Art of Eric Carle* (1996) and the video *Eric Carle: Picture Writer* (VHS, 1993) for more information about Eric Carle's art work.)

For smaller projects, look at and read classroom picture books for inspiration. Read *It Looked Like Spilt Milk* by Charles G. Shaw (1947) and let children make their own white splotches by painting on a piece of brightly colored construction paper and then folding it in half. Just like in the book, children can use their imaginations to determine what their white designs could be.

✳ **Study an artist, looking at examples of his or her work.** Use books to show children pictures of a famous artist's work, and then try his or her technique. For example, use books to display examples of Jackson Pollock's well-known paintings. Talk with children about his work. Ask children what the paintings make them think of. Explain that some artists are not interested in making paintings that look exactly like "real-life" objects but rather are interested in colors, designs, patterns, and just having fun playing with paint. Then, tarp the floor and roll out a big piece of butcher block paper. Let children take turns splatter painting, and create a class mural inspired by Pollock's work. Don't forget to help your class give their work a title!

✳ Sing and read picture books of popular children's songs. Teach favorite children's songs by following along in a picture book. You can sing the songs and can also talk about the illustrations. Some song picture books are true to the words while others create new silly verses for children to enjoy. See the list below for suggestions of titles.

PICTURE BOOKS OF CHILDREN'S SONGS

A You're Adorable by Buddy Kaye, Fred Wise, Sidney Lippman (Candlewick Press, 1994)

Roll Over!: A Counting Song by Merle Peek (Houghton Mifflin, 1999)

There Was an Old Lady Who Swallowed a Fly by Simms Taback (Viking, 1997)

Books by Iza Trapani (Charlesbridge Press) Titles include *The Itsy Bitsy Spider* (1993), *I'm a Little Teapot* (1993), *Row, Row, Row Your Boat* (1994), *Baa Baa Black Sheep* (1997), *How Much Is That Doggy in the Window* (2004), *Twinkle, Twinkle, Little Star* (1997), *Mary Had a Little Lamb* (2003), and *Shoo Fly!* (2004)

SONGS, RHYMES, AND WORD PLAY

The chants, poems, rhymes, and songs that you incorporate during all parts of your day promote children's phonological awareness and support their education in music and movement. As children's ability to listen to music grows, they are strengthening the same skills that they will later use to listen to the sounds in words. Teach children to focus on sound and to differentiate between sounds that are loud and soft, fast and slow, high-pitched and low (this one takes lots of practice!). To help children concentrate on sounds, try the following:

* **Beat out the rhythm.** Clap, tap, or stomp to the beat of a song. Try slowing songs down to help children learn to find the beat. This may be difficult for children at first. Some children can hear the rhythm but struggle to coordinate their movements on time, while others need practice to hear the rhythm of a song. Children can also use musical instruments to bang along with the music. Try maracas, triangles, or small drums. If musical instruments are not available, create your own (see box), or use common objects that make interesting noises (e.g., bang on old pots with wooden spoons).

* **Move to the music.** Play music and encourage children to dance. Help children listen carefully to the music as they move. Teach them to listen to the tempo of the music and to use fast movements when the music moves quickly and slow movements when the music slows down. Talk to children about how the music feels. Does the music feel happy or sad, exciting or peaceful? Encourage children to

---

Make Your Own Musical Instruments

Let children create homemade musical instruments!

* Construct shakers by filling empty plastic bottles or cartons with uncooked rice or beans.

* Make drums by banging on empty hollow containers (cans or tubs work best).

* Stretch rubber bands over an empty tin can, your fingers, or over a board with nails to form instruments that children can pluck.

Although you can provide examples, it is most fun to supply children with a variety of materials so that they can invent their own musical instruments. Allow plenty of time for children to use their special instruments when your class sings together.

match their movements to the "feel" of the music.

Try the CD *Kids in Motion* by Greg and Steve for great movement songs including a perennial favorite, "Animal Action," which instructs children to move like various animals throughout the song.

Play games like Freeze Dance. Children dance while the music is playing and freeze when the music is paused. Children have to listen carefully to the music to know when it is time to dance and when it is time to stay still.

Add hand motions to songs. Hand motions serve several purposes. They help children to remember song lyrics; they make singing a dramatic experience as children act out the song with their hands and facial expressions; and they reinforce phonological awareness as children listen to the music to determine when to perform an action. Teach well-known hand movements such as the motions for "The Itsy Bitsy Spider" or let children invent actions that fit with the lyrics to almost any song or rhyme.

DEVELOPMENTAL WRITING

In preschool, we encourage children to communicate through their artwork. At first, we ask children to tell us about their work, and we take responsibility for recording their words. As children learn more about letters and sounds, we encourage them to add their own "words" to their pictures by labeling their artwork. The transition from representing ideas in pictorial form to more abstract and symbolic written language takes place gradually over the preschool and early elementary school years. The picture books that preschoolers cherish provide a model for communicating through art. Although picture books usually contain text, they often provide additional information and detail through the illustrations. Use wordless picture books such as *Pancakes for Breakfast* by Tomie dePaola (1978) or books with very few words such as *Good Night, Gorilla* by Peggy Rathmann (1994) to instill the idea that children can "write" with their artwork, even if they don't yet know how to write letters or words.

To enhance the connection between writing and drawing (sometimes we call this "driting"), it's important to engage children in conversations about their work. Try to do the following:

* **Talk to children about their drawings.** Encourage children to tell you about their drawings by asking open-ended questions. Say, *What's happening in your picture?* or *Tell me about your work.* If children provide brief or one-word answers (*It's a house*), prompt further by asking follow-up questions: *I wonder whose house it is?* Suggest that children "revise" their work by adding detail to their drawings. Point out the detail that picture book illustrators provide for their readers. At times, you may want to record children's words as they talk about their work. Always read children's words back to them and ask if they would like to add or change anything. Paste children's dictated words on the back of their work or staple the writing to the bottom of their picture.

* **Have a storytelling center.** Let children tell stories while you transcribe their words. For preschool children, this works best in a one-on-one situation. Record children's words exactly

as they say them. Try not to edit children's stories or their grammar. Act as a scribe rather than as an editor. Prompt children to expand on their ideas and to create a beginning, middle, and end without telling the story for the child. Use open-ended questions to encourage creative story telling: *What do you want to tell me about today? What happened next? Who else was there? How did it all end?* Children may tell stories about their real experiences, or they may invent fantasies. Often, preschool children interweave the two. It is important to continually read children's words back to them. Ask if you have it right and if the child wants to make any changes or add any details. Although children cannot write words for themselves, they will have the experience of "writing" as they dictate their stories to you. After children have finished their stories, they should add detail to their work with illustrations. Create times for children to share their work with the class. You can read the story while the child shows his or her pictures. One benefit of sharing is that it encourages other children to participate in storytelling (so that they can have a turn to share as well). Sharing also demonstrates that the goal of writing is communication with others. Children learn that once their words are recorded in writing, their stories are saved and can be read to new people at a later time.

* **Art develops fine motor development.** Artwork also promotes children's fine motor development. The more that children use their hands to cut, color, tear, and paint, the stronger and more coordinated they become. Although preschool is really too early for handwriting practice, children who engage in artwork on a regular basis gain more control over their writing implements, which facilitates an easy transition to writing letters. Note that some children develop this type of coordination more quickly than others, and the range is most visible in the late preschool years. One child may be able to produce neat drawings while another has difficulty forming a circle that closes. This range narrows during the early elementary school years, and most children are able to form clear (even if not always neat and tidy) letters by the end of first grade.

The preschool years are the time to notice the way that children grip their pencils (or crayons, colored pencils, and markers) and hold their scissors. Although kindergarten teachers usual-

The more children use their hands to color, paint, and shape clay, the more fine motor skills they develop.

ly do not expect children to arrive at school with perfect grips, we need to move preschoolers away from grasping writing implements in their fists. Guide children's hands and explain gently that you are going to teach them a "stronger" way to hold their crayons. Say, *I'm going to help your hand to hold that colored pencil in a strong way. When you hold it like this, you will be able to make the pencil go just where you want it to go.* Children will regularly slip back into their more familiar grips, but in time, most children make the transition to a regular grip because they are eager to gain more control. Work on holding scissors as well. In particular, show children that it is easier to cut shapes by turning the paper rather than by turning their hand or arm in awkward directions. You can model scissor use (and scissor safety!) at circle time, but many children need regular reminders and your guidance in correctly placing the scissors in their hands.

PLAY

Plenty of time for dramatic play, both in the classroom and on the playground enables preschoolers to engage in drama and make-believe. Children of this age enjoy replaying "real-life" scenarios ("I'm the doggy and you're my owner") as well as pretending to be fictional characters (a fairy, a king, Spider-Man, a character from a favorite picture book). If you stand back and watch, you'll notice children's fantasy play throughout the day. Even drawing can be a dramatic experience for young children. Often, preschoolers act out their play on a piece of paper. As you watch children drawing, you may hear them talking aloud as they work.

> Adam is sitting at a table drawing. "He's gonna get the bad guy," he says aloud as he draws two stick figures on the page. "Get the net! Fooosh! He gotted him in a net." We watch as Adam scribbles over one of the stick figures to show that the bad guy is caught in a net.

Teachers can learn a lot from observing children as they engage in socio-dramatic play. You can gain insight into children's language skills as they narrate their play and discuss the progression of their play with peers. Watching play will enable you to gain knowledge about children's ability to negotiate with peers and solve conflicts when disagreements occur. You will also be able to tell what children are learning at school and at home as they weave their knowledge and experiences into their dramatic play. Free play is one of the best times for intensive kid watching and note taking, allowing you to gather an anecdotal record of children's learning and development. Try to use free-play times for careful observation rather than for classroom prep and organization.

Provide times for children to play with various art materials. Let children explore with modeling clay, play dough, tempera paint, water colors, crayons, colored pencils, markers, and crayons. Let children build by gluing three-dimensional objects together or by gluing craft sticks or wooden shapes to paper. Also, children love to collage. They can cut or tear construction paper, magazines or newspapers, or use a variety of three-dimensional objects (feathers, beads, colored noodles, buttons) to create artwork. Simply place art materials on a table, and children will get to work! Free art time enables children to use their creativity to make their own projects without the structure of adult direction.

Taking Stock

Portfolios are a wonderful way to keep track of children's creative activities and to observe how children progress throughout the year. Portfolios are a helpful way of organizing various examples of children's work and a great way to share what they are learning with their families. Artists use portfolios to demonstrate their skills and achievements; teachers can use portfolios in a similar manner to portray the creative work and progress of each child over a period of time.

Portfolios typically include samples of children's writings, favorite activities, and drawings that represent their most unique or interesting work. Try to involve children in selecting materials for their portfolios. Consider including the following examples:

✳ Special art projects that represent their creative abilities

✳ Dritings (drawing and writing) that demonstrate their fine-motor capabilities

✳ Recording retellings of favorite stories

Taken together, these work samples provide a picture of children's progress toward becoming readers and writers and their growing capacity to use their creative abilities in many different ways.

Closing

*T*wo girls are painting flowers using watercolors. "We can use scribble-scrabble to make 'em pretty," says Mauni to Jessie. Then a big glop of paint drips from the tip of a paintbrush onto Jessie's beautiful flower. "Oh! No! It is sinking," says Mauni. More big glops of paint drip-drop. "It's sinking . . . sinking . . . The flower is sinking, Jessie. Oh! Oh! It sinked."

When young children make art, they are, in the words of Anne Haas Dyson, "symbol weaving." Preschool children practice a kind of performance art as they talk and gesture. They make provocative observations, share insights, ask questions, and state curiosities as they are inspired to create. It is the intensity of the child's involvement in creative arts and enterprises that makes the child aware that there are many ways to explore the world, many ways to inquire and to convey one's emergent understandings in a life made more colorful and memorable through creative expression.

CHAPTER 11

Linking Literacy and Physical Health and Development

*P*hysical activity is the foundation of good health in life, and no curriculum in early childhood should be without it! For young children, movement is at the very center of their lives. We often think about physical activity as gross movement skills, such as walking, running, galloping, jumping, hopping, skipping, throwing, catching, striking, kicking, and balancing. However, physical activity also includes fine motor skills such as cutting, constructing, drawing, and writing. All are important for learning (Sanders, 2004).

Children experience a real sense of accomplishment when they can move, exercise, and fully involve themselves actively. You'll find there are so many ways to link literacy and physical health and development to enrich your curriculum and support children's development and learning. The more you promote children's participation in physical activities, the better they'll do.

What Children Need to Learn in Physical Health and Development

Gross Motor Activity

Children learn through movement. Because they are naturally active learners, children use physical activity to gather and apply information about their ever-expanding worlds. They manipulate objects in play; skip, leap, and hop to rhymes and rhythms; and play games that involve throwing and catching. With practice, these activities help to expand children's worlds and language development.

The American Academy of Pediatrics (2001) notes the following:

* Cognitive, social, emotional, and physical development should not be compartmentalized; rather, there is a vital interaction between all these developmental skills.

* Teachers of young children should serve as guides or facilitators in children's learning.

* Planned movement experiences enhance children's development.

Preschoolers demonstrate gross motor skills in early learning standards when they do the following:

Gross Motor Skills	Show increasing levels of proficiency, control, and balance in walking, climbing, running, and jumping
	Demonstrate increasing abilities to coordinate movements in throwing, catching, and bouncing balls

Fine Motor Activity

Young children need lots of opportunities to handle and manipulate different objects. Three-, 4-, and 5-year-old children are just beginning to gain increasing control of the small muscles in their arms, hands, fingers, feet, and toes. Fine-motor activities involve developing hand-eye coordination to hold implements (brushes, crayons, pencils) and exercising control over the marks they make. You'll find that activities involving folding, cutting, sewing, stringing beads, punching holes, inserting pegs, stacking blocks, and moving pedals will help to improve children's coordination and strengthen their dexterity.

Handwriting skills are just forming (Neuman et al., 2000). Children will gain increasing dexterity with large pencils or markers to drite (draw/write). It's important, however, to keep these activities fun and pleasurable. Long sessions practicing letters on lined paper are really quite difficult for children's hands at this age. As these muscles develop—usually by kindergarten—you'll find children are more ready to practice handwriting as a skill.

Also, be sure to include on your resource list large-sized pencils, fat crayons, and big markers (with washable ink!). These tools are easier for children to use.

Preschoolers demonstrate fine motor skills in early learning standards when they do the following:

Fine Motor Skills	Develop growing strength, dexterity, and control needed to use tools such as scissors
	Develop hand-eye coordination in building with blocks, putting together puzzles, and reproducing shapes and patterns
	Progress in ability to use writing, drawing, and art tools

Good Health

An important part of your job is to encourage children to make healthy choices about diet and physical activity. Be sure to include healthy snacks, and observe carefully all health standards and precautions. Remember that many children have food allergies (Welch, 2000). When considering cooking activities, be sure to consult families first to determine if children may be lactose intolerant or have any allergies.

Working together to keep children healthy, the American Academy of Pediatrics (2001) recommends that parents and teachers share the daily responsibility for making sure children:

* Are served nutritious meals and snacks
* Are engaged in physical activities
* Get plenty of rest
* Are protected from harm

Although we often think of health and physical activity as separate focuses, in truth, good health, activity, self-esteem, and learning are integrated. When children feel good about themselves, they are fit, happy, and motivated to learn.

Preschoolers demonstrate health in early learning standards when they do the following:

Health Status and Practices	Progress in their physical growth, strength, stamina, and flexibility
	Participate actively in games, outdoor play, and other forms of exercise
	Show growing independence in their hygiene, nutrition, and personal care
	Build ability to follow basic health and safety rules

Essential Literacy Practices in Physical Health and Development

Just about every essential literacy practice can be incorporated in outdoor and indoor play. No other subject area is quite so varied. Children delight in sand and water play and in swinging and sliding on outdoor equipment; they love to ride tricycles and make nature trails. All of these activities involve children in language, as they work and play together through physical activity.

This section discusses how you can create a supportive learning environment, use shared book reading, engage in word play and developmental writing, and encourage active play to build young children's understandings of their own physical growth and development.

Of course, literacy opportunities arise as a natural outcome of children's physical activity. However, they should never take the place of the physical activity itself, which all children very much need for healthy development and growth.

SUPPORTIVE LEARNING ENVIRONMENT

What better place to build a supportive learning environment than on the playground! Even small play yards will do. Outdoor space is precious in many early childhood settings. Plan your outdoor space carefully so that children can challenge themselves and take risks without any worries of serious injury (see sketch on the next page).

Try not to waste space. You'll need places for active motor play—swinging, sliding and rolling, climbing, jumping, and balancing. You'll also want to establish retreats for pretending, wondering, building, and creating. And you'll probably want to consider places for growing things, collecting things, measuring things, and watching things.

After outdoor playtime, you can involve children in posting signs, rules, guides and descriptions in various areas, such as Watch Out for Frogs! Don't Ride on the Grass! Dig Here for Worms. The Very Leafy Trail. Writing tools (sticks, chalk, markers) are a must, along with sturdy cardboard (or wood scraps) for making signs and marking even the tiniest of trails. Don't forget tags for labeling flowers and plants, and notebooks for recording. *How much rain fell last night? How tall is the sunflower today? Here's what the bug I saw looked like . . . and it had twenty-four legs!*

Space can be created indoors for large-motor activities, too. Whether in the classroom or somewhere nearby, these places should contain equipment and materials to promote the development of physical skills. Flexible, multiuse equipment is best, such as a house-gym or nesting climbers that can be stacked out of the way when not in use. Running, jumping, or hopping pads can be included for exercising in a small area. Balance or walking boards should be available along with places to bend under, crawl through (e.g., cloth tunnels), and creep in and out of (e.g., a small tent).

Use lightweight, nonbouncing objects, such as beanbags, sponge balls, yarn balls, foam balls, and plastic balls for children to practice throwing underhand and overhand. You can set up a throwing booth in the gross-motor area for children to practice throwing skills on their own. Catching is a harder skill for many preschoolers than throwing. To provide practice, set up a catching coop for two children to use together. They can throw balls against a wall and catch them as they bounce back or toss the balls between each other.

Just like the outdoors, fill the gross-motor areas with signs, directions, pictures of children involved in physical activity, charts with pictures, and action chants (for example, *Janie is a jumper/See her hop, hop, hop* [jump in place three times]*; Lakiel is a bumper/See him bop, bop, bop* [jump forward three times]*; Philip is a flier/See him loop-the-loop* [turn in place with arms outstretched]*; I can go still higher/Watch me fly-the-coop!* [run away, flapping arms like wings]. Sign-in charts are good motivators, along with children's artwork and books, like Robert Kalen's *Jump, Frog, Jump* (2003), for inspiration!

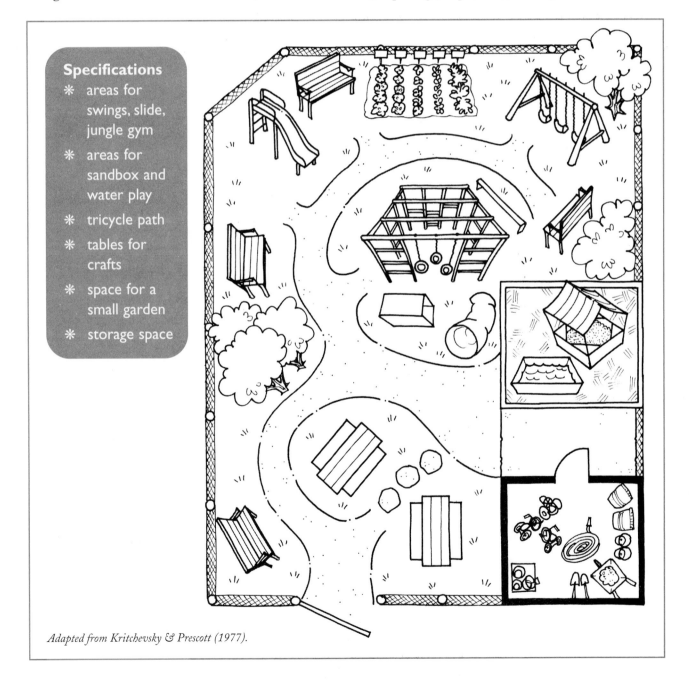

Specifications
* areas for swings, slide, jungle gym
* areas for sandbox and water play
* tricycle path
* tables for crafts
* space for a small garden
* storage space

Adapted from Kritchevsky & Prescott (1977).

PHYSICAL HEALTH AND DEVELOPMENT RESOURCES

BOOKS

Playing on the Playground by Dorothy Chlad (Children's Press, 1987)
A little girl and her friends play on the playground and obey the safety rules.

Playing Together: 101 Terrific Games and Activities That Children Ages 3–9 Can Do Together by Wendy Smolen (Fireside, 1995)
Collection of indoor and outdoor games and activities to engage children.

Be a Frog, a Bird or a Tree: Rachel Carr's Creative Yoga Exercises for Children by Rachel E. Carr (HarperCollins, 1977)
Clearly explained and illustrated introduction to yoga for children.

Other books about fitness, building, collecting, water, safety, crafts, gardening, tunnels, nature, camping

MATERIALS

Large motor
  * swings
  * slide
  * jungle gym or play structure
  * tricycles, wagons
  * cardboard tubes
  * balance beam
  * step exerciser
  * hula hoops, jump ropes
  * tunnel
  * large blocks
  * mats with shapes or the alphabet
  * tents
  * boats
  * parachute
  * mini-trampoline
  * ribbon wands, scarves

Small motor
  * easels
  * fingerpaints
  * water play toys
  * boxes for collecting
  * blocks
  * construction materials
  * paintbrushes, writing tools
  * gardening supplies
  * bubble wands, spinners
  * scrapbooks, notebooks, signs, labels

Generally lagging somewhat behind gross motor development are fine motor skills, and children also need places and spaces to try these out. Setting up an office play setting with writing tools, small objects to manipulate, scissors (with supervision), and clothespin activities helps children begin to use and coordinate the small muscles in their hands and wrists. Making tools like crayons, markers, pencils, and paper easily available to children creates a wonderful opportunity to link literacy and psychomotor development.

Talking About Physical Fitness

Talk about health and fitness starts early with young children. Conversations about healthy habits are a natural part of the preschool day and will give you many opportunities for expanding vocabulary, keeping charts, and improving social skills as children work (and exercise) together. Here are some ideas related to health and nutrition you may want to try.

* **Snack-Time Snippets.** Lots of conversation about healthy eating habits can happen at the snack table. Introduce the vocabulary of nutrition, using terms like *protein*, *carbohydrate*, *fats*, and *serving size*. It is appropriate for preschool children to learn about trying new and interesting foods, the different food groups (*Why is bread a grain? What is a grain? Where does it come from?*),

the importance of eating fruits and vegetables (the benefits of having a "colorful plate"), and the fact that some foods are "junk foods" because they are very sweet or very greasy, and we should eat only a little of these.

Use this time to describe different types of foods—vegetables, fruits, grains (crackers and bread), meat, poultry, eggs. Take taste tests and use lots of delicious words, like *sweet*, *tangy*, *spicy*, *sour* (purse your lips!), *bitter*, *bland*, *cottony* (cotton candy!), *crispy*, *crunchy*, and so on. Invite the children to talk about their favorite foods—and provide food facts and introduce related foods. Also, consider integrating snack-time foods with current themes or the seasons, as a way to expand children's knowledge of food items and names.

＊ **Fitness Facts and Figures.** Many children have heard discussions about exercise and physical fitness on television or other places. Build on these experiences by discussing the benefits of regular exercise. Include favorite books that address fitness topics, such as *Bicycle Race* by Donald Crews (1985) or *I Went Walking* by Sue Williams (1992). Invite trainers from local fitness centers or gyms to visit and engage children in a "training program." Use "fitness" vocabulary like *muscles*, *aerobics*, *stretching exercises*, *pulse rate* (*Let's feel our pulses—blop, blop, blop!*), *scales*, *jog*, and *workout* (*How about a workout before we get started today?*).

＊ **Safety—First, Last, and Always.** Take the time to talk about safety with children. Point out the safety rules of the room and discuss why they are so important: *We store the blocks on the shelf when we are done playing, so we don't trip over them and fall down.* Use terms like *precaution*, *prevention*, *safety equipment*, *safety goggles*, *seat belts*, *helmets*, *sunscreen*, *hand sanitizer*, *hand washing* to explain ways to be safe, to protect our bodies, and to prevent injuries.

Remind children of basic safety rules to follow out of doors, and at crosswalks. It is appropriate to teach children of this age about road safety. *We cross the street holding an adult's hand. We look both ways, we wait for the light, and we never run out in the street even to get something like a ball. What do red lights, yellow lights, and green lights mean? What do stop signs mean?*

Emphasize how we can help each other stay safe by picking up after ourselves, giving a helping hand, washing our hands, buckling up, and being alert to what is around us.

THREE SAMPLE LESSON PLANS

Lesson 1: Learning About Physical Health and Development

Learning Objectives

＊ To develop hand-eye coordination and coordinate movements through throwing, catching, and bouncing balls

＊ To participate in games, outdoor play, and other forms of exercise

Whole Group: Learn together

  ＊ Read the book *Sports* by Gallimard Jeunesse and Pierre-Marie Valat (1998) to the class.
    What do you think we're going to see inside of this book? Can you name any sports?

  ＊ After reading, draw the children's attention to the sports listed in the book, such as skiing, soccer, fencing, and martial arts. *Have you ever played any of these sports? Which sports needed a ball? Can you think of a sport we saw in the book that a person does alone?*

✳ Refer back to the text to make points and illustrate responses.

Small Group: Explore together and check

✳ In small groups have the children rotate to sport stations:

- Basketball Toss: Have the children toss a ball into a basket.
- Obstacle Course: Set up an obstacle course that children can crawl under, through, and over.
- Tennis: Have the children play with flyswatters and balloons.
- Soccer: Have the children dribble a soccer ball with their feet.
- Bicycling: Have children take turns riding a stationary bike.

✳ Award Olympic Certificates to each child.

✳ Have children print their name on the certificate.

Lesson 2: Movement

Learning Objectives

✳ To experience movement through space

✳ To participate in games and forms of exercise

Whole Group: Learn together

✳ Make a large quantity of homemade liquid bubbles in front of the class, following a recipe that is posted on chart paper (see box right).

✳ Have helpers assist you as you measure ingredients and stir the mixture.

✳ Take the children outside and give them time to experiment with the bubbles, using all different kinds of "wands" (cookie cutters, bent pipe cleaners and hangers, plastic straws).

> **Bubble Recipe**
>
> - 6 parts water
> - 2 parts Joy dishwashing liquid
> - 3/4 part corn syrup

✳ After they have had time to experiment, have them sit down and watch as you blow bubbles into the air. Tell them not to reach for them! *What happens when the bubbles touch something?*

✳ Next, have children pretend they are inside of a bubble that will not pop and where they cannot touch anyone else. *Remember not to touch anything so you don't pop! Now stand up and reach all around. Can you feel the sides of your bubble? Can you reach really high and touch the top of your bubble? Now lie down and stretch out in your bubble as far as you can. Float around the room in your bubble. Let the wind blow you around.*

✳ Finish the activity with children's bubbles floating gently to the ground. *Now you are floating to the ground, slowly, slowly . . .*

Small Group: Explore together and check

* Write the recipe for bubbles onto a piece of paper and make a copy for each child.
* Allow children to draw a picture of themselves in their bubble on the page.
* Have each child dictate a sentence to you about how it felt to be inside the bubble.
* Write the sentence at the bottom of the page.

Lesson 3: Basic Nutrition

Learning Objective

* To learn about basic nutrition for physical health

Whole Group: Learn together

* Retell the story *Lunch* by Denise Fleming (1992), using a flannel board and flannel objects (mouse, turnips, carrots, corn, peas).
* Following the story, engage children in a discussion about healthy foods. *What foods did the mouse eat that you like? What is your favorite fruit? Vegetable? What do you eat for a snack after school? Why does your body need fruits and vegetables like the mouse ate?*
* Allow children to sample foods from the book, such as turnips, oranges, carrots, corn, peas, blueberries, grapes, apples, and watermelon.

Small Group: Explore together and check

* Have pictures of healthy foods from magazines available for the children.
* Encourage children to select some pictures to glue onto a paper plate. Encourage conversation about the foods. *What is your favorite food? Do you like broccoli?*
* Have each child talk about the foods they selected and glued to their plate. *I see you have corn. Vegetables are very healthy for your body, so that was a good choice.*

SHARED BOOK READING

Encourage children to learn about health and nutrition by selecting read-alouds that address these themes. Choose books that teach children about physical activity and good hygiene. Children are particularly interested in books that provide fascinating information about their bodies. They are eager to learn how their bones and muscles work, why we eat food, and why we need to wash our hands and take baths. Preschool children can also be cautious eaters who would prefer not to try foods that are new or different. Discussion about storybook characters, like Lola in *I Will Never Not Ever Eat a Tomato* and Francis in *Bread and Jam for Francis* (see box on page 178), who both learn to try new foods, can help children to understand the benefits of eating a variety of healthy foods. Books provide a wonderful starting point for conversation around almost any physical health issue, and they can help you teach children healthy habits that will start them on the right track.

PICTURE BOOKS OF CHILDREN'S SONGS

Bread and Jam for Frances by Russell Hoban (HarperTrophy, 1993)
Frances the badger is a picky eater who only wants to eat bread and jam. After her parents give her bread and jam for every meal, she realizes that she feels better when she eats a variety of different foods.

I Can Move by Mandy Suhr (Penguin, 1992)
In this book, a child talks about how we move our bodies. The book addresses growing, bones, muscles, and joints in a simple and clear way and includes humorous illustrations that are appealing to young children.

I Will Never Not Ever Eat a Tomato by Lauren Child (Candlewick, 2003)
Charlie's younger sister Lola is a fussy eater who refuses to eat healthy foods, especially tomatoes. Charlie convinces her to try a variety of vegetables by referring to them by new names: carrots are "orange twiglets from Jupiter" and mashed potatoes become "cloud fluff from the pointiest peak of Mount Fuji." Once Lola realizes that these foods taste good, she is even willing to try a "moonsquirter" (a tomato!).

On the Move by Deborah Heiligman (HarperCollins, 1996)
This energetic book shows children doing all sorts of movements, from climbing to forward rolls to walking on a log. The text even encourages listeners to participate: "Can you waddle like a duck?" The book also addresses movement over a lifetime—a baby crawls and a grandpa uses a cane—and movement by a child in a wheelchair whose "arms are strong" allowing her to do lots of pull-ups.

The Busy Body Book: A Kid's Guide to Fitness by Lizzy Rockwell (HarperCollins, 2004)
In this book, children are encouraged to keep their bodies busy. In addition to the text, the book contains simple diagrams of the systems of the body. Children learn that "a body that gets busy each day stays strong, healthy, and happy."

Your Skin and Mine by Paul Showers (HarperCollins, 1991)
This book explains the importance of skin for keeping us cool in summer and for keeping out harmful dirt and germs. It also deals with the need for sunscreen and for washing to keep our skin clean.

SONGS, RHYMES, AND WORD PLAY

There are many songs, chants, and games that encourage children to move their bodies. Since young children need lots of time to move about, teachers can use these songs and games throughout the day. Songs like "Head, Shoulders, Knees, and Toes" or "The Hokey Pokey," which require children to stand up and be physically active, are particularly valuable before or after times when children need to sit and concentrate. If at any point you notice that children are becoming wriggly, why not take a quick break to sing and move? This enables children to "work out" their energy in an appropriate and productive way, and it usually allows children to refocus after the movement break. Also, listening and moving to the music enhances children's phono-

MOVEMENT SONGS, GAMES, AND FINGERPLAYS

101 Movement Games for Children: Fun and Learning with Playful Moving by Huberta Wiertsema (Hunter House, 2002)

Movement games include:

- Head, Shoulders, Knees, and Toes
- Freeze Dance
- I'm a Little Teapot
- Ring Around the Rosie
- London Bridge
- This Little Piggy

- Duck, Duck, Goose
- If You're Happy and You Know It
- Little Bunny Foo Foo
- The Hokey Pokey
- Simon Says
- Where Is Thumbkin?

Experiences in Movement by Rae Pica (Delmar, 2003)

Games Children Sing Around the World: 12 Singing Games for 12 Countries by Paul Ramsier (Warner Brothers, 1997)

logical awareness, so while children are enjoying a chance to be active, you are addressing an essential literacy goal.

Fingerplay rhymes like "Where Is Thumbkin?" and "This Little Piggy" are silly and they make children laugh, but they also work on fine-motor development. It is not simple for preschool children to coordinate singing or chanting words, listening to the words in order to know which finger to move, and actually moving the correct fingers. For many children, these games require lots of concentration.

As with other types of rhymes and songs, when you teach movement games, it helps children if you begin slowly:

❋ Model the activity for children by singing the entire song and doing all of the movements so that children can get excited about the song they are about to learn. Ham it up! There is nothing that preschoolers love more than laughing at their teacher when he or she is being silly.

❋ Then, teach a few words at a time. After you've added a new part, sing or chant the whole song from the beginning.

❋ After children are familiar with the words, add movements. Again, just a few at a time, and then repeat the whole chant from the beginning.

❋ When you introduce a new song, keep the tempo slow so that children can keep up. Particularly with fingerplays, you may have to move around and guide some children's hands to help them feel how their fingers need to move.

❋ Repeat, repeat, repeat. The more often that you repeat movement songs, games, and fingerplays, the better children become at participating.

DEVELOPMENTAL WRITING

While all writing and drawing activities support children's fine motor development, we can also connect writing to themes of health, nutrition, safety, and hygiene. Cooking healthy foods and recording the recipes is the perfect activity for integrating writing and health goals. As we have mentioned, 3- to 5-year-olds can be fussy eaters. Children at this age like routines and feel comfortable with things that are familiar. Children may feel tentative and uncomfortable about trying unfamiliar foods (and participating in other unfamiliar experiences).

One way to address this cautious behavior is to include children in the process of cooking. Teach children about various foods (*What is a carrot? How does it grow? How can eating carrots help our bodies?*), and let them participate in preparing the foods they will eat. Children are usually much more willing to try foods that they are proud to have cooked themselves. Not only does cooking support health and nutrition goals, but it advances literacy and math skills as well. Children learn mathematics as they measure and slice ingredients (*How many cups of flour do we need? Let's cut the strawberries in half for our fruit salad.*), and they learn about reading and writing as they follow and record recipes. (*To make our soup, we added six carrots and one onion.*) Invite parents and other relatives in to cook with the class. Record their recipes as well.

To help children follow recipes, use lots of pictures. If you need to add three eggs, draw three eggs next to this direction. Soon, children will be able to "write" recipes in the same way. Keep track of the recipes that your class has made and create a recipe book to photocopy and send home. Or send recipes home on a regular basis so that children can "teach" their parents to cook healthy snacks at home.

As you learn about healthful behaviors, involve children in labeling the classroom (or the whole school!) with reminders for themselves and their friends. Ask children to think of reminder signs that will help to keep everyone safe and healthy. Children can draw pictures and label, and if necessary, you can add their dictated text. In the bathroom, include signs such as "Don't forget to wash your hands with soap!" or "Throw your paper towels in the garbage!" or "Remember to flush the toilet!" The children in your class will be able to think of many more creative tips for one another (e.g., "Wipe your nose if it is runny!" "Be careful of the slippery wet boots!").

Giving children time to move and exercise supports growth across all areas of their development.

PLAY

As we work to ensure children's development in all areas of the preschool curriculum, we should never underestimate the value of outdoor play. Giving children plenty of time to run, jump, swing, and climb outside is one of the best ways to support their growth across all areas of their development. As we have already mentioned, outdoor play is important for children's gross motor development. Over the year, you will watch children grow in confidence and coordination as they master new tasks, whether it is climbing a little higher on the jungle gym, learning to pump on the swing, or inventing a new game to play. Outdoor play is also crucial for social and language development as children discuss their play (*You be the mommy and I'm the baby*), narrate their play (*Vrrrooom, vrrooom. Beep, beep. My race car is fast!*), and negotiate conflicts (*But I'm using the trike first*).

Outdoor play bolsters more than just gross motor and social development; it is essential to support children's focus and participation in all areas of the preschool day. Just as regular exercise helps adults feel more energetic and able to focus during other parts of the day, exercise helps children stay more energized, focused, and alert. If you want to help the children in your classroom to listen to a story, to think carefully about sorting shells, to negotiate sharing toys with words rather than by grabbing or pushing, to participate actively in singing and chanting, or to be engaged in any of the activities that we have suggested throughout this book, *give children plenty of time to run and play outside!* It can be surprising how much more ready children are to tackle the social and academic challenges of a preschool classroom after they have had time to "work out" their energy by getting some fresh air and exercise. Don't let the cold weather stop you. The time it takes to bundle everyone up is well worth the result of a classroom full of happy and productive children.

Taking Stock

You'll want to observe children and document their progress in physical activities through developmental checklists. Try to observe and record children's progress in different settings—during activities on the playground and other kinds of outdoor exercises and games, as well as their developing fine motor coordination in drawing and writing. Checklists might include the following items:

* Does he or she grasp and manipulate writing tools?
* Write his or her own name?
* Handle books properly?
* Engage in regular routines of hygiene?
* Play actively in games?
* Participate in other forms of exercise?

Using a simple rubric such as "Usually," "Sometimes," or "Never," you can chart children's progress toward meeting benchmarks of development in literacy and physical health and development.

Closing

*P*aul, like so many other children, is experiencing the delights of movement. And in this vivid display of his writing, he is demonstrating an important principle: Movement influences and is influenced by all facets of development, including motor, cognitive, and affective development. To deny children the wondrous opportunities to engage in physical activity, therefore, is to deny them the opportunity to experience the joys of healthy development.

CHAPTER 12

Making Literacy Connections to Parents

*I*n this chapter, we've included material you may want to share with the parents of the children you teach. In the first section, we describe and explain for parents the five essentials we explored in the earlier chapters of this book with you. Following this section are common questions parents might have and answers to them.

The Five Essentials

As parents, every day, we come face to face with a wonderful mystery. How does that tiny tot figure out how to sit up, talk, crawl, and, eventually, walk? How does that young toddler begin to learn all those words and put them together into meaningful phrases? And how do these preschoolers seem to create new inventions that are totally beyond our imagination?

We still don't know the answers to many of these questions, but we can begin to offer helpful guidance, suggestions, and encouragement about one of the great mysteries of early childhood: What is reading, and how is my child going to learn how to do it?

Luckily, there are now plenty of scientifically proven ways to help figure out this puzzle and put your child on the right road to reading. And given the right support, there's a lot you can do to help. In fact, there are five essentials that will help motivate your child to become a reader. These essentials might seem like typical everyday activities, but the research shows they have enormous potential to help children read. Very simply, they are: Talking, singing, playing, reading, and writing.

Your child's path to reading begins at birth. He begins to learn about language the first time you gaze into his eyes, say his name, whisper that you love him. Talking to your baby and smiling when he coos conveys the message that communication is meaningful, loving, and fun. And that discovery continues to unfold as a child approaches the task of beginning to read.

Talking with your child plays a pivotal role in language development, and you can do a number of things to help it along. You may occasionally want to include sophisticated words in your conversations, with explanations as needed. You may ask questions and encourage her to think aloud with you. Simply put, the more words you use, the more words your child will know. And the more words she knows when she gets to kindergarten, the more likely she will become a skillful reader. That's why it's important to go on errands together even if it takes a bit more time—it's a great conversation starter, a time to chat informally with your child. And you'll find mealtimes a special moment to share events from your day and learn what's most important to her.

Even if you don't have a great voice, it's easy and fun to do the next essential—singing. If you've ever sung the ABC song, or played "This little piggie went to market," you may not have realized it at the time, but you were doing something very important. Activities like these help strengthen your child's ability to hear and pay attention to the sounds and rhythms of speech. This kind of play reinforces the concept of words and tunes your child's ear to differences and similarities in how words sound. Putting an activity to rhyme helps children remember sounds and helps them to discover common word patterns (e.g., Jack be nimble, Jack be quick). Try to find as many opportunities to sing to your child as you can—and feel free to make up silly rhyming songs of your own too. There are also wonderful silly songs on the market that children just love (e.g., Marlo Thomas's, "Free to Be You and Me"). These memorable songs will become a family tradition.

Representing an important piece of the learning-to-read puzzle, a third essential involves playing with your child. Play, as you well know, consumes much of young children's time and energy. But for many children, play is where reading actually begins. Play appears to have two potential links to the development of reading: it allows children to develop and refine their capacities to use symbols or props to represent experiences and construct imaginary worlds, and it helps children develop a sense of narrative. Those brief play scenarios that you and your child engage in help your child take on new character roles, with events unfolding much like the narrative in a story. And many times, when you enter into play with your child, you can extend the vocabulary, or add a new wrinkle to the story, encouraging solutions to new problems. Sometimes adding a new prop, like a menu to a child's restaurant play brings about fresh new ideas and new language. Save your old Halloween costumes for hours of special play. But always remember that play ultimately belongs to your child, so be careful not to take over too much. Enter into play, but then exit when the time is right.

Storybook reading and storytelling are the fourth essential in helping your child on the road to reading. The world of stories is the gateway to the world of the written word. But stories aren't always found in books. Stories are your history that you share with your child. Stories are important because they use language to impose a structure on experience. They have a beginning, middle, and end. And a child who becomes attuned to stories develops habits of listening that will ease his transition to school and whet his appetite for learning to read. When you're reading or telling a story together, invite your child to reimagine the story by introducing a new character or coming up with a new ending. *What would happen if the shoe actually fit the wicked stepsister in Cinderella? What if the gingerbread boy got away?* Or you can encourage your child to tell you a new story. And what you will find is evidence of how much he is learning. Many children will use the language they've just heard to make up entirely new stories.

And the final essential in the learning-to-read puzzle is writing. Start simply, by giving him a crayon or a marker and a plain piece of paper. You'll soon see the magic of beginning writing. It will start as a squiggle, perhaps lots of scribbles. But soon your child will probably delight in learning how to write his own name, and from there, many words. Writing is important in these early years because it helps children connect what they hear in words with the symbols that they represent. Especially in these years, let your child simply enjoy the process of writing, and if he expresses interest you can help him form letters the correct way. Start by printing in large capital letters, and let him trace letters if he wants. The act of writing gives a young child the impetus to learn how to read what he's written.

These simple activities—talking, singing, playing, reading, and writing—help unlock the mystery of print. And by entering into that wonderful, exciting, fulfilling world with your child, you are helping him find the pathway into a rich and rewarding lifetime of literacy.

Frequently Asked Questions

What is early literacy?

There has been an explosion of knowledge over the last few years about how infants and toddlers develop, and how a child's earliest experiences set the stage for success in learning to read. Today, we use the term "early literacy" to refer to the skills and behaviors associated with successful reading development. Results of many studies indicate that experiences in the early years, from birth to 5, are critically important and form an indelible blueprint for your child's learning, success, and well-being.

These early behaviors used to be described as "readiness skills." But today we recognize that early literacy is far more than being able to identify colors or numbers or shapes. Rather, early literacy includes such important skills as a child's oral language development, phonological and phonemic development, knowledge of the alphabet, and such common print concepts as knowing that print goes from left to right, and from top to bottom on a page. Another important thing we know is that not all children will be at the same place at the same time when they begin kindergarten. Some children will know all their letters, upper- and lowercase, before they go to school, while others will know only some uppercase letters.

Although we recognize the significance of knowing letters and sounds, probably the most important skill in reading success is your child's oral language development. Language development is the foundation of reading development and is strongly related to a child's growth in reading and writing. For example, research suggests that by about 5 years of age, children have learned approximately five thousand words. But this doesn't come about through magic. In fact, if language development was just about hearing language, then probably television would be our best language intervention. But it isn't. Children's language development is supported through interactions and experiences with you and your extended family as well as your child's immediate caregivers.

Interestingly, studies suggest that the most interactive setting for conversation is mealtime, when families casually get together and talk about daily events in their lives. Though your child may not actively chime in on the conversations yet, clearly she is learning and taking it all in. Probably all of us have had the experience of saying, "Where did she learn that word?" not recognizing that all of these daily informal experiences help form the basis for your child's development.

Early literacy behaviors also include motivation to read and self-regulation. Children develop motivation to read by being read to often, learning firsthand the pleasures that reading will bring to them. They also see how important reading is by being involved in daily chores that involve reading. Going to the grocery store, for example, Heather made sure that her mother included all the ingredients for making muffins. She later writes a note to her dad, asking to make muffins together. Children's uses of print and motivation to read grow out of such adult-child interactions.

Self-regulation involves your child's ability to control his behavior. Attending to a story, sitting still when necessary, and listening to directions are skills that will help your child become a capable learner in a classroom. For those especially active young learners, start with brief activities, such as a very short story, and then slowly extend the time, once you've captured his attention. You'll find that self-regulation is more difficult for some children than others and will be learned only through your patience and persistence. But believe me, your child's teacher will appreciate all of your efforts!

While it's important to understand preliteracy skills and behaviors, you don't have to directly teach them. In fact, for some children, direct teaching may be counterproductive. Instead, try to take your child's lead. For example, interesting experiences like grocery shopping, bank visits, and trips to the veterinarian encourage children to talk. These informal occasions allow them to take risks using language, particularly in new and creative ways. They play with familiar words, explore new meanings, and test uses of language in different settings. Sometimes they'll even invent new ways to use well-known words, and begin to start writing about these events (through scribble writing, letters, and phonic spellings). All of this happens in interactive settings with a devoted adult who listens and responds in positive ways to their language play.

What are appropriate expectations for early literacy skills by the time your child enters kindergarten? For the most part, the teacher will expect your child to be able to carry on a brief conversation, to attend and react to stories, to know some letters of the alphabet, the sounds that these letters make, and some basic print concepts, such as knowing that print has meaning and where on each page print actually begins. If you believe that the expectations for what your child should know and be able to do have dramatically changed from when you went to school, you're absolutely right. Given recent evidence from brain research, we know that literacy for life is nurtured and supported in these earliest years.

How can I increase my child's vocabulary?

Vocabulary development—understanding words and their meanings—is a key factor in your child's success in learning to read and write. From infancy on, children are learning an amazing number of words. In fact, vocabulary expands between 18 months and 6 years at the rate of six to nine words a day, or three thousand words per year. By the time your child is 6 years old, his vocabulary is likely to range from about ten thousand to fourteen thousand words.

As you know, most children do not use all these words in their daily conversations or activities. There is a difference between what children know and what they say. Children's receptive language, commonly known as listening vocabulary, is larger than their expressive language or speaking vocabulary. But don't be fooled by your child's limited utterances in the early years. Most likely, he or she knows far more words that it appears.

Before children reach about 2 years old, they learn most of their words through informal teaching. Parents and others point to specific objects, label them, and discuss their meaning. Research suggests that talkative parents, particularly in these early years, influence the number of words infants and toddlers acquire—just by the sheer number of words they hear. After 2 years of age, children learn most new words by inferring their meanings from daily activities. They pick up word meanings when parents, caregivers, siblings, and friends join together to play with toys, ride in a car pool, or do chores. Children also learn new words from television programs like *Sesame Street* and, of course, from listening to stories.

You'll notice an interesting phenomenon as your child picks up new words. Young children learn lots of words, sometimes from only one exposure (we call it "fast-mapping"). But what you'll notice is that while fast-mapping works well enough to make it possible for children to understand words, it often is not sufficient for them to use the new word correctly. So you'll see them use a novel word in ways that do not necessarily fit the situation. But don't fret; children are merely revealing their budding skills in playful ways. The more you give them opportunities to talk, the better they'll get.

Exposure to a rich language environment, therefore, affects your child's vocabulary growth. Be sure to talk frequently to your child, even in the first weeks of infancy. Soon you'll begin to see her first efforts to take a turn. Sometimes it might be short vocalizations, moves, or smiles. Then it becomes a pattern in which your child begins to respond more frequently to the pauses you provide. This turn taking is conversation in its nascent form.

Another way to support your child's vocabulary is to focus on a common object or event that is meaningful to your child. Spend time trying to help her learn more about it. For example, asking lots of questions about the worm she's discovered in the backyard is a helpful way to focus her interest and help her learn new words associated with her interests.

And of course, storybook reading is an ideal word-learning strategy for many reasons. Regular rereadings of your child's favorite stories provide repeated exposure to new words. Books with beautiful, detailed illustrations typically provide a wonderful opportunity for explaining new words.

What are the indicators of significant language and vocabulary delay? We know for example that some children say their first words at 8 months, while others wait until their first birthday or later. Most diagnostic indicators suggest that the production of less than 50 words by age 2, or a difficulty combining words into simple sentences by age 2 may be used as a benchmark of language delay. But specialists also point out that some children who have very small vocabularies at age 2 may turn out to be very talkative by age 5. Therefore, watch, listen, but by all means, talk to your child. It will help to create the special bond between parent and child that will last a lifetime.

How do I help my child make letter-sound correspondences?

Probably the single most important insight for your child to develop in the kindergarten year is the recognition that letters and sounds are related. We often call this insight "the alphabetic principle," the notion that speech sounds can be mapped onto letters in a predictable fashion. It involves the basic understanding that letters represent speech sounds, that letters go together to make words, and that changing the letters changes the sounds and the words.

It's not an easy concept for young learners to grasp. Unlike many other languages, English has far more sounds (what we traditionally call phonemes) than letters. This means that many of our letters make more than one sound. The letter *e*, for example by itself can stand for as many as eight different sounds in English. Just try this sentence: *The smell of the fern reeked despite our efforts.* Because English has incorporated words from different languages, we also have many sounds that can be spelled in more than one way—for example, the sound /ow/ in *now* and *out*, or /f/ in *cuff* or *cough*.

Also, many words sound alike but are spelled differently, such as *bear* and *bare*.

Our vowel sounds alone can produce lots of confusion for young children. In fact, many educators will stay away from teaching vowel sounds until later on in first grade. At last count we have about 19 different vowel sounds, and only five or six letters to spell them with (a, e, i, o, u, and sometimes *y*). We have long *a* as in *cake*, short *a* as in *bat*, and r-controlled *a* as in *bark*. No wonder it takes children two to three years to learn how to match sounds to their letter names!

There are plenty of specific activities to help children learn to make letter-sound correspondences. Try to stay away from workbook-like tasks, since they can make the joys of learning the alphabetic principle seem deadly dull. Rather, encourage children to notice the shapes of letters when they do alphabet puzzles or use letter-shaped cookie cutters in damp sand or dough. Magnetic letters and alphabet blocks allow children to explore letter-sound connections, arrange and rearrange letters to form words, and become more aware of the sequences of sounds within words.

And don't forget that young children love to look at photographs of themselves and their friends. By displaying snapshots of your child and friends in his or her class and having your child match up faces to names, you can create an activity that provides experience in letter recognition and naming and in noticing the initial sound (phoneme) in a name.

Once children start to make connections between letters and sounds, they'll be able to begin to read some very simple texts. First they'll sound out the words very, very slowly as if they're "glued to print." But then, they'll begin to polish their new-found skills, recognizing letters and sounds very quickly and connecting them to smooth, flowing, meaningful reading.

You can see that one of the more important skills for children to develop is the alphabetic principle. But don't try to rush it. Lots and lots of experiences with print will get them on track toward learning and loving to read.

Are there some multisensory ways to learn the alphabet?

Learning about letters is an important part of the puzzle of learning to read. But it can be a bit more challenging for a young child than you might originally think. First, it involves learning the names of all 26 letters. Next, it involves connecting the name with the letter shape. And for the young child, letter shapes can be somewhat confusing since several letters have different print styles (like *g* and *a*), and forms (uppercase and lowercase), and different "scripts" (and sizes), depending on the person who is writing them.

Some children will just take a little bit longer to learn the alphabet. But it is certainly true that this skill is important in learning to read. The best way to help, however, is not by using flash cards or some other contrivance for drilling your child on the alphabet. You can help by having fun with letters.

The easiest way to begin is to sing the alphabet song. In early childhood classrooms, we used to tell children to sing it loud, with great spirit, so that everyone in the school would know what we were learning. Sing it often, and you'll find that your child will join in spontaneously, learning the alphabet in a playful way.

The alphabet song will begin the process of learning the letter names. But it's not the sole answer. Many children who memorize the alphabet song develop the "elemeno" problem. Instead of hearing distinct letter sounds, such as "l-m-n-o," children hear these letters together, as if they were one word. This is relatively simple to solve. Write out the letters in block print and then point to each letter as you sing the song very slowly. The song will remind your child of the letter that comes next, and your pointing will help him focus on the particular letter shape that's associated with it. You don't have to tell him what you're doing; just do it and you'll find that the "elemeno" problem goes away.

Alphabet books also offer many wonderful opportunities for reviewing and revisiting the alphabet, and savoring its sounds. These books come in a host of formats, and many feature the wonderful, rare vocabulary words you want your child to hear. My favorites, are those that play with language, like Bill Martin Jr. and John Archambault's *Chicka Chicka Boom Boom* (1998), or books like Giles Andreae's *K Is for a Kissing Kangaroo* (2003), which associates memorable words (kissing kangaroo) with letter names (*k*).

You can also draw letters almost anywhere. Use a stick in sand in the playground; spell out words with plastic letters; use chalk on the sidewalk or a paintbrush with water. Play with shaving cream or soap foam in the bathtub; draw letters or trace a letter in soap on your child's back, and then ask him to guess which one it is. You can buy magnetic letters and put them on the fridge—to leave reminders or to spell out a special message (*I love you*) or just to play around with words.

The simplest toys, too, can be more playful than lots of pricey electronic gadgets that are currently on the market. Games such as Alphabet Lotto and alphabet puzzles are always great, but also think about modeling clay or play dough, and alphabet stencils with construction paper. As your child plays with these materials, playfully point to the letters and ask him to tell you their name. You'll notice, of course, that the first letters he delights in learning are those in his own name.

You can also begin to help your child play with writing. Start by printing his name for him in large, uppercase letters. I always begin with uppercase since it's easier for a child to print in large strokes at this age. Let him trace over your letters to get a better feel for them, and then let him practice copying the whole word. Giving him a small whiteboard with an eraser will keep him busy for many hours.

Keep markers, crayons, large pencils, and paper in a spot where he can easily reach them. Some friends even have a small table in the kitchen set up with all these materials, and they encourage their child to play with them at moments when he's looking for something to do. You can put up a small board in the kitchen for menus and family reminders that your child helps you write.

And when you go on daily errands, or on trips with the family, be sure to point out the letters in various signs that you see. Sometimes you'll find that while your child seems to know the letters in the alphabet, he may not be able to identify a letter in a word. It may take a little time before he's confident, but you can start by saying, *Look David, there's a* d *in the MacDonald sign, just like the* d *in your name.*

If your child expresses an interest, show him how to form the letters. But don't push—especially if he resists. Remember that children's fine motor coordination at this age is not well formed. Long periods of attempting to write may be uncomfortable for their little hands. What's more important than striving for perfect form is to help your child develop curiosity and enthusiasm about letters. Ideally, your preschooler will see writing, like reading, as one more way to play and have fun.

By offering your child lots of opportunities to explore the world of print, you'll have done more for him than all the flash cards in the world could ever do. And you'll know as he goes off to school, that you've done a great job in getting him ready to read.

Why do children ask "why"?

Children are active seekers of information. Their curiosity and desire to learn about their world often leads to what authorities describe as "passages of intellectual search"—long, seemingly endless "why" and "how" questions to their parents.

Sometimes it might seem like a series of challenges, as we see in the case of Christopher and his mother. You might have experienced something like this with your preschooler:

MOTHER: What do you want to drink?

CHRISTOPHER: Apple juice.

MOTHER: Okay, you can have one glass of apple juice, but that's all for now.

CHRISTOPHER: Why?

MOTHER: Because it's close to dinner and I don't want to spoil your appetite.

CHRISTOPHER: Why would a drink spoil my appetite?

MOTHER: Because it's filling and it has a lot of sugar.

CHRISTOPHER: Why can't I have sugar?

MOTHER: Because it will make you more thirsty.

And so the conversation continues as the mother attempts to satisfy the puzzled mind of the young child. But while a child's many questions might seem frustrating at times, these questions illustrate his intense need to make sense of apparent anomalies in his limited knowledge base. Analyses of conversations have consistently revealed the logical, albeit extremely persistent, ways in which children are attempting to make sense of their world.

Children learn so much from these conversations. These "why" and "how" questions really play a vital role in learning. Children will pick up words you use in the course of your explanations, and gain great amounts of general knowledge through these exchanges. In fact, for every word or concept you carefully define for your child, there are dozens more he'll pick up by hearing you use them in context and later try to use them on his own. For this reason, you may occasionally want to include sophisticated words in your conversations along with the explanations if needed.

Of course after a while, you might want to turn your child's questions back to him by asking what he thinks, and why he thinks so. *Why do you think that a drink would spoil your appetite?* Having your child explain things to you will give you a wonderful window into his world. It will create a problem that he'll need to solve. It will also encourage him to use more descriptive language, and sentences that grow longer and more complex. And the more your child knows about words and knowledge networks when he starts kindergarten, the more likely he is to become a skillful reader.

Helping your child engage in these glorious "passages of intellectual search" is one of the most valuable things you can do as a parent to lay the groundwork for literacy. That's why it's important to use these constant "why" questions as an opportunity to extend your conversations. It's a great way to strengthen language, reasoning, and problem-solving skills.

How do children learn about writing?

Just as young children may pretend to read at an early age, they also begin to pretend to write. Children often begin by making marks on paper and calling it writing as early as the preschool years—scribbling a list, drawing circles and lines, filling an entire page with marks and calling it a story. As they move to kindergarten, these behaviors become more purposeful, less random, and more recognizable as writing. By the end of the year, most kindergartners will be able to write their names, as well as a few phrases, such as "I love you."

Children often begin writing by using random marks, or scribbling, in their pretend play. They'll pretend to write traffic tickets, receipts, and bills and take phone messages and orders from a menu. They'll experiment with the visual features, formats, and conventions of writing, exploring and playing with the way language looks on the page. Many of these inventions will not look conventional by any means. But that's okay for now. You'll want to focus more on what they're trying to write than on how they're writing it. The desire and motivation to write is what counts, not perfect spelling in these early years.

Sometimes drawing and writing, or "driting," is common in the preschool years. Children make pictures that combine letter or letter-like shapes and drawings. Some of children's earliest stories are told mostly through drawing, probably because drawing is more familiar and easier to control than writing. They may use a "mixed medium" of pictures, shapes, and words to playfully engage in writing. You can support your child's writing by asking her to tell you about her story. Let her point to some of the pictures and marks and tell you what they are. Sometimes you might write a sentence below the "driting" to help her remember her story.

Through kindergarten and first grade, children will use a lot of "invented spellings," writing *bs* for *bus* or *kat* for *cat*. Parents sometimes worry that if they permit invented spellings, their children will never learn to spell correctly. Yet these spellings are very useful because they provide a valuable window on children's learning. Children don't randomly pick letters to stand for a sound. Instead they seem to work hard to pick ones that make some kind of sense to them. You can see from their writings, then, what sounds they are hearing and what sounds they are not. Saying a word slowly will help them begin to connect new sounds with letter names.

There are lots of ways that you can strengthen your child's natural interest in writing. Bring along paper and crayons wherever you go. Read a story and then write a new ending for it together. You might even write a letter to your favorite author. To develop as writers, children will need to find a balance between "doing it myself" and asking for help. Remember to offer prompts and encouragement, but use a light touch and follow your child's lead. As noted researcher Anne Haas Dyson puts it, "We want to guide but not smother the emerging voices of our children."

American Academy of Pediatrics. (2001). *Promoting optimal health for America's child.* Grove Village, IL.

American Association for the Advancement of Science. (1993). *Benchmarks for science literacy: Project 2061.* New York: Oxford University Press.

Andress, B. (1995). Transforming curriculum in music. In S. Bredekamp & T. Rosegrant (Eds.), *Reaching potentials: Transforming early childhood curriculum and assessment* (Vol. 2, pp. 99–108). Washington, DC: National Association for the Education of Young Children.

Aram, D., & Levin, I. (2004). The role of maternal mediation of writing to kindergartners in promoting literacy in school: A longitudinal perspective. *Reading and Writing, 17,* 387–409.

Beatty, A. (2005). *Mathematical and scientific development in early childhood: A workshop summary.* Washington, DC: National Academies Press.

Biemiller, A. (2003). Oral comprehension sets the ceiling on reading comprehension. *American Educator,* Spring, 23–24.

Bloodgood, J. W. (1999). What's in a name? Children's name writing and literacy acquisition. *Reading Research Quarterly, 34,* 342–367.

Bodrova, E., & Leong, D. J. (1996). *Tools of the mind: The Vygotskian approach to early childhood education.* Columbus, OH: Merrill.

Bodrova, E., & Leong, D. (2005). *Tools of the mind kindergarten curriculum research project.* Denver, CO: Center for Improving Early Learning.

Both-de Vries, A. (2006). *It's all in the name—early writing: from imitating print to phonetic writing.* Amsterdam: Rozenberg.

Bransford, J., Brown, A., & Cocking, R. (Eds.). (2000). *How people learn.* Washington, DC: National Academy Press.

Brophy, J. (1990). Teaching social studies for understanding and higher-order applications. *Elementary School Journal, 90,* 351–417.

Bruner, J. (1972). The nature and uses of immaturity. *American Psychologist, 27,* 687–708.

Bruner, J. (1983). *Child's talk: Learning to use language.* New York: Norton.

Bruner, J. (1984). Vygotsky's zone of proximal development: the hidden agenda. In B. Rogoff & J. Wertsh (Eds), *Children's learning in the "zone of proximal development."* San Francisco: Jossey-Bass.

Cazden, C. (1976). Play and metalinguistic awareness. In J. Bruner, A. Jolly, and K. Sylva (Eds.), *Play: Its role in development and evolution.* New York: Basic Books.

Center on the Social and Emotional Foundations of Early Childhood. (2006). Resources. Retrieved May 8, 2006, http://www.csefel.uiuc.edu/resources.html.

Chaille, C., & Britain, L. (1997). *The young child as scientist: A constructivist approach to early childhood science education.* New York: Longman.

Christie, J. (1991). *Play and early literacy development.* Albany, NY: SUNY Press.

Christie, J., & Enz, B. (1991). *The effects of literacy play interventions on preschoolers' play patterns and literacy development.* Paper presented at the American Educational Research Association, Chicago, IL.

Clements, D., Sarama, J., & DiBiase, A. M. (Eds.). (2004). *Engaging young children in mathematics: Findings of the 2000 National Conference on Standards for Preschool and Kindergarten Mathematics Education.* Mahwah, NJ: Erlbaum.

Cohen, D. K., Raudenbush, S. W., & Ball, D. L. (2002). Resources, instruction, and research. In F. Mosteller & R. Boruch (Eds.), *Evidence matters: Randomized trials in education research* (pp. 80–119). Washington, DC: Brookings Institution Press.

Dickinson, D., & Neuman, S. B. (2006). *Handbook of early literacy research.* New York, NY: Guilford Press.

Dickinson, D., & Tabors, P. (Eds.). (2001). *Beginning literacy with language.* Baltimore: Brookes.

Dunsmuir, S., & Blatchford, P. (2004). Predictors of writing competence in 4- to 7-year-old children. *British Journal of Educational Psychology, 74,* 461–483.

Dyson, A. H. (1982). The emergence of visible language: Interrelationships between drawing and early writing. *Visible Langua*ge, 16, 360–381.

Dyson, A. H. (1993). *Social worlds of children learning to write in an urban primary school.* New York: Teachers College Press.

Eckler, I., & Wininger, O. (1989). Structural parallels between pretend play and narratives. *Developmental Psychology. 25,* 736–743.

Edwards, C., Gandini, L., & Forman, G. (1993). *The hundred languages of children.* Norwood, NJ: Ablex.

Ehri, L., & Roberts, T. (2006). The roots of learning to read and write: Acquisition of letters and phonemic awareness. In D. Dickinson & S. B. Neuman (Eds.), *Handbook of early literacy research* (pp. 113–134). New York: Guilford Press.

Eisner, E. (1988). *The role of disciplined-based art education in America's schools.* Los Angeles: Getty Center for Education in the Arts.

Fernandez-Fein, S., & Baker, L. (1997). Rhyme sensitivity and relevant experiences in preschoolers from diverse backgrounds. *Journal of Literacy Research, 29,* 433–459.

Ferreiro, E., & Teberosky, A. (1984). *Literacy before schooling.* New York: Heinemann.

Gardner, H. (1980). *Artful scribbles: The significance of children's drawings.* NY: Basic Books.

Gelman, S., & Brenneman, K. (2004). Pathways to science for young children. *Early Childhood Research Quarterly,* Vol. 19, 150–158.

Geography Education Standards Project. (1994). *Geography for life: National geography standards.* Washington, DC: National Geographic Research and Exploration.

Gmitrova, V., & Gmitrova, J. (2003). The impact of teacher-directed and child-directed pretend play on cognitive competence in kindergarten children. *Early Childhood Education Journal, 30*(4), 241–246.

Greenman, J. T. (1988). *Caring spaces, learning places: Children's environments that work.* Redmond, WA: Exchange Press.

Hart, B., & Risley, T. (1995). *Meaningful differences in the everyday experience of young American children.* Baltimore: Brookes.

Heath, S. B. (1983, 1996). *Ways with words: Language, life, and work in communities and classrooms.* New York: Cambridge University Press. p.421.

Johnson, J., Christie, J., & Wardle, F. (2005). *Play, development, and early education.* New York: Allyn & Bacon.

Karmiloff-Smith, A. (1992). *Beyond Modularity.* Cambridge, MA: MIT Press.

Kilpatrick, J., Swafford, J., & Findell, B. (Eds.). (2001). *Adding it up.* Washington, DC: National Academy Press.

Kritchevsky, S., & Prescott, E. (1977). *Planning environments for young children: physical space, 2nd edition* (p. 20). Washington, DC: National Association for the Education of Young Children.

Levin, I., & Bus, A. G. (2003). How is emergent writing based on drawing? Analysis of child products and their sorting by children and mothers. *Developmental Psychology, 39,* 891–905.

Maclean, M., Bryant, P., & Bradley, L. (1987). Rhymes, nursery rhymes, and reading in early childhood. *Merrill-Palmer Quarterly, 33,* 255–281.

Malaguzzi, L. (1993). *The hundred languages of children.* In C. Edwards, L. Gandini & G. Forman (Eds) (p. 151). Greenwich, CT: Ablex.

Mardell, B. (1999). *From basketball to the Beatles.* Portsmouth, NH: Heinemann.

Mason, J. M. (1984). Early reading from a developmental perspective. In P. D. Pearson, R. Barr, M. L. Kamil, & P. Mosenthal (Eds.), *Handbook of reading research Vol.1,* (pp. 505–543). New York: Longman.

Morrow, L. M. (1990). Preparing the classroom environment to provide literacy during play. *Early Childhood Research Quarterly, 5,* 537–554.

Morrow, L. M. (2002). *The literacy center: Contexts for reading and writing* (2nd Ed.) Portland, ME: Stenhouse.

Morrow, L. M. (2005). *Literacy development in the early years: Helping children read and write* (5th ed.) Boston, MA: Allyn & Bacon.

National Association for the Education of Young Children/National Council of Teachers of Mathematics. (2002). *Early childhood mathematics: Promising good beginnings.* Washington, DC: National Association for the Education of Young Children.

National Council of Teachers of Mathematics. (2000). *Early learning standards in mathematics.* Washington, DC: National Council of Teachers of Mathematics.

National Reading Panel. (2000). *Report of the National Reading Panel: Teaching children to read.* Washington, DC: U.S. Department of Health and Human Services, National Institute of Health.

Neuman, S.B., et al. (2001). *Access for all: Closing the book gap for children in early education.* Newark, DE: International Reading Association.

Neuman, S. B., Copple, C., & Bredekamp, S. (2000). *Learning to read and write: Developmentally appropriate practice.* Washington, DC: NAEYC.

Neuman, S. B., & Dickinson, D. (2001). *Handbook of early literacy research.* New York: Guilford.

Neuman, S. B., & Roskos, K. (1992). Literacy objects as cultural tools: Effects on children's literacy behaviors in play. *Reading Research Quarterly, 27,* 202–225.

Neuman, S. B., & Roskos, K. (1993). Access to print for children of poverty: Differential effects of adult mediation and literacy-enriched play settings on environmental and functional print tasks. *American Educational Research Journal, 30,* 95–122.

Neuman, S. B., & Roskos, K. (Eds.). (1998). *Children achieving: Best practices in early literacy.* Newark, DE: International Reading Association.

Neuman, S. B., & Roskos, K. (2005). The state of state prekindergarten standards. *Early Childhood Research Quarterly, 20,* 125–145.

O'Brien, C. (2005). *Final Report: Cuyahoga Community College W. K. Kellogg Home Based Child Care Literacy Training Project.* Cleveland, OH: Department of Early Childhood, Cuyahoga Community College.

Olds, A. R. (1987). Designing settings for infants and toddlers in spaces for children. In C. Weinstein & T. G. David (Eds.) *Spaces for children: The built environment and child development.* New York: Plenum.

Olds, A. R. (2001). *Child care design guide.* New York: McGraw-Hill.

Owocki, G. (2005). *Time for literacy centers: How to organize and differentiate instruction.* Portsmouth, NH: Heinemann.

Panksepp, T. (1998). Attention deficit hyperactivity disorders, psycho-stimulants, and intolerance of childhood playfulness: A tragedy in the making. *Current Directions in Psychological Science, 7* (3), 91-98.

Pellegrini, A., & Galda, L. (1993). Ten years after: A re-examination of symbolic play and literacy research. *Reading Research Quarterly, 28,* 162–177.

Phyfe-Perkins, E. (1980). Children's behavior in preschool settings: A review of research concerning the influence of the physical environment. In L. Katz (Ed.), *Current topics in early childhood education* (Vol. 3, pp. 91–123) Norwood, NJ: Ablex.

Piaget, J., & Inhelder, B. (1969). *The psychology of the child.* New York: Basic Books. (Original work published 1966)

Prescott, E., & Jones, E. (1984). *Dimensions of teaching-learning environments*. Pasadena, CA: Pacific Oaks College.

Ravitch, D. (1995). *National standards in American education: A citizen's guide*. Washington, DC: The Brookings Institute.

Read, C. (1971). Pre-school children's knowledge of English phonology. *Harvard Educational Review, 41*, 1–34.

Richards, R., Collis, M., & Kincaid, D. (1987). *An Early Start in Science*. London: MacDonald Educational.

Roskos, K., & Christie, J. (Eds.). (2000). *Play and literacy in early childhood: Research from multiple perspectives*. Mahwah, NJ: Erlbaum.

Roskos, K., & Christie, J. (2004). Examining the play-literacy interface: A critical review and future directions. In E. Zigler, D. Singer, & S. Bishop-Josef (Eds.), *Children's play: The roots of reading* (pp. 95–123). Washington, DC: Zero to Three Press.

Roskos, K., & Christie, J. (Eds) (in press). *Play and literacy development*, 2nd edition. Mahwah, NJ: Erlbaum.

Roskos, K., & Neuman, S. (1993). Descriptive observations of adults' facilitation of literacy in young children's play. *Early Childhood Education Quarterly, 8* (1), 77–88.

Rowe, D. (2006, April). *Learning social contracts about text: A social practice perspective on two-year-olds' writing*. Paper presented at the annual meeting of the American Educational Research Association, San Francisco, CA.

Saltz, E., Dixon, D., & Johnson, J. (1977). Training disadvantaged preschoolers on various fantasy activities: Effects on cognitive functioning and impulse control. *Child Development, 48*, 367–380.

Sanders, S. (2004). *Active for life: Developmentally appropriate movement programs for young children*. Washington, DC: National Association for the Education of Young Children.

Sawyer, R. K., & DeZutter, S. (in press). Improvisation: A lens for play and literacy research. In K. Roskos & J. Christie (Eds.), *Play and literacy in early childhood: Research from multiple perspectives*. Mahwah, NJ: Erlbaum.

Schickedanz, J. A. (1999). *Much more than ABC's: The early stages of reading and writing*. Washington, DC: National Association for the Education of Young Children.

Seefeldt, C. (1995). Transforming curriculum in social studies. In S. Bredekamp & T. Rosegrant (Eds.), *Reaching potentials: Transforming early childhood curriculum and assessment* (Vol. 2, pp. 109–123). Washington, DC: National Association for the Education of Young Children.

Singer, D., Golinkoff, R. M., & Hirsh-Pasek, K. (Eds.) (in press). *Play=learning: How play motivates and enhances children's cognitive and social-emotional growth*. New York: Oxford University Press.

Smilansky, S. (1968). *The effects of sociodramatic play on disadvantaged preschool children*. New York: John Wiley.

Snow, C., Burns, M. S., & Griffin, P. (1998). *Preventing reading difficulties in young children*. Washington, DC: National Academy Press.

Sonnenschein, S., Baker, L., Serpell, R., & Schmidt, D. (2000). Reading is a source of entertainment: The importance of the home perspective. In K. Roskos & J. Christie (Eds.), *Play and literacy in the early years* (pp. 107–124). Mahwah, NJ: Erlbaum.

Stone, S., & Christie, J. (1996). Collaborative literacy learning during sociodramatic play in multiage (K–2) primary classrooms. *Journal of Research in Childhood Education, 10*, 123–133.

Taylor, A., Aldrich, R., & Vlastos, G. (1988). Architecture can teach. *In Context, 18*, 31.

Teale, W., & Sulzby, E. (1986). *Emergent literacy: Writing and reading*. Norwood, NJ: Ablex.

Tharp, R.G., & Gallimore, R. (1988). Rousing schools to life. *American Educator, 13*(2), 20–25, 46–52.

Tolchinsky-Landsmann, L. (2003). *The cradle of culture and what children know about writing and numbers before being taught.* Mahwah, NJ: Erlbaum.

Tomasello, M. (1999). *The cultural origins of human cognition.* Cambridge, MA: Harvard University Press.

Treiman, R., Kessler, B., & Bourassa, D. (2001). Children's own names influence their spelling. *Applied Psycholinguistics, 22,* 555–570.

Vukelich, C. (1994). Effects of play interventions on young children's reading of environmental print. *Early Childhood Research Quarterly, 9,* 153–170.

Vygotsky, L. S. (1978). *Mind in society: The development of higher psychological processes* (M. Cole, V. John-Steiner, S. Scribner, & E. Souberman, Eds. and Trans.). Cambridge, MA: Harvard University Press.

Vygotsky, L. S. (1966). Development of the higher mental functions (abridged). In *Psychological research in the U.S.S.R.* (Vol. 1). Moscow: Progress.

Wachs, T. (1987). Developmental perspectives on designing for development. In C. Weinstein & T. David (Eds.), *Spaces for children* (pp. 291–307). New York: Plenum Press.

Weir, R. (1976). Playing with language. In J. Bruner, A. Jolly, & K. Sylva (Eds.), *Play and its role in development and evolution* (pp. 609–618). New York: Basic Books.

Weir, S., & Emanuel, R. (1976). *Using LOGO to catalyze communication in an autistic child* (DAI research report). Edinburgh: University of Edinburgh.

Weitzman, E., & J. Greenberg, J. (2002). *Learning language and loving it: A guide to promoting children's social, language, and literacy development in early childhood settings* (2nd ed.). Toronto, Ontario, Canada: The Hanen Centre.

Welch, M. J. (Ed.). (2000). *American Academy of Pediatrics guide to your child's allergies and asthma: Breathing easy and bringing up healthy, active, children.* New York: Villard.

Wells, G. (1985). *The meaning makers: Children learning language and using language to learn.* Portsmouth, NH: Heinemann.

Wolfersberger, M. E., Reutzel, D. R., Sudweeks, R. R., & Fawson, P. C. (2004). Developing and validating the Classroom Literacy Environmental Profile (CLEP): A tool for examining the print richness of early childhood and elementary classrooms. *Journal of Literacy Research, 36*(2), 211–272.

Zigler, E., & Bishop-Josef, S. (2004, April 18). A well-rounded child needs playtime and book time. *New Haven Register.*

Zigler, E., Singer, D., & Bishop-Josef, S. (2004). *Children's play: The roots of reading.* Washington, DC: Zero to Three Press.

INDEX

372.476
N4921

LINCOLN CHRISTIAN UNIVERSITY

128799

3 4711 00219 1759